Mrs John B. Miller

PICTORIAL HISTORY

OF THE

SECOND WORLD WAR

*A PHOTOGRAPHIC RECORD OF A
YEAR OF VICTORY WITH SPECIAL
SECTIONS ON WAR PERSONALITIES,
WEAPONS, AND GREAT BATTLE SCENES*

Vol. 5

New York

WM. H. WISE and CO., INC.

1946

CONTENTS

A YEAR OF VICTORY

	PAGE
STORY, SEPTEMBER THROUGH AUGUST	2055
PICTURE HISTORY, SEPTEMBER-AUGUST	2057
PERSONALITIES OF THE WAR	2241
GREAT BATTLE SCENES	2305
WEAPONS OF THE WAR	2433
INDEX	2497

ACKNOWLEDGEMENTS

Photographs in this publication were obtained from the following sources:

Acme Photo — 2060, 2073, 2090, 2091, 2114, 2137, 2138, 2158, 2242, 2245, 2481

Bachrach — 2279

British Information Service — 2078, 2079, 2441, 2482

French Press and Information Service — 2390

Government of India Information Services — 2378, 2379

International News Photo — 2057, 2061, 2062, 2063, 2064, 2065, 2068, 2069, 2072, 2075, 2076, 2077, 2080, 2086, 2094, 2095, 2107, 2113, 2117, 2122, 2123, 2124, 2125, 2126, 2127, 2128, 2129, 2142, 2148, 2156, 2157, 2168, 2281, 2283, 2284, 2285, 2287, 2289, 2292

Odhams Press — 2342, 2372, 2403, 2408, 2409, 2418

Official Coast Guard Photo — 2279, 2377, 2385, 2422, 2423, 2428, 2458, 2471

Official U. S. Marine Corps Photo — 2070, 2337, 2344, 2351, 2360, 2361, 2382, 2391, 2412, 2413, 2415, 2420, 2427, 2429, 2440, 2446, 2465, 2474, 2479, 2486

Official U. S. Navy Photo — 2059, 2309, 2322, 2332, 2333, 2340, 2348, 2349, 2352, 2354, 2355, 2358, 2368, 2370, 2371, 2375, 2383, 2386, 2387, 2397, 2400, 2402, 2406, 2426, 2437, 2439, 2450, 2457, 2471, 2488

Press Association — 2058, 2066, 2067, 2071, 2074, 2081, 2082, 2083, 2084, 2085, 2087, 2088, 2089, 2092, 2093, 2096, 2097, 2098, 2099, 2100, 2101, 2102, 2103, 2104, 2105, 2106, 2108, 2109, 2110, 2111, 2112, 2115, 2116, 2118, 2119, 2120, 2121, 2130, 2131, 2132, 2133, 2134, 2135, 2136, 2139, 2140, 2141, 2143, 2144, 2145, 2146, 2147, 2149, 2150, 2151, 2152, 2153, 2154, 2155, 2157, 2159, 2160, 2161, 2162, 2163, 2164, 2165, 2166, 2167, 2169, 2170, 2171, 2172, 2173, 2174, 2175, 2176, 2177, 2180, 2181 through 2239, 2242, 2243, 2244, 2246, 2247, 2248, 2249, 2250, 2251, 2252, 2253, 2254, 2255, 2256, 2258, 2259, 2260, 2262, 2263, 2264, 2265, 2266, 2267, 2268, 2269, 2270, 2271, 2272, 2273, 2274, 2275, 2276, 2277, 2278, 2279, 2280, 2282, 2286, 2288, 2290, 2294, 2295, 2296, 2297, 2298, 2299, 2300, 2301, 2302, 2303, 2404, 2407, 2408, 2417, 2419, 2434, 2435, 2436, 2438, 2442, 2443, 2445, 2447, 2448, 2449, 2451, 2452, 2453, 2454, 2456, 2459, 2460, 2462, 2463, 2466, 2470, 2472, 2475, 2476, 2478, 2483, 2484, 2485, 2490, 2491

Sovfoto — 2247, 2261, 2291, 2338, 2339, 2374, 2388, 2389, 2410, 2425, 2430

U. S. Army Air Forces — 2318, 2334, 2335, 2347, 2357, 2359, 2401, 2411

U. S. Army Signal Corps Photo — 2293, 2306, 2307, 2308, 2310, 2311, 2312, 2313, 2314, 2315, 2316, 2317, 2319, 2320, 2321, 2323, 2324, 2325, 2326, 2327, 2328, 2329, 2330, 2331, 2336, 2341, 2343, 2351, 2353, 2356, 2362, 2363, 2366, 2367, 2373, 2376, 2380, 2381, 2382, 2384, 2391, 2392, 2393, 2396, 2398, 2399, 2414, 2415, 2416, 2421, 2424, 2431, 2444, 2448, 2455, 2461, 2464, 2467, 2468, 2469, 2473, 2474, 2477, 2480, 2486, 2487, 2489, 2492, 2493, 2494, 2495

FOREWORD

THIS fifth, and final, volume of the PICTORIAL HISTORY OF WORLD WAR II brings to the reader the story of the first year of victory in a world still technically at war. While the events of that year would perhaps have filled a volume by themselves, it was felt that there was rounding out and polishing off to be done on the story of the earlier years.

For this reason, the fifth volume has been divided into five sections, the first and largest of which is the chronology of the dramatic year just past, from V-J Day to Baker Day in the Bikini Lagoon. The second section is a gallery of the great personalities who led the Allies to victory—in informal studies as they appeared during the war years.

One of the important gaps in the earlier volumes was caused by the necessity for censorship—photographs not being released for publication until security had been satisfied. It has been possible now to go back and collect a number of the most interesting and breathtaking photographs which were released too late for inclusion in their chronological position in earlier volumes. These are gathered into the section on Great Battle Scenes. Likewise, with the section on Weapons. Many of these photographs were not released until after the war.

Not the least interesting section to the reader, it is hoped, is the cumulative index to all five volumes. The index is complete and detailed and should make it easy and quick to locate any subject, be it ship, personality, outfit, or theatre of operations.

There was so much that might have been included in this volume, that the editorial problem was one of leaving out, rather than putting in. If subjects have been omitted or treated too lightly, it is only because of the limitations of space.

THE PUBLISHERS

SEPTEMBER - AUGUST

THE full story of the Japanese surrender was not told on V-J Day. Not only Japan itself remained to be occupied, but her vast stolen Empire, from Singapore to Manchuria, had to be restored.

American troops entered Tokyo on September 5 while the British prepared to occupy Singapore on the same date. Troops of the Chinese Sixth Army began to fly to the coastal provinces of China and to liberate important cities such as Nanking as early as September 6. The situation in northern China was more complicated, with clashes occurring between the Communist and Nationalist armies for many months.

A further complication which plagued the victors was the spread of strong movements for independence, from Egypt to the Dutch East Indies. In Indonesia rebels set up an independent government and declared war against the Netherlands on October 13. Repeated demonstrations, frequently accompanied by bloodshed, occurred in Egypt, Palestine, India, and Indo-China. As the first year of peace ended, revolts were still simmering in these trouble spots.

INSIDE GERMANY AND JAPAN

IN Japan, General Douglas MacArthur moved quickly and efficiently to disarm and democratize the country. Emperor Hirohito proved an effective puppet for carrying out the Allied aims. The key men in the government were shaken up and a progressive, democratic regime under Premier Shidehara was installed. The banks were reorganized, war industries converted to civilian purposes. But Japan was a badly crippled country, her cities had been laid waste by Superfortresses and atom bombs. There was much hunger and misery. It would be a long struggle to emerge from the disaster brought upon the Japanese people by their war lords.

Germany, on the other hand, was scarcely a nation. It had been divided into four administrative zones (English, American, French and Russian) which badly hampered the rehabilitation of the war-weak country. Germany's towns were heaps of rubble. Her people too were hungry. At the Paris Peace Conference in the summer of 1946, Germany was not even on the agenda, well over a year after her defeat. The future was distant and uncertain for the once powerful country which had been the hotbed of nazism and the starting point of the world War II holocaust.

THE WAR CRIMES TRIALS

A NOVEL procedure after World War II was the rounding up and prosecution of those charged with war crimes. The Nuremberg trial of high Nazi officials was unique in history. Opening on November 21 with the arraignment of twenty top Nazis, including Goering, Keitel, Hess, von Ribbentrop and von Papen, the trial continued for nearly a year before the defendants were finally sentenced. The whole extraordinary procedure was calculated to establish a precedent which would help to deter future wars.

Although the war with Japan ended later than the European struggle, the prosecution and punishment of many high Japanese war criminals took place before the Nazi criminals were brought to justice. General Yamashita was taken into custody on September 3 and hung on February 22, 1946. General Homma was arrested on September 15, found responsible for the "Bataan Death March," and shot on April 2, 1946. General Hideki Tojo, Premier at the time of the Pearl Harbor attack, was apprehended on September 11, but attempted suicide and was not arraigned for his crimes until the following summer. Many lesser known but no less ruthless and brutal men were shot or hung in both Japan and Germany in the first year following V-J Day.

THE UNITED NATIONS

IN the first year following the end of World War II, the chief hope for future peace lay in the organization of the United Nations. The first session of the General Assembly opened on January 14 in London and the Security Council met in New York on March 25. From the outset of the meetings, there was a major split in policy between the Western Powers and Soviet Russia. The first test case was Iran, which Russian troops had occupied beyond the agreed date for withdrawal. The question was placed on the Security Council's agenda in the face of Russian disapproval and a satisfactory settlement was finally effected. Progress was also made by the United Nations in lesser matters and the way was cleared for the first peace conclave in Paris where delegates of the twenty-one victor nations gathered on July 29 to see whether the peace of the world could be secured by lawful negotiation in a future dominated by the atomic bomb.

DOMESTIC PROBLEMS

IN the United States, the main post-war headache was economic. Throughout the first winter of peace, management and labor struggled for what each deemed its proper share of profits. Reconversion came to a standstill as all the major industries went on strike, including the automotive, steel, coal and utility industries. But by spring, satisfactory wage levels had been negotiated and the wheels of industry began to grind again. However, the damage had been done and the consumer was still waiting for the goods he did without during the war. After a year of peace there was still a seller's market with prices zooming sky high. In the summer of 1946, the Office of Price Administration was briefly discontinued, then a substitute measure passed which some thought might prevent inflation and disaster. It had been a bitter year for labor, management and consumer.

A bright spot in the picture was the readjustment of the returning veterans. Although millions of men were demobilized, the rate of veteran unemployment was surprisingly low. Many of the younger veterans were taking advantage of the GI Bill of Rights and attending college. They proved to be the best students in the nation's universities.

On the other hand, although veterans were securing employment, salaries were too low for the new high-cost-of-living and many preferred to mark time while collecting their unemployment insurance. Although many veterans proved excellent students, others were unable to enroll because of the crowded conditions in the universities. Worst of all was the housing situation which forced many veterans to live in cold water flats, tents, huts, or with overcrowded "in-laws."

But on the whole, the spirit of America was hopeful. Despite inflation, black markets, and other evils, there was a feeling in the air that the country was headed for a period of unprecedented prosperity.

OPERATION CROSSROADS

OPERATION Crossroads in the summer of 1946 could conceivably change the future course of the world. Costing an estimated $90,000,000, this unique experiment consisted in detonating two atomic bombs, one in the air (Test Able) and one under water (Test Baker), both bombs exploding in the bull's-eye area of Joint Task Force I. There were seventy-three target ships of all types in the first test; about 87 ships in the second test.

Admiral William H. P. Blandy was in command of the tests, with some 42,000 men manning the ships and conducting the experiments. Able Day was July 1, Baker Day, July 25. Of the 160 vessels in both tests, eight warships and two landing craft were sunk, some twenty other vessels seriously damaged.

The blasts indicated that either type of atom bomb detonation would probably sink or badly damage any ship within 500 yards of the explosion point; personnel casualties would be heavy within a four mile radius. In short, the effects were startling and terrible, but less spectacular than expected by many observers. It appeared that the bomb's importance would be strategic, that is, it would be most effective against cities rather than against dispersed ships on the ocean. In any case, the atom bomb was demonstrated to be a potent force to reckon with in keeping the peace so dearly won.

"IT'S OVER, OVER THERE." During the war 7,300,000 soldiers and 126,859,000 tons of cargo were shipped from United States ports. Much of the cargo would never be brought back and more than 250,000 men would never return. Total casualties, including wounded, were 1,069,632. Many of the armed forces would remain overseas for occupation duty, and compulsory conscription continued long after V-J Day. But those thousands who were lucky enough to be immediately demobilized (above) cheered wildly as they came home to their war-dislocated country.

YAMASHITA SURRENDERS. On the day after V-J Day, General Tomoyuki Yamashita came out of the Luzon mountains to surrender to Lieut. General Jonathan Wainwright at Baguio. The arrogant, six-foot-tall Japanese general was the commander of all hostile forces in the Philippines where Wainwright had been forced to capitulate in 1942, and also waged the brilliant drive on Singapore. The general is shown as he grimly enters Bilibid prison a few hours after signing the surrender.

EPIC OF ISLAND ENDS. Wake Island, which was defended so gallantly by 400 marines in the first month of the war, was avenged on September 4, 1945, with the raising of Old Glory and the surrender of 1,200 Japanese soldiers to Brigadier Gen. Lawson S. Anderson, commanding general of the Fourth **Marine Wing.** The American naval base had fallen to the Japanese in December, 1941, after 14 days of furious fighting by the small band of marine defenders.

THE FINAL TRIUMPH. The first American flag to fly over Tokyo is hoisted above the Nippon Times building. Two days later the official flag was raised at the United States Embassy compound in the presence of General MacArthur who remarked as the flag went up: "General Eichelberger, have our country's flag unfurled and in Tokyo's sun let it wave in its full glory as a symbol of hope for the oppressed and as a harbinger of victory for the right." General Robert Eichelberger was commander of the Eighth Army which garrisoned Tokyo.

An embarrassing situation for the Japs September, 1945

POLITENESS PREVAILS. When the Yanks first landed in the Tokyo Bay area, although no shots were fired, the situation was tense and the Japanese reaction was mixed. The two Japanese in the top picture, among the first to be questioned during the early landings, appear openly hostile to the U.S. Marine Corps interpreter, while the Japs, below, are polite, correct and even grateful for the cigarettes proferred by a generous Yank at the Imperial Palace in Tokyo. Other Japanese soldiers, especially those who had run prisoner of war camps, were servile to the point of bowing low before their conquerors.

The Japs bow in defeat—to their Emperor

IT'S AN OLD CUSTOM. When the Yanks first arrived in Tokyo the Japanese were still revering their Emperor as in this picture where they are shown bowing to the Imperial Presence within the Imperial

Palace. Many of the Japs also bowed before their conquerors. This was their way of being politely— and discreetly—correct. Here, the Americans look puzzled.

DEMOBILIZATION PROCEEDS QUICKLY. Beaten Japanese troops await mustering out in a Tokyo street. General MacAurthur was to demobilize about 3,000,000 Japanese homeland troops and 4,000,000 overseas troops within the short space of less than two months. By October 16 MacArthur announced the job was completed.

WANTED: A JOB. Glum war workers crowd a New York State employment office in search of work. They're glad the war is over but one must eat. However, many war workers were tired from their long and faithful ordeal and seemed in no hurry to find work. Many of the women were to be replaced by men in peace-time industry. Some of the older workers would not be needed. Some of the younger would not have experience. All of the workers wanted war-time pay.

Peace at last in China

NANKING CELEBRATES. The various tentacles of the Japanese Army in China were lopped off one by one. United States Army Air Force planes began a vast operation to transport 80,000 Chinese troops to the coastal provinces to disarm and control the rapidly surrendering beaten enemy. Here, joyous natives of Nanking line the highway to the airport to watch the victorious Chinese forces arrive to accept the Japanese surrender there. This greatest airborne movement of troops in Asiatic history was under the direction of Lieut. General George E. Stratemeyer, commander of United States Air Forces in China. Troops of China's Sixth Army, equipped with American material, flew 650 miles to liberate Nanking.

The Marines rescue Formosa prisoners of war

BRAVE MINE FIELDS. A United States task force swept through two mine fields to land marines on Formosa where they rescued 1,200 weak but happy prisoners of war who had spent the better part of the war in three "hell camps." The commander of the rescue force, Rear Admiral Dixwell Ketcham, sent out this radio message: "We are observing darkened-ship regulations, but the glow from within the souls of these men who were Japanese prisoners for almost four years lights up our whole horizon." Most of the prisoners were British, about 200 being Americans. The picture shows emaciated British and Australian soldiers streaming out of Camp No. 6 in Formosa as sullen faced, well-fed Japanese guards turn away.

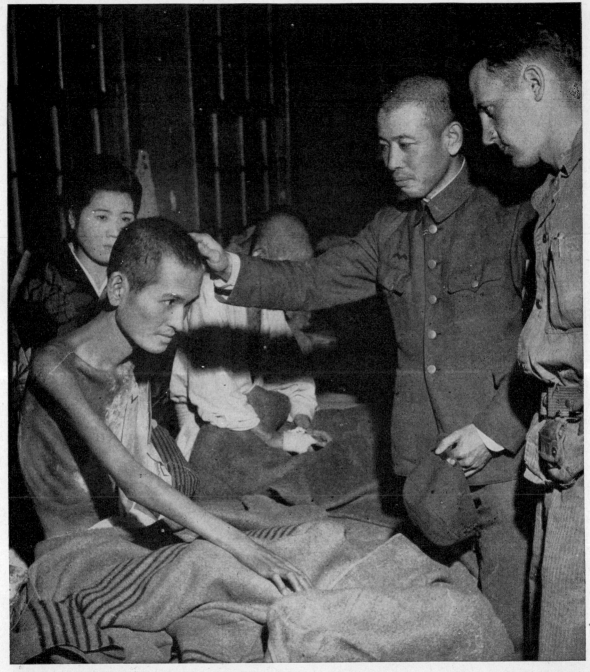

ONE OF THOUSANDS. The dreadful effects of the Nagasaki atom bomb are examined by the head physician of the Saga General Hospital and by a United States Navy lieutenant as a Japanese nurse stands by. On September 3 a Tokyo radio broadcast stated that scientists of the Kyushu Imperial University had classified the effects of the bomb on the human body under three headings: (1) instant death, (2) symptoms like those of dysentery followed eventually by death and (3) throat ulcers, bleeding gums, falling hair and eventual death. All victims showed a marked decrease in blood count and severe damage to bone marrow according to this report. Plant life, on the other hand, the report said, had revived in Nagasaki. Japanese newsmen who visited the Nagasaki region said that persons were paralyzed ten miles from the explosion center and other persons who had originally received only minute wounds eventually perished as a result of the atom explosion.

HER VOICE BARRED. Iva Toguri, the "Tokyo Rose" who broadcast Japanese propaganda to American troops in the Pacific, now blows off steam in a cell in Yokohama. In her broadcasts she attempted to undermine the morale of American GIs. Born twenty-nine years ago of Japanese parents in Los Angeles, Calif., she was charged with treason against the United States.

Japanese war fangs are pulled

GUNS GO OVERBOARD. Japanese small arms and rifles are heaped into an LSM to be borne out to sea off Saishu Island, Japan, where they were dumped into the ocean. The very first task of American occupying forces was to disarm the enemy and render all fighting equipment harmless.

GERMANS FORAGE FOR FOOD. Hungry Germans pick through a garbage dump for scraps of food. GI trucks unloaded waste from army kitchens in this area and people from as far as five miles came to look for edibles. Well-fed during their victories over other European countries, some of Europe's misery now comes home to the German people.

FOREIGN MINISTERS' COUNCIL MEETS. The first post-World War II peace parley opened in London when the Foreign Ministers' Council of the five big powers prepared to grapple with problems of the peace which might take a year or two of negotiation. This first meeting of the big powers who had held together during the war began in an atmosphere of conflict and ended twenty-two days later a complete failure. Nothing had been accomplished. But here, on the opening day, the United States Secretary of State James F. Byrnes, earnestly tackles a problem with an expressive forefinger, while England's Foreign Secretary Ernest Bevin listens lugubriously.

NATIVES CARRY ON. Although most of Hiroshima was obliterated and although the odor of death still clings to the ruins, the survivors of the atom blast in Hiroshima gradually begin to restore their broken lives. These little natives, dressed in the long bloomers that became the wartime fashion in Japan, pick their way through the rubble wearing mouth and noseguards to protect them against the human decay and carrying parasols to guard against the sun.

Tojo attempts suicide

TOPPED WAR CRIMES LIST. When General MacArthur put out a dragnet for forty Japanese militarists and war fomenters, General Hideki Tojo, Premier at the time of the Pearl Harbor attack, sought to cheat a conqueror's court by taking his own life not by the traditional hara-kiri but by a bullet. When MacArthur's men came to take him in custody he beckoned from a window (above) but when the house was entered Tojo had collapsed (picture at right) from a self-inflicted bullet. American blood plasma and medical skill saved Tojo's life for trial as a war criminal.

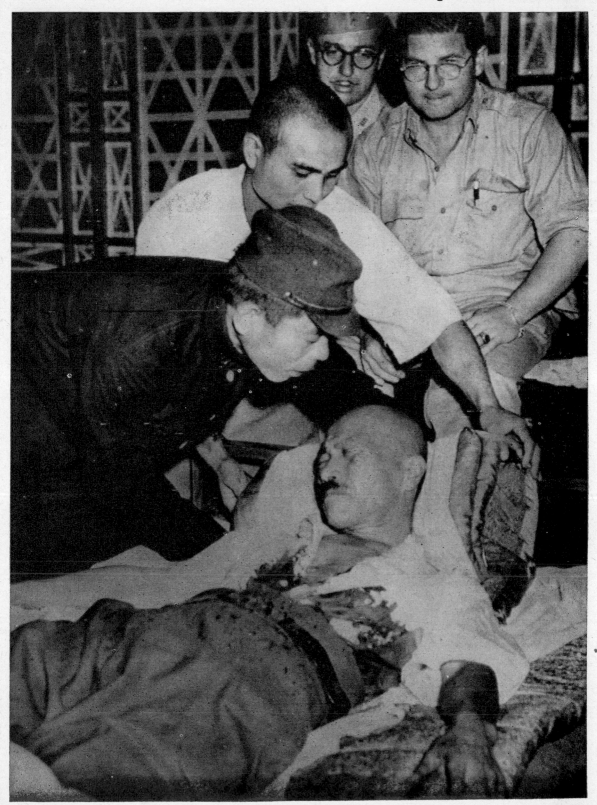

JAPANESE SURRENDER RELUCTANTLY. The huge, unbeaten in battle, southern armies of the Japanese surrendered to Admiral Lord Louis Mountbatten at Singapore on September 12. The capitulating enemy forces included 85,000 troops in the Singapore area and 500,000 troops in southeast Asia and the East Indies. In the picture, Admiral Mountbatten reads the order of the day. At his side is General R. A. Wheeler, deputy Southeast Asia Commander representing the United States.

CELEBRATE WITH A CARNIVAL. Gay processions of gigantic masks, gong beaters and cars with floral decorations wound through the crowded streets of Singapore to greet the returning British. The surrender by the Japanese to the British put the British again in control of 1,500,000 square miles of territory inhabited by 128,000,000 persons and rich in mineral and agricultural wealth, territories extending from Bengal to Hollandia.

2079

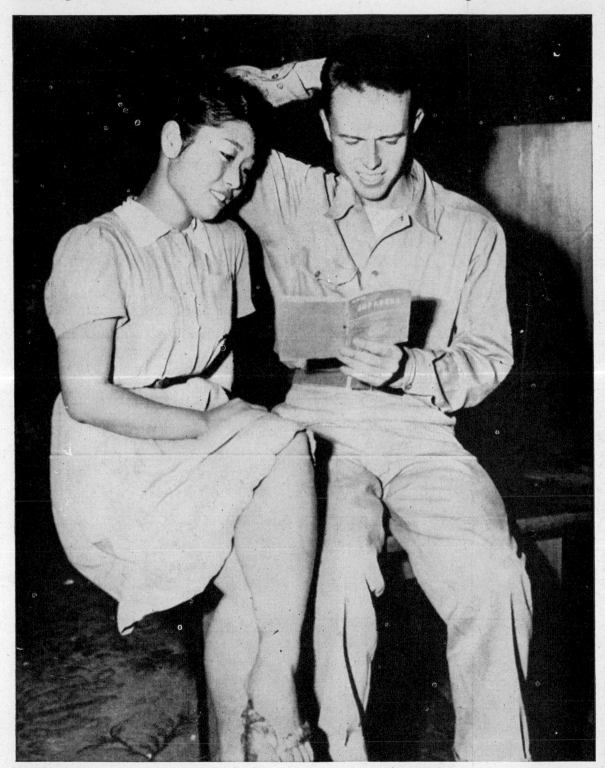

IT'S A TOUGH LANGUAGE. The fraternization ban in conquered Germany had proved impracticable and was not put in force in beaten Japan. Here, a bewildered Yank scratches his head over a difficult first lesson in the Nipponese language. He is aided by a booklet and a pretty Japanese tutor.

SUSPECTED OF BATAAN "DEATH MARCH." When Lieut. Gen. Masaharu Homma was arrested in connection with the "death march" of Bataan he remarked in a British accent that he had been "surprised" to find his name on MacArthur's list of suspected war criminals. Of the infamous "march" he said, "I don't think it was such a tough march." With Homma is Lieut. Gen. Shigenori Kuroda, center, and at the right is an American MP. Kuroda was Homma's successor in the Philippines.

FORD SHUTS DOWN. A bare two weeks after V-J Day Henry Ford II announced a shut-down of virtually all Ford plants because of a series of crippling strikes. Above, young Ford tells a radio audience of layoff of 50,000 employees. A few days later, automotive labor troubles were followed by a wave of strikes in the oil industry. The picture below shows Texas pickets eating refreshments. The wave of strikes, with both management and employes trying to get as big a share of post-war profits as possible, reached a climax in mid-winter. Meanwhile, reconversion dragged, prosperity was far around the corner.

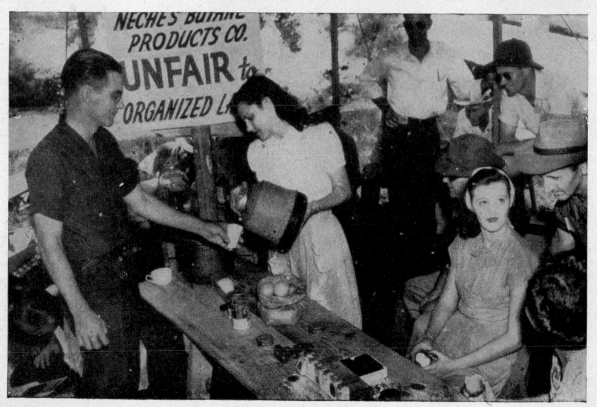

SERVED ON CEBU. Although the Japanese forces on Cebu, in the Philippines, gave up nine days before the general Japanese surrender, this picture was not released until after V-J Day. The girls take their defeat hard as do their brothers-in-arms, in the background of picture. These army nurses served in the field under the same battle conditions as the men.

250,000 DEMONSTRATE. In an unprecedented expression of mass feeling, one quarter of a million Argentinians demonstrated in Buenos Aires against the military dictatorship which had controlled the country for more than 27 months. Bearing banners and placards, the crowds surged through the streets shouting for their liberty and singing, surprisingly, "God Bless America."

THE BOSS AND HIS PUPPET. General Douglas MacArthur, wearing his campaign khaki without medals or necktie, stuffs his hands in his pockets to pose with his visitor, Emperor Hirohito of Japan, at the United States Embassy. The Emperor arrived in a five-car convoy from the Imperial Palace and bowed and tipped his hat to a group of correspondents at the entrance of the Embassy. The foreign ruler of Japan and the man through whom he rules conversed for 35 minutes. The subjects discussed were not made public but the visit was said to be a social one. In any event, the unusual procedure was a powerful symbol to expose the divinity of the Emperor to the Japanese people.

Life stirs in shattered Tokyo

CONQUERED CITY IS DESOLATE. American forces in Tokyo were appalled by the immense stretches of obliterated buildings in Japan's capital. However, residents set to work cleaning away the debris and, in the above picture, a trolley is again in operation. Poorer residents of Tokyo, below, line up for a ration of beans. Note complicated ration documents.

THE GOOD DID NOT BALANCE THE BAD. The top picture shows the hospital ward in the notorious Shinagawa prison camp in Japan. The sick and wounded slept on the wooden platforms or on the floor. In sharp contrast is the picture below depicting an American colonel and the Japanese commandant of a prison camp in Shanghai engaged in a chat before a baseball game. This picture was distributed by the Swedish representative of the YMCA War Prisoner Aid.

The homeless and hungry of Japan

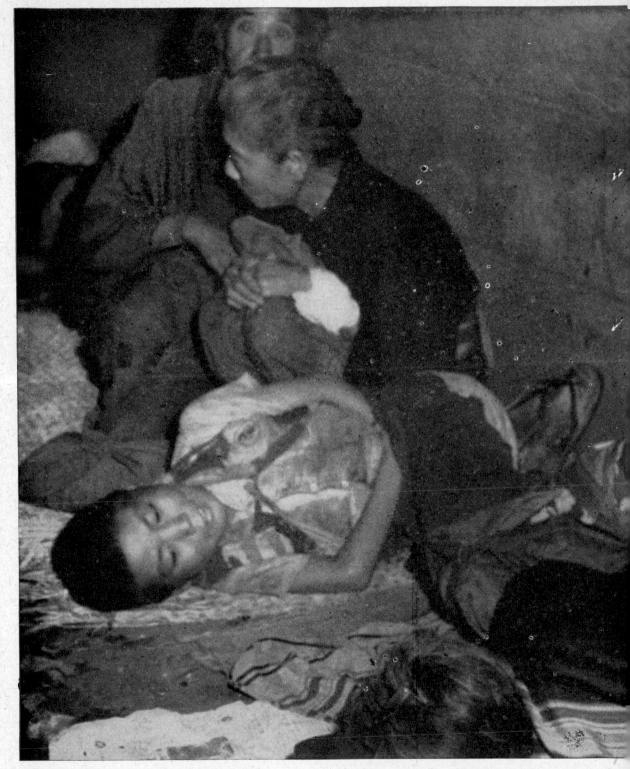

WAR'S VICTIMS. Hundreds of Japan's homeless and hungry people sought shelter in the subways of Tokyo during the windy, fall nights following defeat. Many were bombed out of their homes, others were

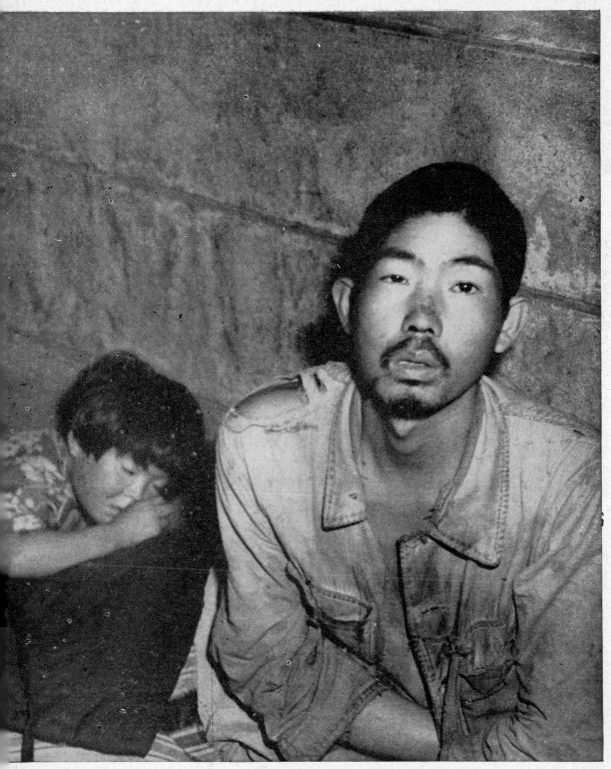

affected by the war's economic dislocations. Reports indicated that the season's crop would be considerably smaller than the previous year's. On October 16 Tokyo had its first "hunger march."

The Marines occupy north China hotspot

SITUATION IS CONFUSED. When the First Marine Division, above, marched into Tientsin the natives were genuinely glad to get the Japanese conquerors off their backs. Note the crowds even on the rooftop. However, Tientsin was uneasy with Chinese Nationalist and Communist forces at bayonet points and a Japanese Army still to be disarmed. Bridges and trains had been blown up and there were many riotings and lootings of dubious origin. North China was far from peace and security.

TRIAL IS TURBULENT. Pierre Laval is shown taking his place in the Paris High Court of Justice on the opening day of his trial on charges of treason and intelligence with the enemy. The very first day of the trial, October 4, was marked by unbelievable outbursts from Judge, jurors, spectators and the defendant. The crafty former Premier of France cajoled, persuaded, argued, acted hurt, contrite insolent and was finally dragged from the stand screaming like a madman.

Japan gets a new Premier

ANTI-MILITARIST GETS POST. When General Douglas MacArthur purged the Higashi-Kuni cabinet it fell apart and Hirohito appointed 74-year-old Baron Kijuro Shidehara as Premier to form a new cabinet. The new Premier is shown, center above, with Chief Secretary of the Government Tsagita, left, and Public Welfare Administrator Ashida, right. Baron Shidehara, anti-militarist who had been in retirement 14 years, is shown flashing his medals in a happier time, lower picture. He promised full cooperation with our occupation forces and freed 3,000 political prisoners.

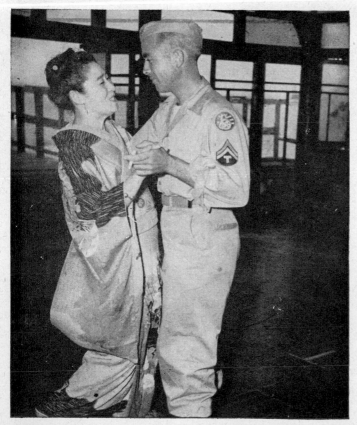

GIs DANCE WITH GEISHA GIRLS. The Army imposed no fraternization ban in Japan and much of the Yank's social life was provided by Geisha girls, trained from childhood in the art of entertainment and dancing. Above, a GI jitterbugs while another Yank, below, prefers ballroom dancing. The Japanese girls quickly adapted themselves to the strenuous American dance steps.

REUNION—ORIENTAL STYLE. There is no "vulgar," western-style kissing as this demobilized Japanese soldier is greeted at the station by his wife and child. They exchange polite greetings. But there is pathos in the intent look they exchange as the little soldier leans forward under the weight of his immense pack and the infant peers timidly over his mother's shoulder.

The Indonesians demand independence

DECLARE WAR ON NETHER-LANDS. The occupation of Java began peacefully at the end of September but the natives were quick to demand their independence and early in October seized control of key cities, declaring war on October 13. The commander of the Indonesian People's Army in the Batavia area called for all-out guerrilla warfare, stating that the weapons would be "poison, poison darts and arrows, all methods of arson and any kind of wild animals, as for instance snakes." In the youth meeting shown here the natives are armed largely with sharpened bamboo poles. The British opened up with fire from their warships and the RAF strafed and bombed the rebels.

Laval, traitor of France, faces firing squad October 15, 1945

TRIED SUICIDE FIRST. Pierre Laval, three times Premier of France, and a notorious collaborator with Nazi Germany, faces the firing squad in the Fresnes prison yard, Paris. A few hours before he was to be shot he swallowed poison which he had carried on his person for the past year, but time had deteriorated the poison and Laval was resuscitated. Wearing the white tie which he had made famous, he stood before the firing squad hatless and without a blindfold, crying out to his executioners, "I do not hold this against you. Aim at my heart. Vive la France!"

Revolution below the border

BLOOD IS SHED IN VENE-ZUELA. Three hundred persons were reported killed and 1,000 wounded when young army officers revolted in Caracas and deposed President Isaias Medina Angarita. The dead officer in the foreground of the upper picture was killed after he had slain those lying in the background. The revolutionary junta which took control of the country, left to right, consisted of Carlos Delgado Chalbaud, Raul Leoni, Dr. Bettancourt (President of the junta), Luis Beltran, Major Vargas, Dr. Eduardo Fernandez and Dr. Gonzalo Barrios.

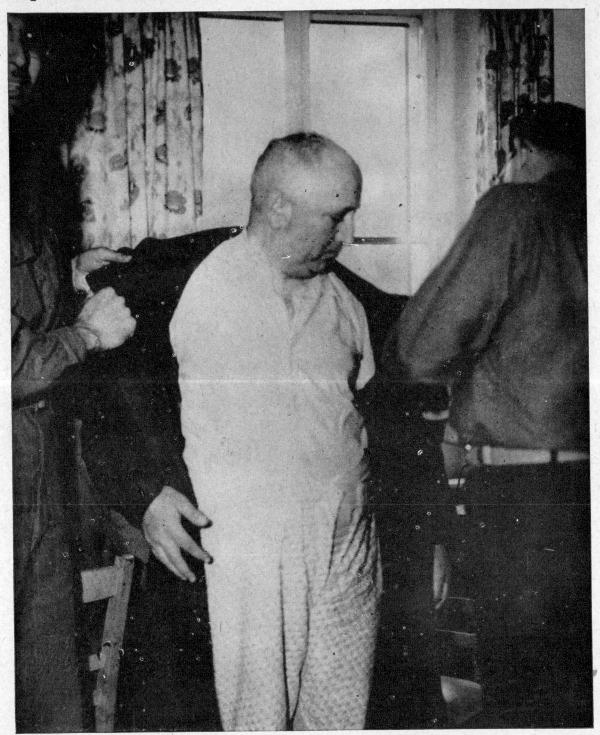

STRANGLES SELF IN CELL. Dr. Robert Ley, former Nazi labor leader who was to be tried as a war criminal at Nuremberg, took his own life with a strip torn from a prison towel which he tied about his neck and fastened to a pipe in the toilet of his cell. He had stuffed his mouth with bits of rag to muffle his death gasps. Ley was first apprehended in May of 1945 while hiding near Berchtesgaden. He had been clad in pajamas (above) and showed signs of mental and physical degeneration.

24,000,000 VOTERS SET RECORD. In the first general elections in France since 1936, 24,000,000 voters expressed their overwhelming support of the Communist, Socialist and Republican Popular Movement parties. All other parties were far behind. Women voted for the first time in a national election (above) and 31 women, 14 of them Communists, won seats in the Assembly.

The Navy has its day

THE PRESIDENT REVIEWS THE FLEET. The greatest fleet in the world assembled a powerful portion of its ships in the Hudson River west of Manhattan Island on October 27 to celebrate Navy Day. Vast crowds swarmed along the shoreline as the great battleships, carriers, cruisers and other craft paraded their might from mid-Manhattan all the way up to the George Washington Bridge. Overhead an armada of 1,200 Navy planes roared in impressive formations. In the picture, President Harry S. Truman stands on the bridge of the Renshaw with Admiral Jonas H. Ingram, commander of the Atlantic fleet, and takes a salute from a cruiser. As the President proceeded up the Hudson 47 other ships each gave him the full 21-gun salute. Earlier in the day he had ridden the length of throng-lined Fifth Avenue and at Central Park another huge crowd (estimated at a million) heard the President address the nation and the world in a speech outlining America's foreign policy for keeping the peace. The President's statement of America's peaceful intentions cheered the troubled world for the moment, with favorable comments coming from all the great capitals.

ACTRESS TESTIFIES. A recital of incredible cruelties was begun on the opening day of the trial of General Tomoyuki Yamashita, first to be tried as a war criminal in the Pacific area. Carazon Noble, Filipino actress, took the stand with her arm in a sling and told of the massacre in the Manila Red Cross building on February 10, 1945. She described in a low voice and with tears in her eyes how she had been shot and bayoneted while holding her ten-months-old baby in her arms. She testified that the infant had been bayoneted to death. Major Robert M. Kerr, chief prosecutor, charged Yamashita with responsibility for not controlling those within his command.

RUB-A-DUB-DUB. These gentlemen are really in hot water. They're top Japanese war criminals awaiting war trials at Omori prison camp in Japan. Their crude tub formerly served American prisoners of war. The gentlemen now being cleaned up are, left to right, former Cabinet Ministers Michiyo Iwamura, Admiral Baron Kantaro Suzuki and Admiral Ken Tereshima.

TOJO'S ONE-ROOM SUITE. After recovering from his attempted suicide, General Hideki Tojo was lodged in a cell like the one shown here in Sugamo Prison, Tokyo. Tojo, who was Japanese Premier at the time of the attack upon Pearl Harbor, was detained for trial as a war criminal.

RETRIBUTION. Major General Saito was commander of all prisoner of war camps in Singapore. When the British returned to Singapore they put the general in one of his own prisons and held him as a war crimes suspect. The general polices his quarters while awaiting trial.

AWAITS WAR TRIAL. Despite the fact that he must face trial as a war criminal, Japanese Lieutenant Colonel Ohta walks gaily along a precarious log at the Omori Prison Camp in Japan. The smiling colonel was charged with ordering Japanese soldiers to massacre Manila civilians with swords,

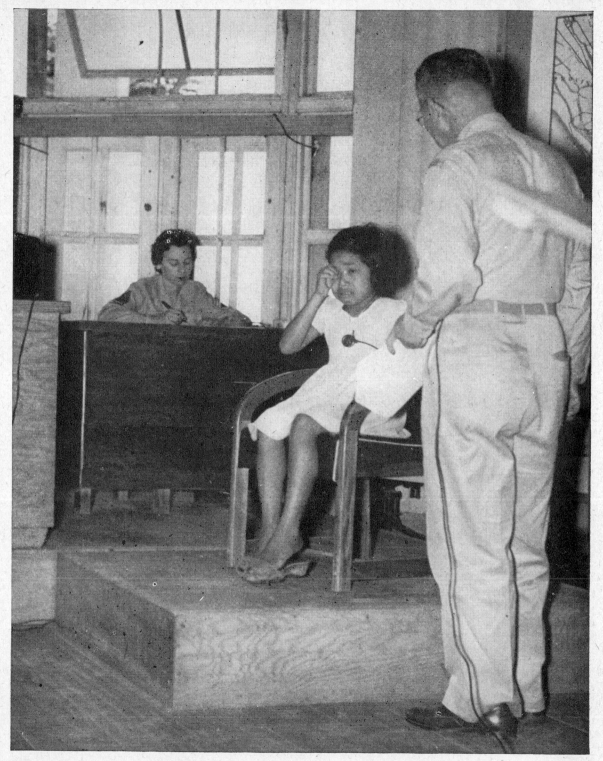

THE JAPS KILLED HER PARENTS. Weeping, 11-year-old Rosalinda Andoy, testifying before court trying Yamashita, describes how she received 38 bayonet wounds and her parents were murdered by the Japanese. Major Gricerio Opinion, of the prosecutor's staff, is at right.

THE CORPORAL IS BOSS. General Sadao Araki, former Japanese War Minister, is escorted into a Tokyo prison by an MP corporal. The general, styled by MacArthur as an "important influence behind Tojo," seems arrogantly reluctant as the husky corporal places a hand under his arm.

HIS CRIME WAS MURDER. Five German civilians were tried and found guilty of the murder of six American fliers who parachuted down upon Germany from a disabled plane in 1944. Johann Seipel, the first to be hanged, has only a few seconds to live. The noose has been fastened about his neck and the hood is being placed over his head preparatory to springing the trap at the Bruchsal Prison, Germany.

DRAWN BY ONE WHO ESCAPED. This crude sketch, presented as evidence at the Yamashita trial, was drawn by Eugene Bayot who received a deep cut in the back of his head but lived through the ordeal. Heads were hacked from victims kneeling at hole in top floor and the bodies tumbled into the room below. The witness said the sketch represented scene at 1195 Singalong Street, Manila.

CAUGHT IN MAC ARTHUR'S DRAGNET. This saucy-eyed, bearded old man was chief of the dreaded Black Dragon Society of Japan. Kuzuu was arrested in a war criminal roundup. Working behind the scenes, he had directed the regime of political assassination and terrorism which reinforced the ultra-militaristic clique in Nippon.

LEADERS DISCUSS ATOM BOMB. After honoring the war dead in Armistice Day ceremonies at Arlington cemetery, President Truman, center, and Secretary of State Byrnes, left, take their distinguished guest, Prime Minister Clement Attlee of England, for a cruise down the Potomac River. The British Prime Minister made the arduous trip to this country for the express purpose of discussing the atom bomb problem. His proposed answer to the problem was to turn the bomb over to the United Nations Security Council, providing that the Soviet Union frankly state its aims and policies.

U.S. starts destruction of Nazi war plants   November 12, 1945

POWDER PLANTS BECOME POWDER PUFFS. Six months after the German defeat the United States began its program of destroying German industries used solely for war purposes. The first plants to go were 59 structures of the Fabrik Kaufbeuren Gunpowder Works. As the destruction begins only smoke is visible, above, as the installations were well camouflaged by trees, roof gardens, and disappearing chimneys. These plants, located in the pine forests of Bavaria at Kaufbeuren, were operated by the titanic I. G. Farben interests. Another Farben plant, below, shows the permanent and expensive structure of these factories, built apparently with a view to many years of world-conquering activity.

TROUBLE SPOT. A train between Tientsin and Chingwantao, China, was stopped by a mine as it was carrying Chinese workmen and U.S. Marines, above. Workmen and Major General DeWitt Peck (standing, extreme left) scamper for cover as marines duck into a ditch, left. After this episode, troops and civilians were fired on from a nearby village, shown in picture below. American planes fly low above the village as a warning. Arrow in foreground guided planes to area.

GOVERNMENT BUILDINGS ATTACKED. On November 13 Britain's Foreign Secretary Ernest Bevin stated that Britain and the United States would form a joint committee of inquiry into the problem of European Jews in Palestine and that in time Palestine would become a trusteeship of the United Nations Organization with eventual self-government as a Palestinian, not Jewish, state. On November 14, terrorists swept through the streets of Tel Aviv, stoning and burning government buildings. Neither the Zionists nor the Arab leaders were pleased with Britain's statement of policy. The soldiers riding in the truck, top picture, were stoned into unconsciousness and the vehicle set afire. In the lower picture, a detachment of the British Sixth Airborne Division clears a street in Tel Aviv.

A page from Eva Braun's diary

DER FUEHRER AND CHILD.
When American intelligence officers found Eva Braun's treasure chest on November 15, they unearthed an album with scores of family pictures showing Adolf Hitler with the mysterious blonde child, Uschi, and with Eva Braun (above). Hitler was supposed to have married the pretty former actress just before both of them died during the siege of Berlin.

The Belsen gang is convicted

GUILTY. Joseph Kramer, the "beast of Belsen," and his hard-faced blonde assistant, Irma Grese, were sentenced to death by hanging for the atrocities they perpetrated at the Belsen and Oswiecim concentration camps. Nine others were sentenced to the same fate by a British Army court at Luneburg. One got life, five got 15-year sentences, 13 got one to ten years, 14 were acquitted. Sixteen of those convicted were women. The crimes committed were mass murder and ill treatment of the prisoners. Sullen-faced 29-year-old Kramer is shown leaving the courtroom, left, followed by Dr. Fritz Klein, who picked victims for the gas chamber. In the picture at the right, Irma Grese, center, leaves the courtroom. The blonde sadist sobbed when she heard the sentence.

The Nuremberg war crimes trial opens

JUDGEMENT DAY. On November 20, months after the European war ended, twenty top Nazis, ragged and dispirited from their long imprisonment, were hailed into the Nuremberg Palace of Justice for the unprecedented purpose of being tried as plotters and planners of aggressive warfare. The prisoners occupy the dock at the extreme left of the picture and are flanked by military policemen at the rear and defense counsel in front. The judges of the High Tribunal are on the bench at the extreme right (former Attorney General Francis Biddle representing the United States) and below and in front of them are the prosecution staffs, with the United States represented by Robert H. Jackson and aides. Vast bundles of evidence were ready—sheaves of documents, transcripts, diaries, letters, and films. When the atrocity films were shown the defendants were visibly shaken, one vomiting upon its conclusion. The prosecution detailed at great length and with scrupulous fairness the whole gigantic plot to seize Austria, Czechoslovakia, Poland. Not one of these once powerful men was left unentangled by the great web of evidence which was spun with such elaborate thoroughness and exactitude.

In the prisoners' dock

THE ACCUSED. Front row, left to right: Herman Goering, former No. 2 Nazi; Rudolph Hess, high Nazi who flew on mysterious mission to England during the hostilities; Joachim von Ribbentrop, diplomat; Wilhelm Keitel, former chief of the German High Command; Alfred Rosenberg, Voelkischer Beobachter editor and propagandist; Hans Frank, former Governor General of occupied Poland; Wilhelm Frick, former Minister of the Interior; Julius Streicher, notorious Jew-baiter; Walther Funk, former Minister of Economics; and Hjalmar Schacht, financier. Rear row, left to right: Karl Doenitz and Erich Raeder, former Grand Admirals; Baldur von Shirach, youth leader; Fritz Sauckel; Alfred Jodl, former Colonel General; Franz von Papen, diplomat; Arthur Seyss-Inquart, Austrian Nazi; Albert Speer, former Minister of Armament and Munitions; Constantin von Neurath, boss of Bohemia-Moravia; and Hans Fritzsche, propagandist.

The International High Tribunal

"FOR CIVILIZATION." Four judges, one each from America, Britain, Russia and France, together with their alternates, presided over the Nuremberg trial. In the top picture are Norman Birkett, British alternate; Lord Justice Sir Geoffrey Lawrence, British presiding judge; former Attorney General Francis Biddle; and United States alternate Judge John Parker. The defense pleaded unsuccessfully against a high tribunal representative of the victors only, claiming that neutral or defeated countries should also be represented. Justice Robert H. Jackson, below, chief prosecutor for the United States, in his opening address emphasized the Nazi determination to wage aggressive war and said that "the real complaining party . . . is civilization." Figure behind Justice Jackson is Sir Hartley Shawcross, British prosecutor.

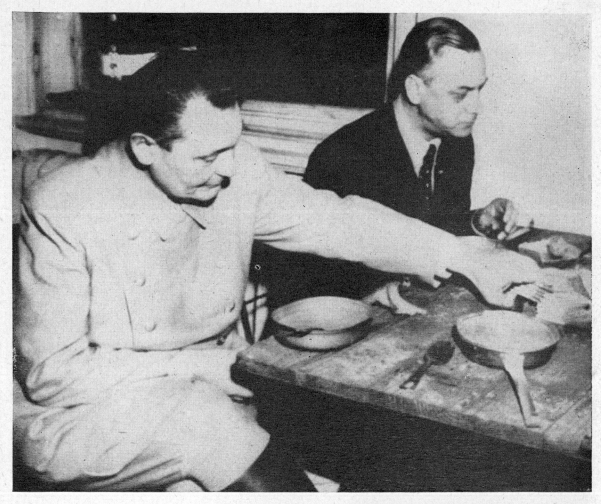

"SLUM AND CRACKERS." Goering's girth attests to his joy in eating, but now it's army stew, regular fare of the GI's, and quite different from the suckling pigs and caviar which Herman formerly wolfed. His dining partner is Alfred Rosenberg, philosopher of Nazism. Below, Rudolph Hess applies himself earnestly to the GI "slum."

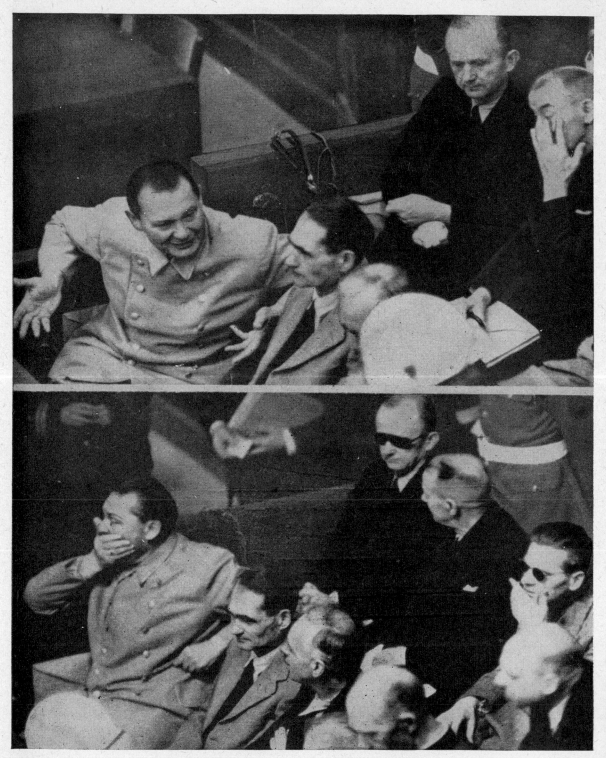

PLAYS TO THE GALLERY. Although the defendants were for the most part a subdued and broken lot, Goering was irrepressible, smiling and bowing to the spectators, guffawing and gesticulating. In the top picture he is talking animatedly past an impervious Hess, while in the lower picture he gets out of hand completely and claps a hand over his mouth after speaking out of turn.

All defendants plead not guilty

INNOCENTS. All twenty of the high Germans accused of war crimes rose and pleaded not guilty. Goering, top picture, tried to use the occasion for a speech but was squelched and said hotly, "I declare myself in the sense of the indictment not guilty." Von Papen, lower left, rises to say, "Guilty not at all," while Keitel, lower right, said, "I declare myself in the sense of the indictment not guilty." Hess, who sits glumly next to Goering, shouted the single word "Nein!" Von Ribbentrop, next to Hess, used the same formula as Goering and Keitel.

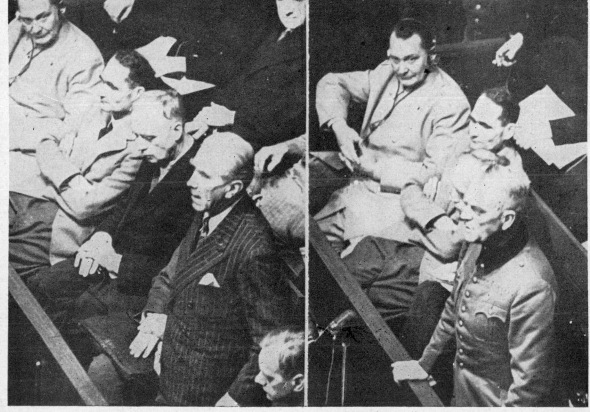

A page from Hitler's book

THE NAZIS IN WARSAW. This photograph, depicting the Nazis "cleaning out" the Ghetto in Warsaw, Poland, was presented as evidence at the Nuremberg trial. The photograph is a copy from a leather bound

book which contained the report of the German commander who was responsible for the Nazi acts in the Warsaw Ghetto. Women and children are herded before the Nazi firearms.

Nation-wide strike cripples car conversion

GENERAL MOTORS' PLANTS SHUT. Members of the United Auto Workers (C.I.O.) Union rush from the plant of the Chevrolet Gear and Axle Division at the start of the longest and most bitter strike of the entire reconversion period. There was little doubt that the workers should get pay rises, but the gigantic industrial organization and the powerful union could not agree upon the amount and as the strike dragged through the winter other problems rose to plague and complicate the negotiations.

HULL TAKES STAND. On November 15 a Senate-House investigating committee began the long-awaited probe of the Pearl Harbor disaster. One of the first major witnesses was former Secretary of State Cordell Hull. The 74-year-old statesman said that on November 25, 1941, he had warned that the Japanese might be expected to attack "anywhere at any time." He emphatically denied that his note to the Japanese on November 26 had been an ultimatum but, in fact, that the Japanese note of November 20 to us had amounted to an ultimatum. When the aging and ill Hull left the inquiry he was given a spontaneous ovation.

WOMEN TO TESTIFY AT NUREMBERG. Women witnesses, waiting at the Nuremberg Jail to testify in the trial of Nazi war criminals are, top, left to right: Johanna Wolf, Hitler's private secretary from 1940 until his death, and Ingeborg Sperr, secretary for Hess from 1934 until 1941. Bottom, left to right: Louise Guyon-Witzschel, secretary at an SS headquarters in Germany, Margaret Himmler, wife of German Gestapo chief who committed suicide, and her daughter, Gudron

The first snow falls in Nuremberg November 26, 1945

COLD COMFORT. What little food there was in Nuremberg often had to be sold in the streets since most of the buildings (background) were wrecked beyond use. Here, German housewives shop for bread amidst debris covered by the winter's first snowfall.

ASKS PEACE AND PROSPERITY. His hands trembling slightly, Emperor Hirohito opens the Japanese Diet with a brief address. He wears a new uniform without military insignia. This was the first time in history that photographs were permitted to be taken in the Diet. When Premier Shidehara addressed the session he was hooted and laughed at and his government was apparently foredoomed.

Hurley resigns as ambassador to China

ASSAILS CAREER DIPLO-MATS. On November 27, President Truman accepted the angry resignation of Patrick J. Hurley, United States ambassador to China, and appointed General George C. Marshall as his special envoy to that country. Hurley had ranted and raved about the career diplomats who had sabotaged our foreign policy but his hearing before Congress soon collapsed. General Marshall, longing for a rest after his war service to his country, nevertheless took off for the highly important job of unifying China and settling differences there. Hurley is shown on the witness stand, above, and General Marshall is shown, below, as he testified before the Pearl Harbor inquiry just before leaving for his tasks in China.

DRAMATIC MOMENT. Rudolph Hess, who had solemnly and steadfastly claimed complete loss of memory, suddenly stunned the Nuremberg court by rising to confess that he had feigned amnesia for "tactical reasons." Not only were medical men fooled by his performance but also his own attorneys. Above, he is excitedly telling the court that he is ready to "bear full responsibility for anything I have done." Below, Goering seems to be poking fun at the poseur, while next to them von Ribbentrop fingers his throat as if in anticipation of a gruesome experience with a rope.

A day with the German generals

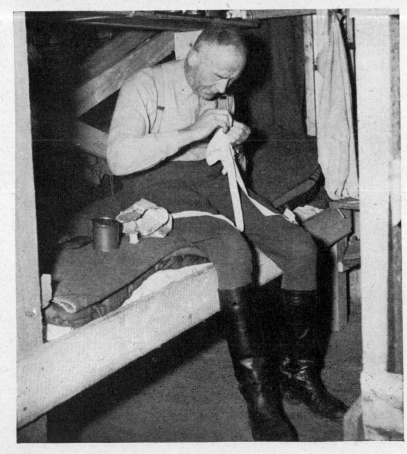

KEEPING HOUSE. At a prisoner of war camp in Hersfeld, Germany, 278 Nazi generals and admirals spent their days as shown on these two pages. Behind the barbed wire, above, the once high ranking brass strolls for an airing. In the picture below, General Karl Theissen, once a member of the General Staff, sits on a crude bunk and sews his own clothing. He must also keep that bunk made up, shine his shoes and brush and care for his clothing. In the picture at the right, General Majors Erich Fiedler (left) and Wilhelm von Kirchenpauer wring out their wash. Fiedler lost his command after the attempt on Hitler's life in 1944. With the conquest of Germany he lost his orderly.

SO SORRY, PLEASE. Major Sakaji Sakai bows politely to his guard as he is removed from his cell for an airing. The guard is impassive for the polite Jap is one of nine soldiers charged with participating in the torture and murder of three American B-29 fliers who crashed near Hankow, China, in November, 1944.

THEY'LL HANG. Lieutenant Commander Soichi Tachibaba, left, and Rear Admiral Shigematsu Sakaibara ordered the execution of 96 American civilians on Wake Island in October, 1943. On trial before a military commission on Kwajalein Island, they read statements in their behalf, above, but were sentenced to die by the hangman's noose.

A German general is paid in kind   December 1, 1945

DOSTLER FACES FIRING SQUAD. In March, 1944, General Anton Dostler ordered the shooting of fifteen American soldiers without trial when they were caught behind German lines on a mission for the Office of Strategic Services. On October 12, 1945, an American military tribunal sentenced General Dostler to "be shot to death by musketry." On December 1, in Aversa, Italy, Dostler was tied to the stake, upper picture, as a chaplain read last rites. In the lower picture, the general slumps as the bullets pierce his body and send up a shower of splinters from the stake. General Dostler was the first officer of the German General Staff to be tried by an American tribunal on a war crimes charge.

Jap die-hards surrender on Saipan   December 1, 1945

FORGOTTEN BATTLE ENDS. It was not until three months after V-J Day that Japanese Imperial Army Captain Sakae Oba and 46 of his soldiers surrendered after hiding 17 months in the coral caves and jungle of Saipan. Captain Oba gives up his Samurai sword to Lieut. Col. Howard G. Kurgis.

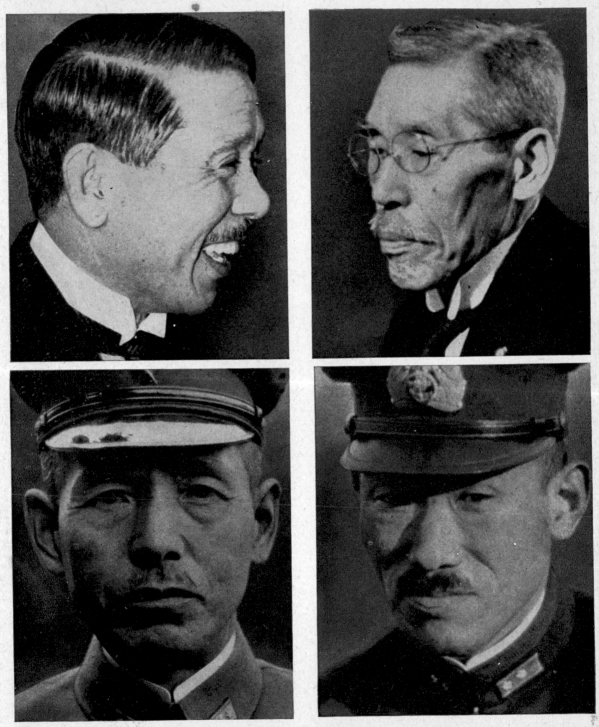

LISTED AS WAR CRIMINAL SUSPECTS. On December 2 General Douglas MacArthur's headquarters published the most extensive list of war criminals to be rounded up since V-J Day. Among the 59 high officials arrested were two former premiers, Koki Hirota (upper left), and Baron Kiichiro Hiranuma (upper right). Important military leaders on the list were Field Marshal Shunroku Hata, Commander-in-Chief of Japanese forces in China (lower left), and Admiral Sankichi Takahashi, former Chief of Staff and Commander of the Combined Fleet (lower right).

HALF A MILLION GO HOME. By December more than 500,000 Japanese living in Korea were repatriated to Japan. Japanese small fry are counted, top picture, by American officers at port, and in the lower picture, Japanese soldiers swab a dock under American supervision. Nips awaiting deportation may be seen crammed aboard ship in background.

DEPOSITED IN NEW YORK. Arriving in New York aboard the Navy transport U.S.S. General A. W. Greely, these brides were married in India by United States servicemen. The young woman at the left was a former WAAF from Aberdeen, Scotland, while the other two are from Karachi and Calcutta, India.

2148

UNRRA LENDS A HAND. These children of the war are fed, clothed, and sheltered at an Allied Commission Camp at Ancona, Italy. The camp was later turned over to the United Nations Relief and Rehabilitation Administration. It was UNRRA's task to prepare children like these to live in a remoulded Europe.

A Japanese war criminal is sentenced

YAMASHITA FACES DEATH. General Tomoyuki Yamashita, the "Tiger of Malaya," listens stonily as he is sentenced to death by hanging by the Military Commission in Manila. The death sentence climaxed weeks of appalling recitals of cruelties and atrocities committed by Japanese soldiers under Yamashita's command in the Philippines. The verdict is being pronounced by Commission President Major General Russell B. Reynolds (seated, lower left). Standing, left to right, are: Colonel Harry E. Carke, chief defense attorney; Hamamoto, interpreter; Yamashita and Major Harry D. Pratt, court interpreter.

A Nazi is hanged for killing American fliers

ONE FOR TWO. Franz Strasser, former Nazi official, is strung up for killing two American fliers who were forced down in Germany during the war. Johann Reichart, German executioner, is just visible behind him. At the far left of picture, Colonel T. N. Griffin, **U.S.** Third Army Provost Marshal, reads the charges against Strasser as other officers and a priest stand by.

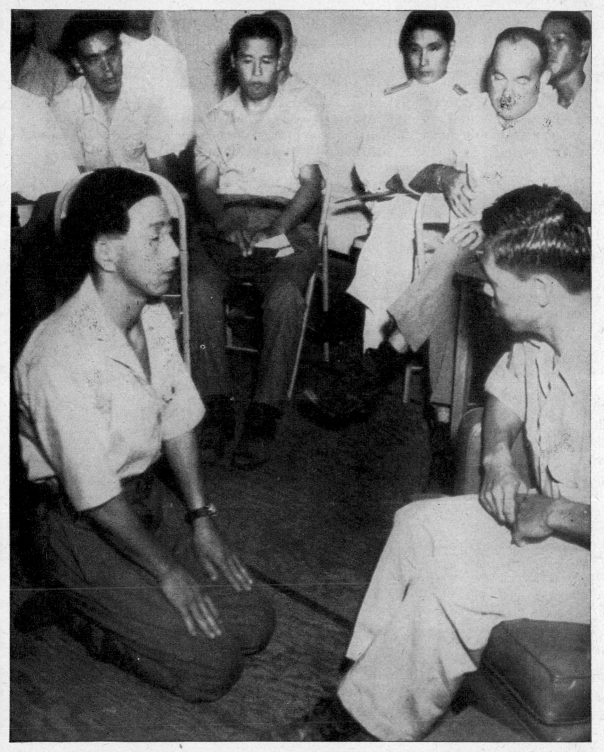

HE'LL HANG FOR IT. Japanese Warrant Officer Tatanichi Manaka illustrates the position he made members of an American B-25 crew assume to be beheaded on Mille Atoll in February, 1944. Manaka and five other Japanese officers were tried in a military court on Kwajalein Island and were sentenced to be hung for their brutal crime.

War still rages in China

COMMUNISTS AND NATIONALISTS CLASH. In Manchuria fighting was frequently on a major scale as Nationalist troops penetrated 210 miles into this region in three weeks. The page at the left shows a railway bridge which the Chinese Communist forces damaged, and, at the right, two Nationalists hold two Communists at gun's-point in Chinchow. Japanese help repair bridge at left.

General Marshall is welcomed to China   December 21, 1945

GREETED BY GENERALISSIMO AND MME. CHIANG. President Truman's special envoy to China, General George C. Marshall, was met at the Nanking airport by Chiang Kai-shek, right, and Mme. Chiang who cast protocol aside to meet the general there rather than have him brought to their residence by officials. The general's difficult task in China was to arbitrate the differences between the Chinese Nationalist and Communist leaders and to make possible a unified and strong China.

INDEPENDENCE MOVEMENT GROWS. While the Indonesians were demanding their independence of the Netherlands, strong factions in India and Indo-China were also clamoring for self rule. Above, members of the Indian National Congress Party halt train service near Calcutta by gathering on the tracks during a three-day demonstration. Below, members of the underground movement in Indo-China brandish swords and pistols in a demonstration to shake off colonial rule.

SCIENCE TAKES A NOSE DIVE. On November 23, American troops raided Japanese scientific laboratories with blow torches and explosives and devastated five costly cyclotrons which had been used in Japanese atomic research. A few days later the mutilated machinery was toted to sea, above, and dumped. The Army's purpose was to destroy the Japanese war potential; some scholars publicly lamented the loss to science.

JAP GETS FIVE YEARS' HARD LABOR. Captain Tatsuta Sotojiro, who gave the firing order in the execution of three grounded Doolittle raiders, bows low before contemptuous Captain Nielsen, Doolittle raider who escaped. The American military commission later gave a surprisingly light sentence of five years at hard labor in view of the extenuating fact that the shootings were carried out in obedience to the orders of higher officials who would be prosecuted in their turn.

A TOUGH BREAK. These soldiers were forced to remain on their ships at San Francisco because of a transportation bottleneck during the Christmas holidays. However, entertainment was provided on the pier and the boys seem to be taking the matter philosophically.

A Russian and a fräulein dance in Berlin December 25, 1945

CELEBRATE CHRISTMAS. A Soviet soldier dances the polka with a blonde, befurred German girl in central Berlin during the Christmas holiday celebration. Note the small fry in the audience of solemn-faced Germans. Celebration was held against background of war-wrecked buildings.

2161

"We want to go home"

GIs DEMONSTRATE IN PARIS. Carrying torches in a night procession along the Champs Elysées, Yanks in Paris shout, "We want to go home!" Other homesick GIs were demonstrating in Germany and in

widespread areas in the Pacific. The President and high-ranking military authorities said that demobilization was proceeding as rapidly as possible and ordered it speeded up still further.

BACK TO THE WALL. General Dwight D. Eisenhower, who led the European invasion, finds himself faced with an "emotionally upsetting" situation, as vociferous wives of service men demand the return of their husbands from overseas. As the clamor for demobilization grew, scenes like the one below also took place, with wives and children demanding "daddies" or punishment for politicians at the polls.

FIRST GENERAL ASSEMBLY CONVENES. The momentous first General Assembly of the United Nations opened in London on January 10 with 51 nations represented. The session, which lasted 37 days, was considered generally satisfactory although the General Assembly was overshadowed by the activity of the Security Council and friction between the Western Powers and Soviet Russia began almost at the outset. In a later New York meeting of the Security Council a climax was to be reached in the matter of Soviet intervention in Iran. Here, in the upper picture, are (left to right) Soviet delegation chief Andrie Vishinsky; Edward R. Stettinius, United States representative; and Ernest Bevin, Britain's Foreign Secretary. Below, the United States delegates are shown upon their arrival in England. Left to right: Senator Arthur H. Vandenberg, Stettinius, Mrs. Eleanor Roosevelt, Senator Tom Connally.

The United Nations look over some real estate

HYDE PARK CONSIDERED. Members of the United Nations site-inspection committee stand on a pleasant knoll and view the rolling country of Hyde Park on the Hudson. The neighborhood of the late President Roosevelt pleased them, but they liked Westchester more. Left to right: François Briere, France; Awyn

Elkhalidi, Iraq; Dr. Shushi Shu, China; Huntington Gilchrist, U.S.; Stoyan Gavrilovitch, Yugoslavia; Major K. S. Younger, United Kingdom; Julio A. Lacarte, Uruguay, and Georgii Saksin, Russia. The chairman of the committee, Stoyan Gavrilovitch, was pleased with "the flat land, so good for building."

LONG SILENCE IS ENDED. Major Gen. Walter C. Short, above, and Rear Admiral Husband E. Kimmel, below, the Army and Navy commanders in Hawaii when the Japanese struck at Pearl Harbor, are sworn in at the Pearl Harbor investigation for their first public opportunity to speak out in their own defense. The late Secretary of the Navy Frank Knox had put the major blame for the Pearl Harbor tragedy on their shoulders. Both commanders denied responsibility, claiming they had received inadequate warning. Other testimony brought out the fact that the Japanese code had been broken, that ample warning of war was received at least in certain quarters. Many weeks of conflicting evidence seemed to indicate that blame for the Pearl Harbor incident was a matter of confusion, misunderstanding, and lack of coordination among several high officials. No one man appeared to blame; the nation had been caught napping.

Man "reaches the moon"

RADAR MAKES CONTACT. The first man-made contact with the moon was engineered at the Evans Signal Laboratories, New Jersey, when a radar signal was beamed at the moon and bounced back in 2.4 seconds. The round-trip signal covered an estimated distance of about 450,000 miles. Lieut. Col. J. H. DeWitt, who supervised the experiment, said he and his associates knew the signal had been echoed from the moon "because there was nothing else there but the moon!" A small group of scientists visited the laboratory and verified the findings. The possibilities for exploring the solar system as well as the war-time use of the experiment were said to be incalculable. Above, the antenna used in the startling experiment. Below, a photograph of a radar scope showing start of impulses towards moon and contact with the moon at a distance calculated at 238,000 miles from the earth.

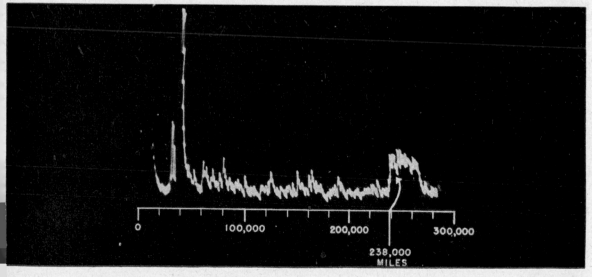

VIOLENCE FLARES. Eleven persons were reported killed and more than 400 wounded when police clashed with supporters of Subhas Chandra Bose, former leader of the Japanese-created Indian National Army. Adherents of Bose staged a demonstration in Bombay and when they were barred from the Moslem sections of the city by police mob rioting began. This was the second outbreak of followers of Bose within two months. Racial problems in India and the movement for independence from Britain were factors in the growing restlessness of the populations. Above, students in a tangle after a foray with police. Below, an Indonesian sailor hurls a basket at police.

FLEW SECRETLY. Dr. Lise Meitner, Austrian physicist whose researches contributed to the development of the atom bomb, arrived at LaGuardia Field from Hurn, England, in a plane whose passengers were kept in ignorance of her presence. On the plane's manifest her occupation was listed as "none," her nationality as "stateless," and her age as 65. She posed for photographers, above, but, asked for a statement, she said, "I really can't. I'm so awfully tired."

FLOWN BY COL. COUNCILL. Streaking from Long Beach, California, to LaGuardia Field, New York, in four hours, 13 minutes and 26 seconds, an Army P-80 jet-propelled fighter plane set a new non-stop transcontinental speed record on January 26. Colonel William H. Councill, who piloted the plane, wore an oxygen mask the whole distance and averaged about 584 miles an hour for the distance of 2,470 miles. He said that at times he reached a speed of 660 miles an hour and flew at a height of from 35,000 to 41,000 feet. Two other planes also made the trip but stopped en route to refuel. The colonel is pictured arriving in New York.

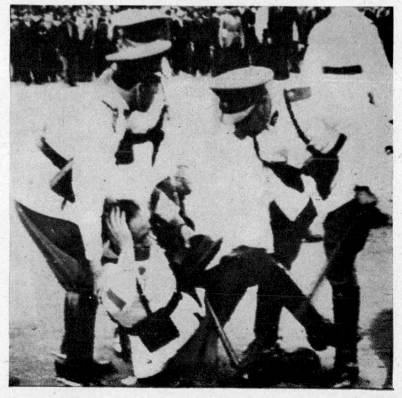

SIX KILLED IN RIOT. Victims of a bloody clash between labor demonstrators and police lie sprawled in a street in Santiago, Chile. In the lower picture, three policemen aid a fellow officer who was wounded. In all, six persons were killed in the rioting.

DUTRA SUCCEEDS VARGAS. Promising a new constitution, a democratic regime and civil rights, President Enrico Gaspar Dutra was inaugurated on February 1 to succeed Vargas as head of the Brazilian government. He is shown here with his daughter, left, and his daughter-in-law.

Homma's wife takes the stand

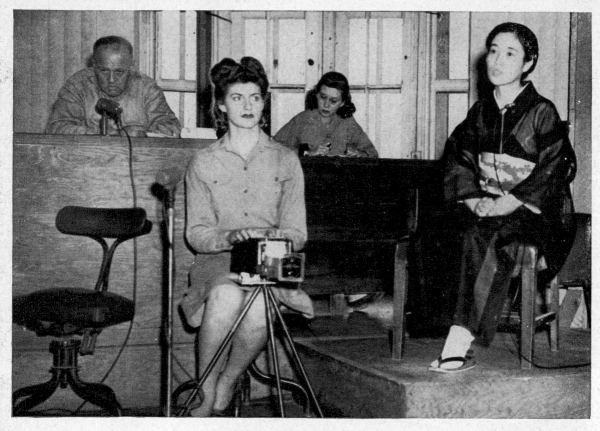

THE GENERAL WEEPS. Japanese Lieut. Gen. Masaharu Homma covers his face with a handkerchief and weeps, lower picture, as his wife testifies in his behalf, above, during his war crimes trial at Manila. The Japanese general assumed full moral responsibility for the Bataan "Death March," for which he issued the order. He was later convicted and sentenced to be shot.

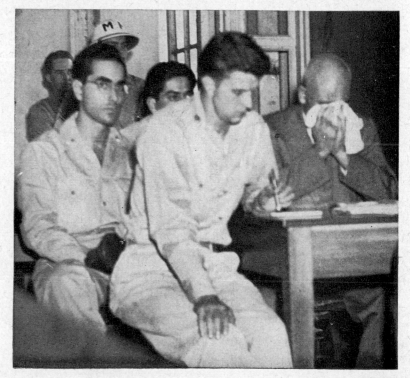

HOMMA HEARS DEATH SENTENCE. Japanese Lieut. Gen. Masaharu Homma stands before a five-man military commission in Manila and hears himself pronounced guilty of war crimes and sentenced to be "shot to death." Homma accepted full moral responsibility for the Bataan "March of Death." Flanking Homma are, left, Major J. H. Skeen, Jr., chief defense council, and on the right is Homma's interpreter. Reading the verdict is Major Gen. Basilo J. Valdes, president of the commission. Members of the prosecution staff are in the background.

America's outer defenses in the Pacific

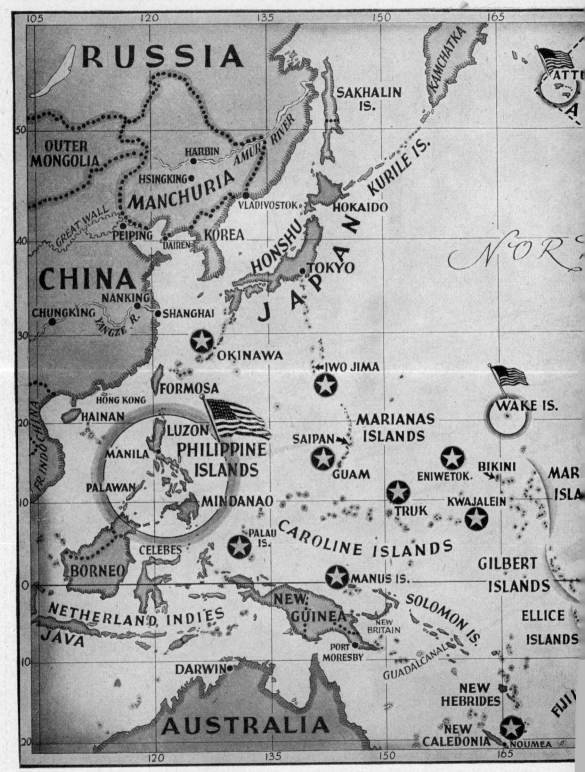

ACTUAL AND PROPOSED BASES. The enormous importance of the Pacific islands in warfare was demonstrated in the conflict with Japan, almost all of which was a battle for these islands, from Hawaii to

Jima. The future fate of many of these bases was left in doubt at the war's end. Here, definite United States bases are indicated by flags; proposed bases by stars. The Philippines later became independent.

Pope Pius XII elevates 32 prelates

February 18, 1946

CONDEMNS IMPERIALISM AS MENACE TO PEACE. For the first time in 400 years Italy became a minority in the College of Cardinals when Pope Pius XII elevated 32 prelates to be cardinals. Only four of the newly created cardinals were from Italy. Eighteen other countries were honored, including the United States with four cardinals. The Pontiff is shown in a recent portrait, above, and the United States cardinals are shown, left to right, below: Cardinal John J. Glennon of St. Louis; Cardinal Edward Mooney of Detroit; Cardinal Samuel A. Stritch of Chicago; and Cardinal Francis J. Spellman of New York. The Pope took the occasion to denounce modern imperialism as a menace to the peace of the world.

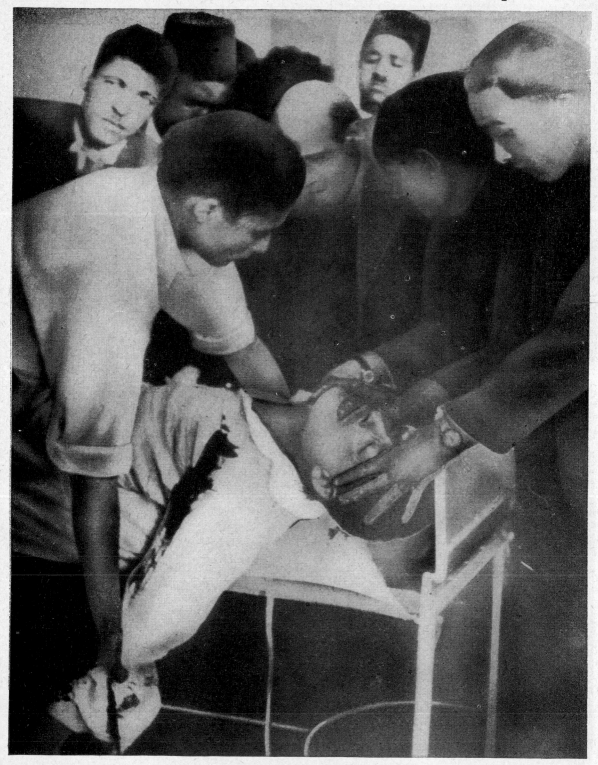

MANY KILLED AND HURT. Anti-British rioting flared in five Egyptian cities on February 21 with twelve dead and more than 100 injured. At the same time clashes occurred in Palestine and India. Above, a young Egyptian receives medical attention after being hurt in the Cairo demonstrations.

Italian war-brides arrive in the U.S.A.   February 22, 1946

BRING JUNIOR GI JOES. Italian brides of American servicemen are wreathed in smiles as they arrive in New York City. Their offspring seem to take a more serious view of the situation. In all, 412 war-brides arrived on the Army transport Algonquin. Other vessels were arriving almost daily with war-brides from England, France, Persia, India, Australia and other countries.

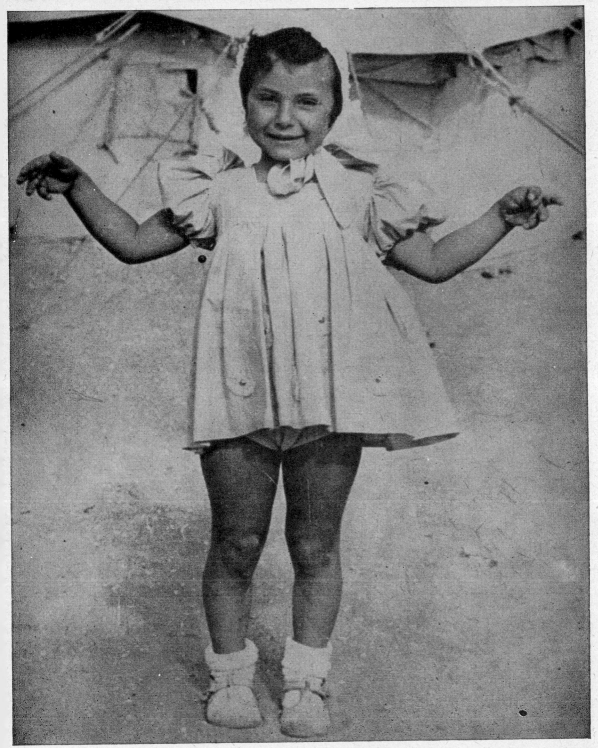

HER FIRST PARTY DRESS. A little Yugoslav girl poses proudly in her first party dress, distributed to her through the United Nations Relief and Rehabilitation Administration. Much of the clothing passed on to the destitute of Europe by UNRRA was gathered together by generous American families in drives held throughout the United States. An UNNRA camp also provides shelter for child pictured here.

"STRONG MAN BEATS TAMBORINI." Three-and-one-half million male citizens of Argentina went to the polls on February 24 to choose between Juan D. Peron (upper left picture) and Jose P. Tamborini (upper right) to succeed President Edelmiro Farrell, shown listening to election returns (below). Farrell had been a figurehead while "strong man" Peron ruled as a dictator and was accused by the American State Department of having flirted with the Nazis. The election was remarkably free of incident and, weeks later, when the returns were in it was found that the people favored Peron, labor candidate, to Tamborini, candidate of the democratic coalition. The elections were considered fair.

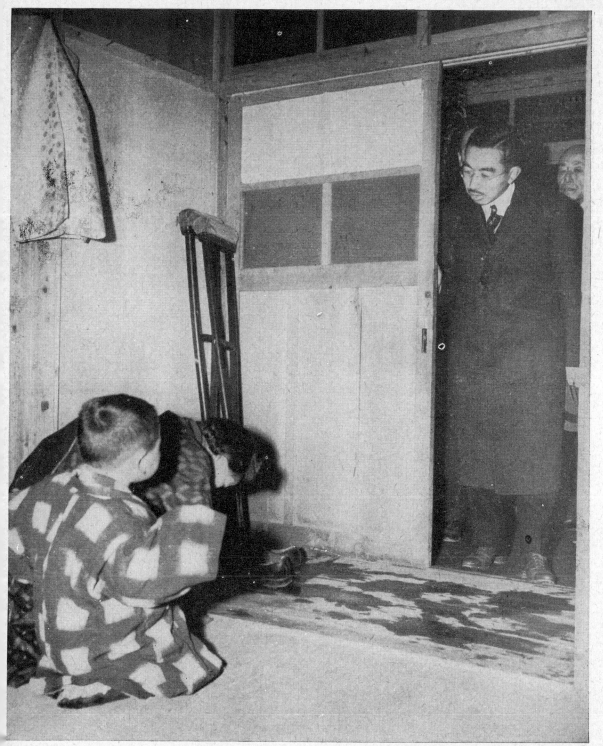

SUBJECTS BOW LOW. A mother, crippled by United States bombing raids, and her son bend low before Emperor Hirohito as he inspects new housing development for homeless Japanese in Yokohama. As the "Son of Heaven" pokes his head in the doorway, "sonny boy" raises his head in curiosity. The mother's crutches are in left hand corner of room.

Former Hungarian Premier is shot

PUNISHED FOR WAR CRIMES. Bela Imredy, former Hungarian Premier and Finance Minister stands before a firing squad, above, in the yard of Marko Jail in Budapest after being convicted for war crimes and anti-Jewish acts. Below, he is shown slumped on the ground after his execution.

FRANCE CLOSES BORDER.
On February 29 France imposed an economic boycott against Spain by closing the border (above), declaring that the Franco regime constituted a danger to international security. The matter was considered for action by the United Nations and popular demonstrations were frequent as in the lower picture. Dancer Sono Osato carries a picket sign in a New York City demonstration directed against Franco for the execution of Spanish patriots in Spain.

PICKETS AND POLICE BATTLE. By midwinter the entire nation was paralyzed by strikes. General Motors, United States Steel, General Electric (pictures on this page), Westinghouse, and many other huge industries came to a standstill, with Ford and Chrysler among the first to break the deadlock between management and labor. By spring a satisfactory formula had been worked out between most managements and labor, only to be threatened by the scuttling of the Office of Price Administration controls. The long and bitter strikes were a hardship to the laborer and his family, costly to management, and a vexation to the consumer itching to buy.

RING CHARGED WITH SUPPLYING INFORMATION TO SOVIET. A gigantic spy ring operating in Canada and the United States, was exposed when several of the suspected agents were arraigned in Ottawa, Canada. Above, left: Kathleen Wilsher, said by Canadian royal commission to have divulged secret documents to Russia. Top, right: Edward Wilfred Mazerall, electrical engineer charged with turning over to Reds confidential radar reports. Lower: Captain Cordon Lunan, left, is booked as leader of spy ring directed by Lieut. Col. Rogov of the Russian Embassy. Meanwhile, Dr. Alan Nunn May, British scientist who worked on the atomic bomb in Canada, admitted disclosing secret atomic information, but would not say to whom he gave the information.

The Russians strip Mukden industry

NEWSMEN INSPECT LOOTED FACTORY. Russian forces in Mukden, Manchuria, were reluctant to leave and when they did leave they took with them large amounts of machinery from local industries to the Soviet. Newsmen inspect one of the stripped factories, above, and Russian soldiers armed with sub-machine guns, below, walk across the main square towards a building decorated with Russian inscriptions and a portrait of Stalin. The Russians admitted taking machinery, saying they did so by Big Three agreement.

Churchill sounds off from America

MISSOURI BLAST STARTLES WORLD. Former British Prime Minister Winston Churchill, speaking as a plain British citizen traveling in America, caused an international furor when he told students of Westminster College, Fulton, Missouri, that "Nobody knows what Soviet Russia and its Communist international organization intends to do . . . or what are the limits, if any, to their expansive and proselytizing tendencies." Since Churchill made his address from the geographical heart of America and in the presence of President Truman, Russian writers criticized him bitterly. In the top picture, Churchill is shown in Fulton with President Truman, left, and in the lower picture the British war leader is shown with Mrs. Churchill, left, and their daughter, Mrs. Sarah Oliver, in New York's Hotel Waldorf-Astoria.

ITALIANS AND YUGOSLAVIANS CLASH. Trieste, with a predominantly Italian population surrounded by Yugoslavians in the hinterland, was a dangerous sore spot in Europe following the end of World War II. The Foreign Ministers' deputies agreed to a four-power commission to study the Italian-Yugoslav border area for the purpose of working out an ethnic frontier and a satisfactory disposition of Trieste, but in the meantime clashes occurred such as the one pictured here. An Italian mother of three children lies dead on a street of Trieste as the result of a skirmish with civil police after a Yugoslav flag was removed from a church.

LONG-DRAWN BATTLES END. Workers of General Motors, above, and General Electric, below, were jubilant when their long fight for an increase in wages ended with acceptable adjustments on March 13. The General Motors strike, lasting 113 days, was one of the most bitter of the reconversion period. The General Electric strike lasted 57 days.

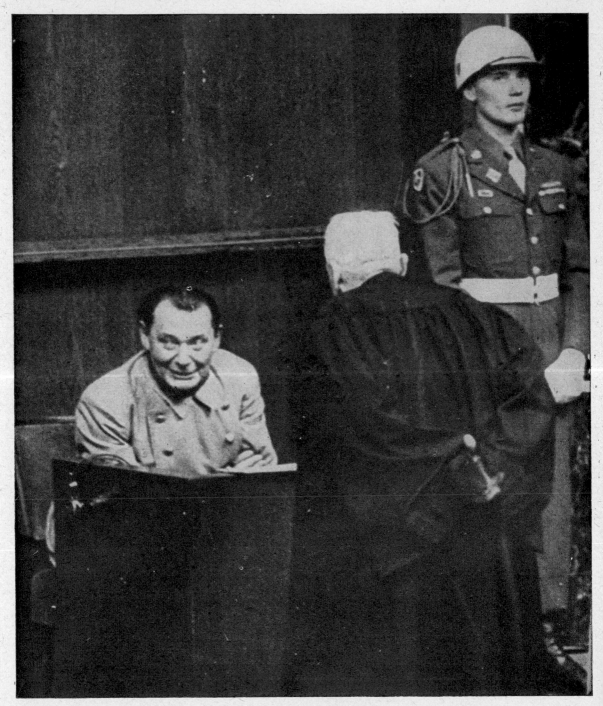

NO. 2 NAZI IS BOLD AND RESOURCEFUL. Hermann Goering proved himself a crafty and enterprising witness when he was called to the stand in the Nuremberg war crimes trial. He boldly proclaimed his Nazi beliefs and aims, proved difficult to trip when cross-examined. He calmly admitted his part in the German plan for seizing living space, but said he had not paid much attention to the master race theory, stating that one is either superior or is not. He said that he had opposed Jewish pogroms for economic reasons and because of their effect on the rest of the world. He admitted drawing up economic laws against the Jews, saying that he scorned to hide behind the Fuehrer's signature. Goering is shown here talking to his attorney, Dr. Otto Stahmer, during a court recess.

FORMER CHETNIK LEADER SEIZED. General Draja Mikhailovitch, who formed the first Yugoslav resistance to the Germans in April, 1941, was captured by Yugoslav authorities in March, 1946, and placed in jail (above) on a charge of treason and collaboration with the Germans. Later, in July, 1946, the former guerrilla leader was tried and found guilty by a Yugoslav military court and on July 17 Mikhailovitch and eight others were shot by a firing squad. The former Chetnik chieftain had been surplanted in his guerrilla efforts in 1943 by the emergence of Marshal Tito's Partisan forces.

FRITZ KUHN GOES TO WORK. The former leader of the German-American Bund, Fritz Kuhn, rustles baggage in an old castle in Asperg, Germany, where he was interned. But by April 25, Fritz Kuhn had been freed and was on his way to join his family in Munich. At the same time that Fritz was freed, General McNarney was improving the morale of American troops in Europe with a nine-point program, including longer training and an 11 P.M. curfew.

SINGS IN JAIL. "Axis Sally," whose voice over the Berlin radio exhorted Allied soldiers to give up the fight, smokes a cigarette and talks to reporters in the United States Counter-Intelligence Headquarters, Berlin, following her arrest. She was born Mildred Gillars, 37 years ago, in Portland, Maine. Note the American tissues and cigarettes in her barracks bag.

NEW YORK CITY IS HOST. The eleven-nation Security Council of the United Nations opened its first session at Hunter College in New York City on March 25. Dr. Quo Tai-Chi of China swings the gavel, above, flanked by New York's Governor Thomas E. Dewey, left, and United States Secretary of State Byrnes. Below, the "Big Three" delegates, left to right: Andrei Gromyko, Russia; Sir Alexander Cadogan, United Kingdom; Edward R. Stettinius, Jr., United States.

RUSSIA UNWILLING TO DISCUSS MATTER. Soviet troops in Iran after the agreed time for withdrawal was one of the first questions suggested for the Security Council agenda. Gromyko (above, left) voices the Russian desire to postpone discussion while (left to right) Cadogan, Stettinius and Byrnes listen. Below, Iranian Ambassador Hussein Ala, center, sits with Akbar Daftari, Iran delegate (right), and John Lord O'Brian, adviser to the delegation.

Gromyko takes a walk

LEAVES SECURITY COUNCIL.
Conflict over the Iranian problem reached a dramatic climax when Andrei Gromyko, Soviet delegate, left the meeting as it became evident that the Iranian question would be discussed over Russia's objection. Poland was the only supporter of the Russian position. Gromyko is shown marching from his position at the extreme left of the council table, while heads turn and expressions register various reactions to the Russian's startling behavior. Later, Russia agreed to evacuate her troops from Iran by a definite date; in Teheran closer economic ties were worked out between Russia and Iran; Gromyko returned to his chair in the Security Council on April 9.

LIEUTENANT IS LATER ACQUITTED. Lieut. Nicolai G. Redin of the Soviet Navy was arrested in the United States by officers of the Federal Bureau of Investigation on charges of buying secret naval information and conspiring to send it to Russia. The young Red officer is shown here with his wife, Galina. Later, on July 17, Redin was cleared by a Federal Court jury. When the verdict was delivered Redin declared, "Ladies and gentlemen of the jury and Your Honor, I'd like to thank you for this fair trial in these United States of America." Redin and his wife were free to go home to Russia.

Death erases a smile

THE LAST LAUGH. Laszlo Endre, former Under Secretary of State in Hungary, smiles broadly as he is put into position to be hung, above. But in death, below, the lips are slack and meaningless. Endre was found guilty of torture and persecution of Jews during the war as was Under Secretary Baky, hung with Endre, upper picture, left.

The war wounded overcome handicaps

ERFORM MIRACLES OF READJUSTMENT. It took heroism to face bullets; it took even more courage face life with the handicaps inflicted by battle. The wounded veterans shown on these pages were ot wanting in spirit or resourcefulness. Upper left picture: M/Sgt. Frederic Hensel, only battle casualty this war to lose parts of both arms and legs, sits behind the wheel of his new car in which he and is wife, Jewell, made a tour of the country. Lower left: Lieut. George L. Sharpnack paints with aid of a and-hook. Above: Elmer Morriss lost both legs, an arm and an eye in the Battle of the Bulge. Newspapers raised money to buy him and his wife, Velma Lee, a home and farm.

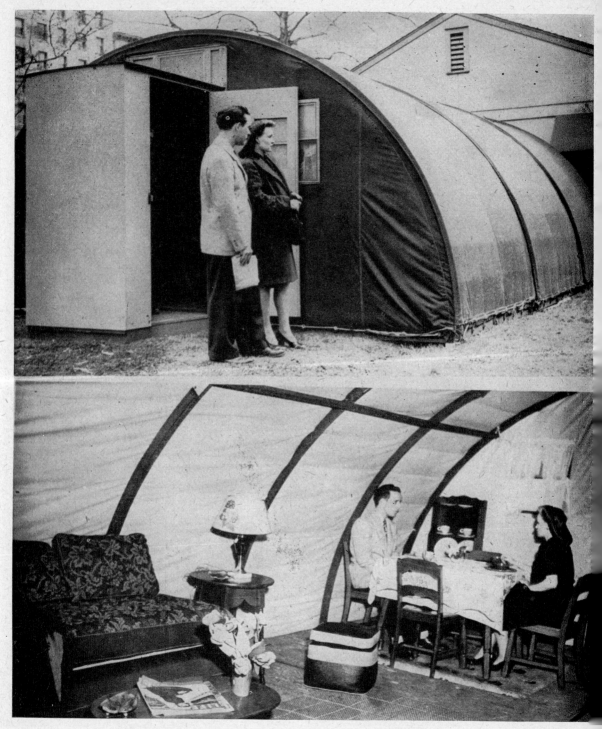

HOUSING SHORTAGE HITS GIs. Many a veteran returning from the foxholes and jungles found himself on the American streets without a roof overhead at the end of the struggle against totalitarianism. Civilians also suffered from the situation but all admitted that the veteran's housing problem amounted to a national disgrace. One makeshift remedy offered was the one-room cottage, above, consisting of a frame on which was stretched a canvas blanket containing spun glass insulation against heat and cold. Soldiers had lived in similar houses in the Arctic and the tropics.

TROLLEYS RUN IN RUBBLE. Almost a year after V-E Day, Dresden, Germany, is still a heap of rubble, most of the damage having been caused in 20 minutes by 2,000 bombers in a mass raid. But out of all the chaos, a semblance of order has been attained, with trolleys running and people boarding them to ride home from their employment amidst the heaps of stone and twisted steel.

The black market in Italy

ITALIANS LOSE THEIR TEMPERS. While black marketeers in the United States were operating in defiance of the Office of Price Administration, similar lawless operators were profiting by the lack of consumer goods in other countries. In Italy an angry crowd takes matters in its own hands by chasing down a black marketeer (arrow, above) and beating him mercilessly, below.

Roosevelt shrine is dedicated April 12, 1946

TRUMAN PAYS TRIBUTE. On the first anniversary of President Franklin Delano Roosevelt's death, crowds gathered at Hyde Park and paid homage, above. The grave-site and homestead were made a national shrine. President Truman, shown, below, with Mrs. Eleanor Roosevelt, pledged himself to fight for the late President's principles, and leaders all over the world joined in paying tribute.

Modern science comes to Bikini

NATIVES MOVE OUT. The location chosen for the most extraordinary scientific experiment in history was the primitive Pacific atoll of Bikini in the Marshall Islands. The picture at the left shows King Juda who cooperated with atom bomb authorities in moving his subjects from Bikini atoll to Rongerik atoll, 109 miles away, to be safe from the explosions of the atom bombs to be dropped in the Bikini Lagoon.

Above, King Juda's subjects are shown moving their possessions to a ship bound for new home.

FOOD FOR THOUGHT. Former President Herbert Hoover, left, is given a royal banquet by Egyptian King Farouk, right, in Cairo, while on a tour of the world's hunger areas. Hoover did not find conditions in Europe as bad as in Asia where he said that unless the world rushed supplies to the stricken peoples of India "tens of millions" would be "in jeopardy of life."

ROXAS DEFEATS OSMENA. Manuel A. Roxas, who defeated former President Osmena at the polls, to become first president of the Philippines Republic after July 4, visits this country after his election in May. He chats gaily with President Truman (left, above). With him is Paul V. McNutt, High Commissioner to the Philippines, right. Below, Maria Rosario Roxas, daughter of General Roxas, sits on a bench at Vassar College, Poughkeepsie, N. Y., where she is a student.

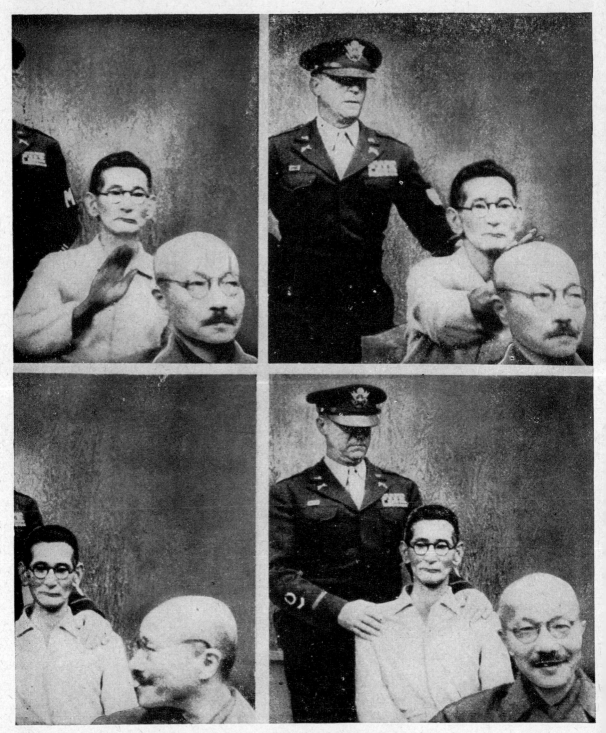

CURIOUS COMEDY AT START OF WAR CRIMES TRIAL. When Japan's wartime Premier Hideki Tojo finally came before the nine-nation International Military Tribunal for the Far East on May 3, he played an involuntary role of comedian, above, when Shumei Okawa, a co-defendant, solemnly slapped the top of his very bald head. The stern-faced former war chieftain seems to enjoy the joke at his expense. Okawa, suspected of cracking up, was taken away for observation. Tojo and twenty-five other defendants stayed to face charges of war crimes.

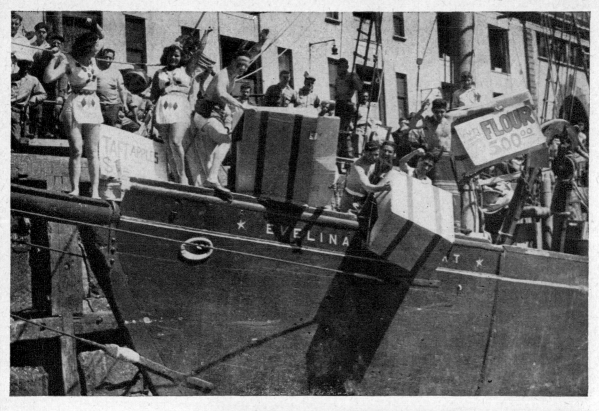

GROUPS FIGHT FOR OPA. Although the Administration favored extension of price controls to prevent inflation, Congress was doing everything it could to weaken controls. Despite demonstrations by the majority of the public for extension of the Office of Price Administration as it stood, Congress submitted such an emasculated bill to President Truman that he vetoed it, saying it was worse than no control at all. Demonstrators pictured on these pages lost their fight and OPA died on June 30. After a short period of no price control, Congress sent another compromise measure to President Truman who signed it into law as the best possible measure he could get out of an unwilling Congress. The rest was left to the future.

INVASION RELICS. Landing craft which carried Allied troops to the German-held Normandy Beach in June, 1944, lie rusting, in 1946, in their former battle positions, upper picture. In the lower picture, amphibious ducks, wrecked airplanes and other war materiel litter a field along the St. Lo-Carentan road where they were left behind by the advancing Allied armies of the great invasion.

REMOTE CONTROL TO CLICK CAMERAS. Because of the widespread and deadly effects of radioactivity, human observers would not have ringside seats for the atom bomb blasts, but would depend upon radio-controlled cameras. The remote-control cameras in the above picture were to be mounted on steel towers ringing Bikini Atoll. The drone planes, below, would fly near to the bursts, with cameras and scientific instruments gathering close-up data by radio control.

Pacific Ocean

Lagoon

South

BIKINI

BEFORE THE ATOM BLASTS. The primitive atoll of Bikini (above), flanked by the Pacific Ocean on the left and a lagoon at the right, became the Crossroads of the world's interest as the United States prepared to atom bomb Joint Task Force One in the peaceful Pacific lagoon. Below, the quiet atoll is shown before the natives abandoned it to the atom bombs.

PILOT AND BOMBARDIER START FOR PLANE. Major Woodrow P. Swancutt, left, pilot of "Dave's Dream," B-29 carrying the fatal atom bomb, leaves hangar at Kwajalein, July 1. With him is Major Harold Wood, bombardier. They dropped the bomb somewhat too high and to one side of the target ship, Nevada, but Admiral Blandy termed the mission "successful."

A single atom bomb blasts a fleet

45 VESSELS DAMAGED IN TEST "ABLE". A cloud of atomic fury bursts over Joint Task Force One, boiling up into the sky and forming a gigantic mushroom of death. This extraordinary photograph was taken from a camera mounted on a steel tower on Bikini atoll, and controlled by radio. If an observer had stood upon the seemingly peaceful beach he would have been in mortal danger from invisible radio-activity. The radio-controlled camera gives a view of the ships on the horizon flaming and smoking.

Preliminary reports showed a score of five ships sunk (two destroyers, a cruiser and two transports); nine ships heavily damaged (including two battleships); at least 45 vessels damaged. The total number of target ships was 73. Many of the test animals aboard the vessels were not immediately killed but died later and it would be weeks, perhaps even months, before the complete story would be told of an aerial atom bomb's potency against a naval fleet dispersed in a harbor area.

A movie "short" of the atomic burst

FROM FISSION TO FINISH. This moving picture sequence depicts the explosion of the first Bikini atom bomb from the moment the nuclear split-second fission detonated the bomb (upper left picture) to the

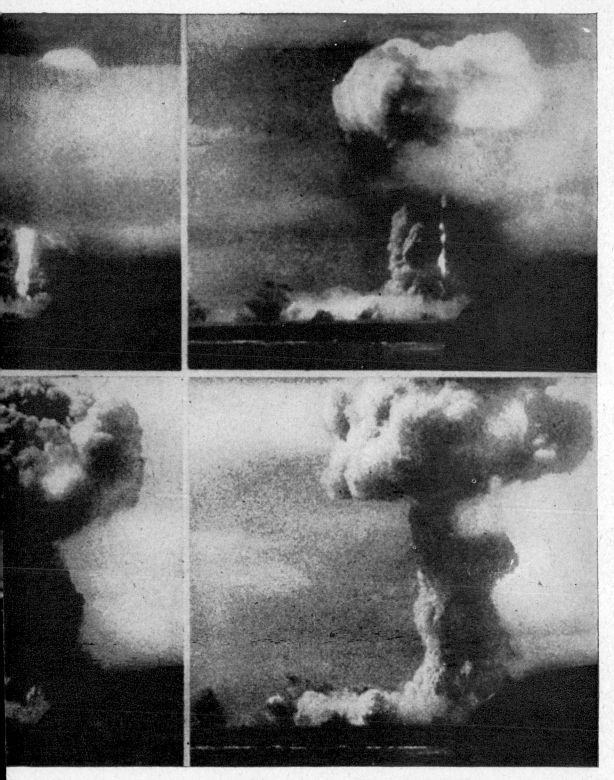

30,000 foot pillar of fiery cloud in the lower right corner. Two tremendous concussions accompanied the burst which flashed light ten thousand times brighter than the sun.

RINGSIDE SEATS ARE TEN MILES DISTANT. Although the flagship U.S.S. Mt. McKinley is a safe ten miles from Bikini, the towering atomic pillar seems to overshadow these observers on her deck. This photo was made aboard Vice Admiral W. H. P. Blandy's flagship just a few seconds after the detonation.

The Independence takes a licking

NEVADA ESCAPES. Although the target ship Nevada remained afloat after the first atom bomb at Bikini, the light aircraft carrier Independence was convulsed by internal explosions and belched fire and smoke (center, above) many hours after the bombing. The superstructure was blown off the carrier's flight deck, which was also heavily damaged, below.

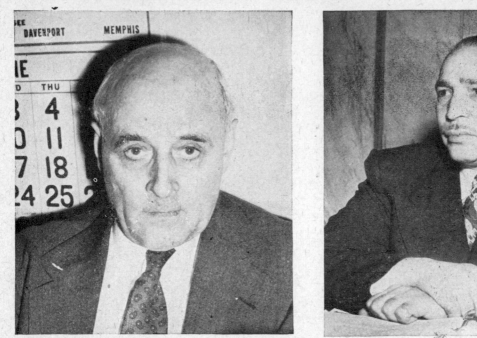

PROFITS PROBED. When the Senate War Investigating Committee took the lid off munitions profiteering, an unsavory odor was exuded. Such high figures in Washington as Representative Andrew J. May, chairman of the House Military Affairs Committee (left, above) were asked to explain their interest in huge munitions combines. May first could not find time to testify, then developed a reported illness. Henry Garsson (above, right) was a central figure in a huge industrial combine under investigation by the Mead Committee. Neither he, however, nor Benjamin F. Fields (lower left, with wife) could be procured for questioning, both standing on their constitutional rights. But pretty Jean Bates (lower right), former secretary in the munitions combine, willingly testified that she had been asked to be "hazy" on the stand. She preferred to be honest. Big names and well known companies were involved in wartime profits grab; "everybody and his brother seemed out to get the government."

The stage is set for Baker Day

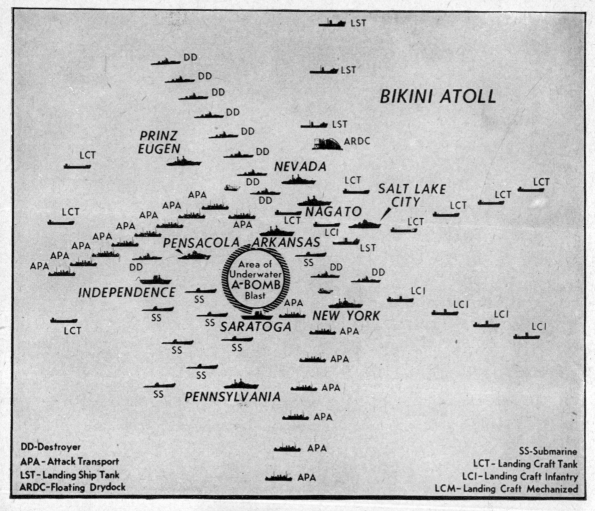

BIKINI ATOLL

LST
LST
DD
DD
DD
DD
DD
PRINZ EUGEN
LST
ARDC
LCT
DD
NEVADA
LCT
SALT LAKE CITY
LCT
LCT
DD
DD
APA
NAGATO
LCT
LCT
LCT
LCT
LCI
APA
APA
LCT
LCT
APA
APA
APA
PENSACOLA ARKANSAS
LST
APA
Area of Underwater A-BOMB Blast
SS
DD
DD
LCI
DD
SS
INDEPENDENCE
SS
LCI
LCI
LCT
SS
SS
APA
NEW YORK
LCI
SARATOGA
APA
SS
SS
APA
APA
SS
PENNSYLVANIA
APA
APA
APA
APA

DD–Destroyer
APA–Attack Transport
LST–Landing Ship Tank
ARDC–Floating Drydock

SS–Submarine
LCT–Landing Craft Tank
LCI–Landing Craft Infantry
LCM–Landing Craft Mechanized

BLANDY BROADCASTS EVENT.
The diagram, above, shows the disposition of target ships for the second Bikini atom bomb test. This time the bomb was placed under shallow water in the area indicated by circle. The dramatic event was broadcast from the U.S.S. Mt. McKinley by Admiral William H. P. Blandy, director of the experiment, below, speaking into microphone held by Sergeant Dave Simmons, of San Francisco.

The world's first underwater atom bomb explodes

GIGANTIC POISON MUSHROOM BLOOMS AT BIKINI. As the second Bikini bomb burst under wate
it sent up a huge water spout, which expanded to one half mile at its base and went seething upward

altitude of one mile. Ten warships were sent to the bottom, including the Arkansas which some observers thought caused the gap at the right side of water column, visible in this picture.

A tree grows in Bikini Lagoon

THE ATOMIC CLOUD HURTLES SKYWARD. This amazing photograph, taken by an automatic cam
on Bikini atoll, shows the underwater atomic explosion in a second stage. The mushroom effect of

...re on the previous page is now roiling up into an immense tree of lethal radioactivity, with the ...rget ships near its huge trunk beginning to become engulfed by the wave of radioactive water.

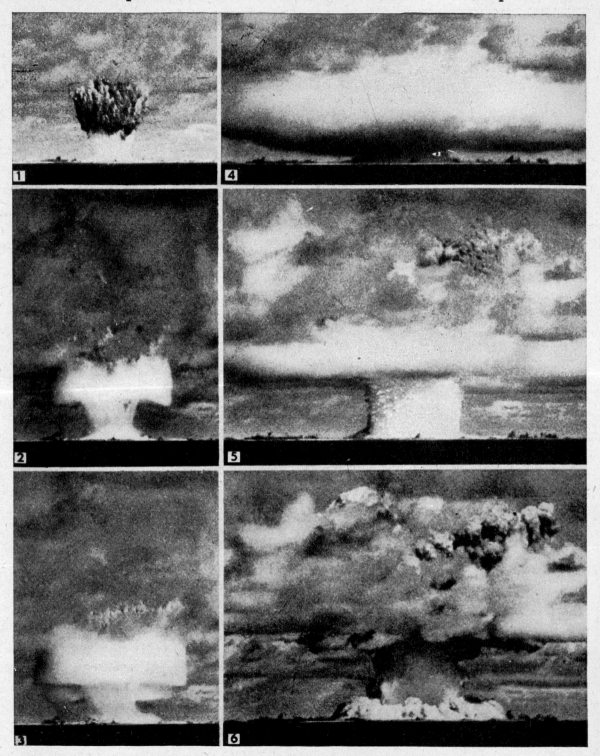

SPLIT-SECOND CATACLYSM. This remarkable series of photographs shows the development of the underwater atomic blast at Bikini from the moment of detonation (Figure 1) to the towering fury in Figure 6, only a minute fraction of a second later. The bomb used was said to be of the same type and power as the one which created such havoc at Nagasaki when exploded in the air, nearly a year earlier.

SINKS SEVEN HOURS AFTER BLAST. The U.S.S. Saratoga, her island showing (above) and her flight deck flopping over (below), goes to the bottom of Bikini Lagoon seven hours and thirty-two seconds after the underwater atomic bomb was detonated. The underwater test sank more than four times the ship tonnage destroyed by the aerial burst. Ten warships were sent to the bottom.

BYRNES ADDRESSES PARIS CONFERENCE. As the first year of victory drew to a close, 21 nations gathered at Paris to start to grapple with the peace treaties. American domestic problems had largely been settled: the wave of strikes was ended, price structures had been agreed upon, employment was at an all-time high of 60,000,000, and production had gone into high in July. Now America was turning with determination to the negotiation of a just and equitable peace. The map on the opposite page indicates the main problems to be thrashed out in the Paris Peace Conference.

Areas under debate at Paris conference   August, 1946

EUROPE'S FACE CHANGES. The Big Four peace treaty drafts, under discussion at the 21-nation Paris Peace conference, affected the shaded and numbered regions on the above map. No. 1—Finland to lose Arctic port and province of Petsamo to Russia. No. 2—Hungarian-Czech border to be restored to pre-Hitler line, Transylvania to go to Russia. No. 3—Bessarabia and Northern Bukovina to go to Russia. No. 4—Italy loses to France five small boundary areas. No. 5—Trieste and environs to be "Free Territory" under United Nations supervision, with Italy losing most of Venezia Giulia to Yugoslavia. No. 6—Bulgaria gets Southern Dobruja from Rumania. No. 7—Italy to return Dodecanese Islands to Greece.

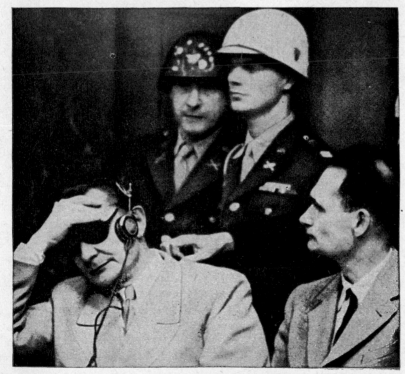

THE VERDICT IS HEARD. A general view of the courtroom as the War Crimes Tribunal read the verdict. The defendants are seated in the prisoners' box in the upper left. Below, Hermann Goering (left) rests his head on his hand and Rudolf Hess (right) stares into space as they listened to their fate.

The Nuremberg trials end

SENTENCES ARE METED OUT. The sentences imposed are listed with each defendant's name in this view of the prisoners' box, below. Rudolf Hess who is hidden behind Goering received life imprisonment. Above, Hjalmar Schacht, who was acquitted, told newsmen, "First I have no money. Second I have no ration card. Third I have no home. So where do I go?"

THE ARMY'S HANGMAN. No photographs of the hangings at Nuremberg prison were made public, the Allied Control Commission having decided that the two photographs of each of the prisoners, one clothed and one nude, should remain "top secret." Above, Master Sergeant John O. Woods of San Antonio, Texas, who was in charge of the hangings.

ANNOUNCING GOERING'S OUTWITTAL OF JUSTICE. Colonel Burton C. Andrus, Chief Security Officer at Nuremberg prison, announces that Hermann Goering committed suicide by swallowing a phial of potassium cyanide several hours before he was to be executed. An Army investigation board was immediately convened to inquire into how he obtained the poison.

PERSONALITIES
OF THE
SECOND WORLD WAR

The Big Three

THEY LED THE ALLIES. The top personalities of the Allied war effort were, for the greater part of the war, left to right (above): Marshal Joseph Stalin of Russia, President Roosevelt, and Prime Minister Winston Churchill of Great Britain. They are shown at the Teheran Conference. In the closing weeks of the war Roosevelt's death and Churchill's defeat at the polls brought two new members into the Big Three meeting at Potsdam, below. Left to right: Prime Minister Clement Attlee, President Harry S. Truman, and Marshal Stalin.

THE WAR'S NO. 1 PERSONALITY. The late President Franklin Delano Roosevelt successfully led the world's greatest nation through the hardest years of the tragic world conflict. He was denied the final victory, dying April 12, 1945, less than a month before victory in Europe and less than six months before Japan's defeat. But his work was done and a free world was grateful. There were many who disputed his politics but few who could deny the great victories at arms that were won by the American forces under the inspiring leadership of the Commander-in-Chief.

2243

Stalin turned the Nazi tide

HITLER UNDERRATED HIM. When Hitler struck his surprise blow at the mighty Soviet Union in June of 1941 the Russian armies reeled back and immense areas were overrun by the German hordes. But at Leningrad, Moscow, and Stalingrad the Russians made their famous stand and slowly, under the leadership of Marshal Joseph Stalin, the German forces were pushed back across their own frontiers and finally crushed in the very heart of their own country. Stalin—and the Russian people—had triumphed in the greatest test of arms in the history of their country.

"THERE WILL ALWAYS BE AN ENGLAND." It was Prime Minister Winston Churchill who more than any other one man inspired the British to defy, withstand, and eventually crush the Nazi onslaught against the tight little isle of England. "Winnie" is shown here wearing his fighting look in the early days of the war when France had fallen, the British had evacuated Dunkirk and the black days of the battle of London were still to be endured.

DeGaulle and the Free French

HEROES OF DEFEAT. When France fell in the early summer of 1940, Petain and others concluded with Germany what they termed "an honorable peace." But tall French General Charles DeGaulle refused to admit defeat, escaped France and formed in England an army of free Frenchmen, consisting of both men and women who wished to continue the fight against the Nazis. The general is shown, above, with a band who rallied to the standard of stricken France.

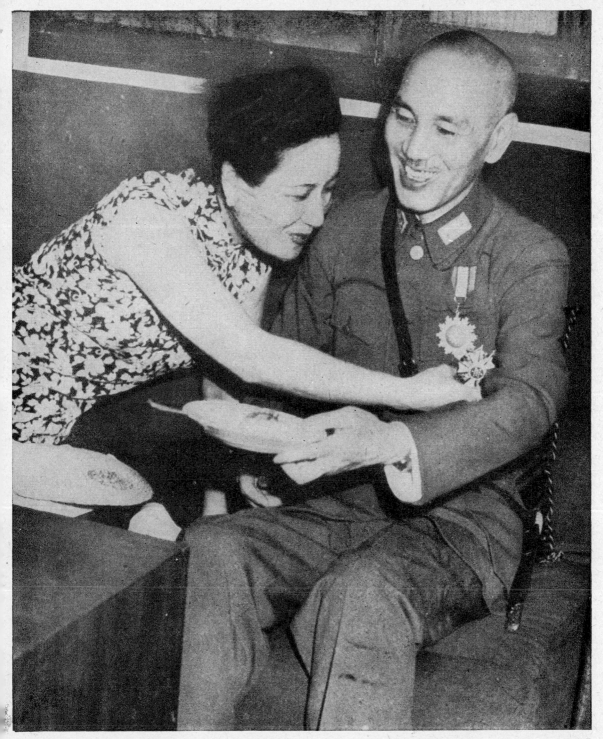

A MEDAL FOR THE LEADER. China had been embroiled with the Japanese long before the Allied entry into the war and the Chinese people had suffered tremendous hardships. China's leader was Generalissimo Chiang Kai-shek shown at lunch with Mme. Chiang, his loyal partner in China's cause. Mme. Chiang fingers a Legion of Merit medal which was presented to the smiling Generalissimo by General Joseph Stilwell, former American commander in the China, Burma, India theater.

Secretary Forrestal tours the front

SUCCEEDED KNOX. Navy Secretary James V. Forrestal, who succeeded Secretary Knox in April, 1944, tours the Marshall Islands in a jeep during the period when he was Undersecretary of the Navy. In the jeep with Forrestal is Admiral Raymond A. Spruance, center, of Fifth Fleet fame. The Marines had just occupied Namur and Roi Islands.

HE SAW THE JOB THROUGH. Secretary of War Henry L. Stimson held the important top post in the War Department from July, 1940, when the nation was mobilizing, until shortly after V-J Day when the 77-year-old Secretary resigned. He is shown here with his wife at the end of his long and arduous war job.

Admiral King and General Marshall

TOP DOGS. Admiral Ernest J. King, left, and General George C. Marshall leave the White House on June 6, 1944, after a conference with President Roosevelt on the progress of the invasion of France. Admiral King was made Commander-in-Chief of the entire U.S. Navy after the Pearl Harbor disaster to replace Admiral Husband E. Kimmel, and in 1942 he became also Chief of Naval Operations. General Marshall, Chief of Staff, served in the Army's highest post throughout the conflict.

REVIEWS PEARL HARBOR DISASTER. One week after the sneak attack on Pearl Harbor Navy Secretary Frank Knox was back from a personal inspection to tell reporters what he saw in the Hawaii area. Calmly smoking his pipe, he leans back in his chair and tells reporters that at least one battleship and five other warships were lost at Pearl Harbor. His aide, Captain Frank E. Beatty, stands beside him. Knox was appointed Secretary in June, 1940, and served until his death in April, 1944.

MacArthur returns to the Philippines

WADES ASHORE AT LEYTE. When General Douglas MacArthur's forces were driven out of the Philippines by the Japs in 1942 he said, "I shall return." Above, he is shown wading ashore with his troops as they invaded Leyte in a major amphibious operation. MacArthur is at the left and next to him is Lieut. Gen. Richard Sutherland, his aide. Below, MacArthur is shown in the early days of the war at Corregidor with Mrs. MacArthur at his side. Later they were evacuated to Australia at the President's order so that the brilliant general could direct the campaign to hit back at the Japs.

A TOUGH COMBINATION. Field Marshal Sir Bernard L. Montgomery, left, Commander of British ground forces, and General Dwight D. Eisenhower, Supreme Commander of the Allied forces in Europe, charted a path from the Normandy beachhead to the heart of Germany. General Eisenhower was the man responsible for the overall plan of the invasion forces; Monty directed the British ground forces against the Nazis.

Army Air Chief "Hap" Arnold

STAR GAZING. General Henry Harley Arnold, who moulded the Army Air Forces into the most powerful in the world, gives a five-star greeting to child admirers at an air show at the end of the war. A West Pointer, "Hap" Arnold got into aviation early and was one of the Army's first four military aviators. In World War II General Arnold brought air power to its peak.

AWARDS GOLD STAR. Fleet Admiral Chester W. Nimitz's brilliant performance as naval commander in the Pacific was recognized in special Nimitz Day ceremonies held on the White House Lawn shortly after V-J Day. President Truman, left, pins on the Gold Star award while Mrs. Nimitz smiles her pride. Nimitz took command of the Pacific Fleet after the Pearl Harbor disaster, built it up, and set it on its course towards Tokyo and victory.

General Vandegrift of the Marines

TOP DEVIL DOG. General Alexander Archer Vandegrift, Commandant of the United States Marines, is shown here in the early days of the war on Guadalcanal. The general telephones from a jungle outpost with his bayonet and rifle handy. Although Vandegrift was in his fifties he scrambled up and down cargo nets, took cover in foxholes and withstood the same battlefront hardships as his men.

HE HARRIED THE NAZIS. Early in the war years Mihailovitch was the chief Nazi stumbling block in Yugoslavia. Later, however, Marshal Josip Broz Tito emerged as the most potent proponent of guerrilla warfare in the Balkans. Tito's importance was political as well as military, for his loyalty was to Moscow and England was no longer master of the Balkans, astride the Empire life-line.

Hero worship

A BOY AND HIS GENERAL. When General Omar Bradley, United States 12th Army Group Commander, came home following the European victory a tumultuous welcome was given him. Here, a small boy sneaks between a policeman's legs and, kneeling, gets a handshake from the Great Man. After V-J Day Bradley was put at the head of the Veterans' Administration.

FORTUNATELY HE WAS WRONG. Admiral Jonas H. Ingram once predicted that it was "possible and even probable that the Germans will attempt to launch bombs against Washington." It did not take place largely because the head of the Atlantic Fleet took effective steps to prevent it. Admiral Ingram's biggest job was to get the soldiers and supplies safely across the Atlantic.

Major Bong gets Congressional Medal

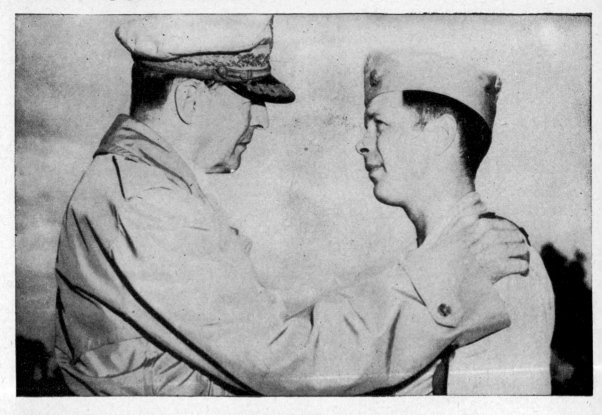

DIES IN TEST FLIGHT. General Douglas MacArthur (above, left) congratulates the Army's Pacific flying ace, Major Richard I. Bong, after presenting him with the Congressional Medal of Honor at ceremonies on an airstrip on Leyte Island in the Philippines. Major Bong led Army fighter pilots with a total of 40 Japanese planes shot down in combat. Shortly afterward in August, 1945, the youthful hero died tragically in a test flight at Burbank, California, when an army P-80 jet-propelled plane exploded. Mrs. Marjorie Bong, widow of the famous flier, poses below with sketches she made of her husband.

HE OUT-GENERALED THE GERMANS. Marshal of the Soviet Union Gregory Zhukov was the most famous of the Russian generals. It was he who directed the defense of Moscow; it was he who led the way back to Berlin. As Deputy Commander of all Soviet forces Zhukov ratified at Berlin the terms of the Nazi surrender at Rheims. He is shown here, his chest sparkling with medals, at a victory celebration in Berlin.

The Russians toss "Texas Bill"

HONOR GENERAL SIMPSON. Lieut. Gen. William Simpson of the U.S. Ninth Army is tossed in the air three times by the Russians, a signal honor in the Soviet. General Simpson led the famous Ninth Army in the conquest of Germany. When he arrived home at the end of the European victory, he was given a hug by his 87-year-old mother, Mrs. Elizabeth Hood Simpson.

Admiral Mitscher swings to safety from the Bunker Hill

SURVIVES TRAGEDY. On board ship there is no distinction between the brass and the enlisted men in combat. A Kamikaze plane does not discriminate. But Admiral Marc A. Mitscher was lucky and when two Kamikazes struck the U.S.S. Bunker Hill, taking a toll of 392 dead or missing, Mitscher was one of the fortunate ones to be swung to safety, above, in a boatswain's chair. The imperturbable Admiral wears the baseball hat which he made famous.

Chennault and Halsey

PERSONALITY PLUS. Maj. Gen. Claire Chennault, of Flying Tiger fame, left, meets Admiral William F. Halsey, of Pacific fame, for the first time at a party after V-J Day. Chennault's 14th Air Force in China and Halsey's Third Fleet exploits became legendary. It was the Third Fleet that helped rout the Japs in the Second Battle of the Philippines and pasted the Jap mainland in the summer of 1945; it was the Fourteenth Army Air Force that finally cleared the Japs from the air over China.

"VINEGAR JOE." Lieut. Gen. Joseph W. Stilwell, Commander of the American armies in the China, Burma, India theater, turned a losing battle of the jungles into a winning one for the Allies. In 1942, badly beaten by the Japs, the peppery general led the famous retreat from Burma through 140 miles of dense jungles and malaria-infested swamps. He is shown at the head of his band, above, and below he is pictured plotting a battle in 1944 when the tide was turning in favor of the Allies. With him at the right is Maj. Gen. Liao Yau Siang, Commander of one of his divisions.

The Allied boss of the Mediterranean

THE BRAINS BEHIND THE BATTLES. As Supreme Allied Commander-in-Chief in the Mediterranean, General Sir Henry Maitland Wilson was not so well known to the public as his field chiefs—Generals Alexander, Clark and others. But he was pre-eminently qualified by brains and background to control the vast theater of operations extending from Gibraltar to the Dardanelles, from Africa to the southern shores of Europe. Of an aristocratic family, Wilson was a professional soldier, trained in the tradition of Empire.

VIEWING THE ADOLF HITLER LINE. General Sir R. L. G. Alexander was the Allied Commander in Italy. His Anglo-American team was composed of General Clark's Fifth and General Sir Oliver Leese's Eighth Army. Before taking over from Eisenhower in Italy, Alexander had distinguished himself in Africa and Burma and when he took charge of the evacuation of Dunkirk he was one of the last off the beaches. Educated at Harrow and Sandhurst, he went over the top 30 times in World War I, was wounded twice.

King George and the British Second Army Commander

IN THE NORMANDY BEACHHEAD. Lieut. Gen. Sir Miles Christopher Dempsey led the British Second
Army onto the Normandy beaches, across France and into northern Germany. It was his difficult assign-
ment to hold the anchor at Caen while Bradley's forces made their spectacular breakthrough into France.
Both he and King George (shown together, above) were veterans of action in World War I.

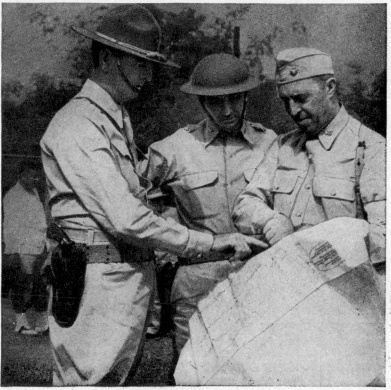

BEFORE AND AFTER. To Lieut. Gen. Jonathan Wainwright went the heartbreaking assignment of surrendering to the Japs at Corregidor in the Philippines. Following this defeat General Wainwright spent the rest of the war in Japanese prison camps. When he was rescued in August, 1945, he was gaunt and emaciated from his long ordeal. But he received a hero's welcome, above, and was presented the Congressional Medal of Honor by President Truman. The lower picture shows the general, wearing campaign hat, directing war games in the Philippines just before the Japanese attack.

"Front line general"

CLARK OF THE FIFTH. Lieut. Gen. Mark Wayne Clark's Fifth Army had in Italy one of the toughest assignments of the war. It was not until the last few days of the war that the Fifth, with the British Eighth Army, was able to push the Nazis up the Italian boot and overwhelm them in the Po Valley. The six-foot-two general is shown here touring the front lines in a jeep, one of his long legs astride a fender. Clark graduated from West Point, was wounded in World War I, and first became famous with his submarine mission to Africa to enlist the aid of French patriots prior to the invasion.

HE REFUSED DEFEAT. General Jacques LeClerc was one of the French military men who helped lift France from her defeat of 1940. He came back to Paris fighting. He is shown here as he inspected one of the units of the Second French Armored Division of which he was commander. Paris is again free and the French armor and men are drawn up in a victory celebration under the Arc de Triomphe.

Merrill and two of his Marauders

JUNGLE GENERAL. Brigadier General Frank D. Merrill was the leader of the first American infantrymen to see action in Asia. Training his forces along the lines developed by Wingate's Raiders, Merrill took his band deep into the swamps and jungles, penetrating behind the enemy and cutting his supply lines. Merrill's forces were dropped supplies by plane. Merrill is shown here, flanked by two of his aides. Later, Merrill became General Stilwell's aide.

'MISS SPARK-PLUG.'' Head woman of the United States Women's Army Corps was Colonel Oveta Culp Hobby. The wife of a newspaper publisher and former governor of Texas, Mrs. Hobby had been a lawyer and also a newspaper executive vice-president. Colleagues on the Houston Post nick-named her Miss Spark Plug. Smart, efficient Colonel Hobby's WACs served in every major battle theater.

An amphibious team watches Leyte invasion

ZERO HOUR. During the opening stage of the invasion of Leyte in the Philippines, Lieut. Gen. Walt Krueger, left, Commander of the U.S. Sixth Army, and Vice Admiral Thomas Kinkaid, Commander of th U.S. Seventh Fleet, grimly watch the action from the deck of an invasion ship. Both commanders playe an important part in the winning of the war in the Pacific.

FROM THE SOLOMONS TO SOUTHERN FRANCE. Lieut. Gen. Alexander M. Patch, a West Pointer and World War I veteran, was Commander of the United States Seventh Army which invaded southern France and then coordinated with Patton's Third Army and the French First Army in the final defeat of Germany. Patch's first battle command in World War II was in the Solomons, where he is here shown congratulating a group of Army privates who captured the first Japanese officer to be taken in the Solomons.

Jimmy Doolittle and his raiders

THE FIRST TO BOMB TOKYO. The first spectacular raid on Tokyo in April, 1942, was led personally by Colonel (later Lieut. Gen.) Jimmy Doolittle. A group of his fliers who landed in China are shown, above, outside a shelter carved from a mountainside in China. After the famous raid both the raiders and Doolittle went on to greater exploits and when the war ended all were adulated by the American public, part of which dances with the general, below, in a Chicago theater.

HELPED FREE FRANCE. The First French Army, under the command of General de Latre de Tassigny, helped roll the Germans back at the southern end of the Western Front. Here, de Tassigny, left, is shown inspecting the famous FFI Alpine Regiment. He compliments a 19-year-old farm boy as others in background sneak glances. Note that the general smokes while making inspection.

A general and his mother

HOMECOMING. General Carl Spaatz, who distinguished himself as Commanding General of the U.S. Tactical and Strategic Air Force, comes home after the victory to pin an orchid on his 87-year-old mother, Mrs. Anna Spaatz. Early in the war Spaatz had headed the Eighth Air Force and a few months after the war ended he succeeded retiring General Arnold as Chief of the Army Air Forces.

LEADERS IN WAR EFFORT. In addition to the large organization of Wacs, there were other important services in which women helped to win the war. The Women's Reserve, United States Navy (WAVES), was directed by Captain Mildred H. McAfee, USNR, upper left picture. The Director of the United States Marine Corps Women's Reserve was Colonel Ruth Cheney Streeter, upper right; Captain Dorothy C. Stratton, USCGR(W), picture at lower left, was Director of the United States Coast Guard Women's Reserve (SPARS); and Captain Sue S. Dauser (NC), lower right, was Superintendent of the United States Navy Nurse Corps.

An amphibious expert

"HOWLIN' MAD" HOLLAND SMITH. Lieut. Gen. Holland Smith laid much of the groundwork for amphibious training of American troops. But truculent Holland Smith ached for combat and got it when he was given the Central Pacific combat corps command. It was on the Pacific atolls that General Smith and his men wrote history—in the Gilberts, the Marshalls, Kwajalein, Namur, and Tarawa.

ALLIED COMMANDER IN ASIA. Admiral Lord Louis Mountbatten, an English aristocrat of royal blood, first captured the popular imagination by heading the British Commandos in the early months of World War II. He later took over in the Far East and it was he who signed the Jap surrender treaty in Singapore in September, 1945. By this treaty the Japanese southern armies in Singapore, southeast Asia and the East Indies gave up to the Allies. The admiral is shown with General Ho Yin-Chen, China's Minister of War and Chief of Staff in 1943 when Mountbatten became the new Allied Commander in South East Asia.

Portrait of a hero

CAPT. COLIN KELLY. The nation's first hero of the Second World War was Captain Colin Kelly who died a hero's death in sinking a Japanese battleship in the Philippines during the first days of the war in December, 1941. Captain Kelly's widow stands beside a portrait which later was hung in the Military Academy at West Point. The whole nation paid tribute and Captain Kelly was decorated posthumously.

BUILDERS OF MacARTHUR'S AIR POWER. To General George C. Kenney goes the major credit for building General Douglas MacArthur's huge southwest Pacific air force. Here, General Kenney, right, chats with his Deputy Chief Major Gen. Ennis Whitehead. In the First World War General Kenney enlisted as a private in the Signal Corps, later got into flying and was twice shot down.

Britain's top soldiers before Dunkirk

GORT AND IRONSIDE. General the Viscount Gort, left, and General Sir Edmund Ironside were considered England's leading military strategists when they studied this map in September, 1939. Ironside was Chief of the Imperial Defense Staff and Gort was Commander-in-Chief of the field forces. It was Gort's lot to lead the B.E.F. before the fall of France and Dunkirk. Later he was made Governor of Malta, Mediterranean island which suffered thousands of Axis air raids.

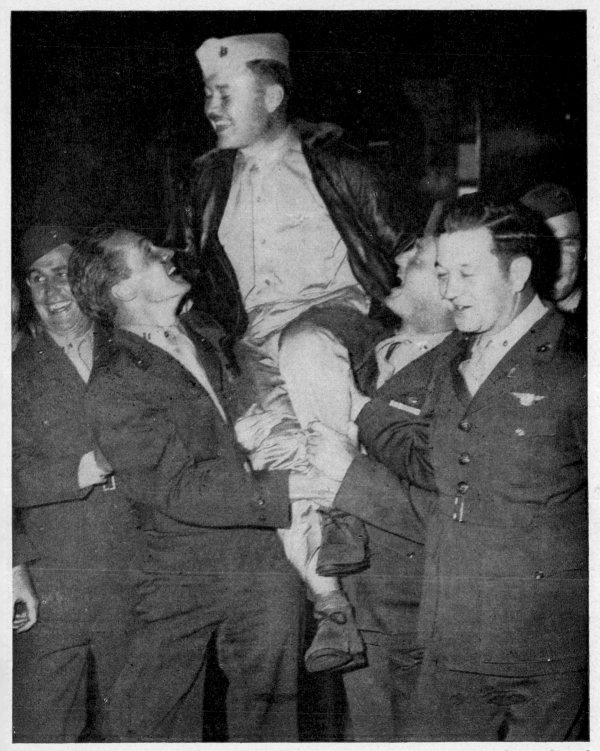

"BLACK SHEEP" WELCOME HIM. Lieut. Col. Gregory ("Pappy") Boyington is held aloft by members of his famous Black Sheep Squadron which he trained and led in battle. The occasion is Pappy's return to the States after spending 20 months in a Japanese prison camp. The famous marine flying ace got his nickname from his three small children.

An American general meets a Russian

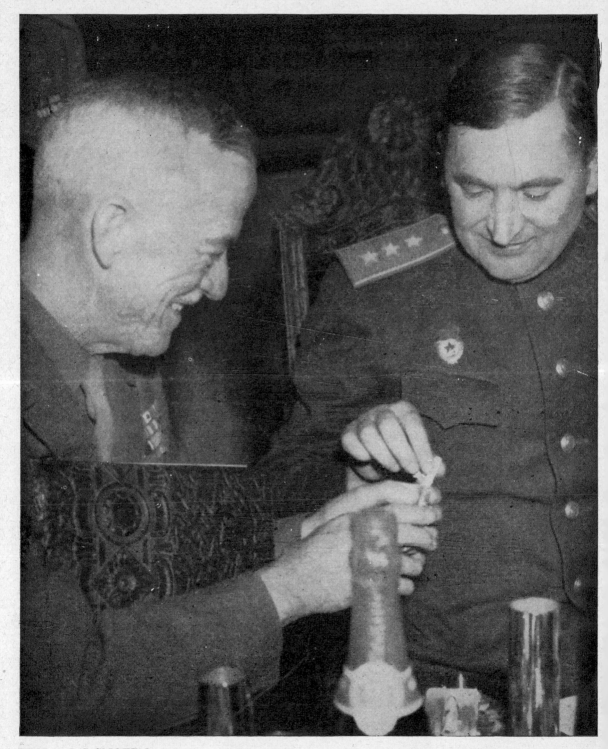

TIME FOR A SMOKE. It was a long, hard road, but now Lieut. Gen. Courtney H. Hodges, Commander of the United States First Army, and Russian General Jardov can relax and smoke as they celebrate link-up in the heart of Germany. Hodges' great First Army fought its way across France, ran head-on into von Rundstedt's counteroffensive, drove on to victory in the inner Reich.

Canadian and British leaders in France

WATCH ACTION OVER NORMANDY. In the top picture, Admiral Sir Bertram Ramsay, left, Allied Naval Commander, and Air Chief Marshal Sir Arthur Tedder, Deputy Supreme Commander, crane their necks to watch Allied planes "go over" the Normandy beaches during invasion. Ramsay and Tedder tour the beaches in a "duck." Below, Lieut. Gen. H. D. G. Crerar, Commander of the First Canadian Army, holds a dress inspection of his men in France. Crerar's Canadians played a big part in the battle against the Nazis in the northern sectors of the European battle front.

Capt. Rickenbacker survives Pacific ordeal

ADRIFT THREE WEEKS ON A RAFT. The famous flier Captain Eddie Rickenbacker drifted for 22 days in the Pacific Ocean aboard a life raft after his plane was lost while on a survey flight from Hawaii. Four others were rescued with him, three were picked up later from a small island, one perished. Rickenbacker is shown above, center, as he is helped to a jeep just after his rescue. Below, left, he is shown with Secretary of War Stimson, to whom he made a report on the ill-fated survey flight.

EXPERT IN JUNGLE WARFARE. Major Gen. Orde Charles Wingate (right, above) created a fabulous legend with his exploits in Burma during the early stages of the war there. As leader of the Imperial airborne Commando forces in Burma, he raised hob with the Japs by dropping men behind their lines to ambush and massacre when least expected. Scholar-soldier Wingate died in the Burma jungle when his plane crashed in March of 1944.

Foxhole generals

"BLOOD AND GUTS." Lieut. Gen. George S. Patton, Jr., above, follows the battle action in Africa during the early days of the war from a foxhole up front. Below, in the same theater, he is joined by Brigadier Gen. Theodore Roosevelt, Jr., left, and Major Gen. Terry Allen, center. After distinguishing himself in Africa and Italy, Patton went on to even more spectacular victories in the invasion of Europe and the routing and defeat of the Nazi armies in the west. Patton was killed as a result of an automobile accident shortly after V-J Day; General Roosevelt died of an illness before the war ended.

THEY LED THE RUSSIANS TO VICTORY. The four Marshals of the Soviet Union pictured here were the geniuses of the Russian victory. Marshals Ivan Konev (upper left) and Konstantin Rokossovsky (upper right) directed the great Russian armies in the mighty offensive which culminated in victory near Berlin. Marshal Alexander Vasilevsky (lower left) led the successful campaign in East Prussia, and Marshal S. K. Timoshenko (lower right) directed early field campaigns, later was member of General Staff.

Airman Eaker gets high honor

DEVERS PRESENTS LEGION OF MERIT. Major Gen. (later Lieut. Gen.) Ira Eaker, Commanding General of the Eighth Air Force, is awarded the Legion of Merit by Lieut. Gen. Jacob L. Devers (left). Eaker was the driving genius behind the famous Eighth Air Force's smashes against Germany. General Devers directed the Sixth Army Group in its task of helping to overwhelm Germany in the west.

TOP NEGRO OFFICER. Brigadier Gen. Benjamin O. Davis, highest ranking Negro officer in the Army, watches a Signal Corps crew in action just after the Normandy breakthrough. Negro troops and officers served valiantly in every major theater of war.

Generals watch assault on Naha

ACTION ON OKINAWA. The high ranking brass on Okinawa were often under fire and several were killed. Shown here are, left to right, Lieut. Gen. Simon Bolivar Buckner, Jr., Commanding General of the Tenth Army; Major Gen. Lemuel C. Shepherd, Commanding General of the Sixth Marine Division, and his assistant commander, Brigadier Gen. William T. Clement. From their rocky ledge they follow the movement of their troops against Okinawa's capital, Naha. Later, General Buckner was killed in action by an enemy shell fired during the final phase of the battle of Okinawa.

HE'S QUITE A DAD. Since Major Joe Foss of the Marines knocked 26 Japanese planes out of the skies it is natural for his daughter, Cheryl June, to look up to him. She's 3½ months old and they're meeting for the first time. With them is Mrs. Foss. Major Foss was the first to top Rickenbacker's World War I record. Later, Major Bong surpassed all records with 40 planes to his credit.

Carney of the Third Fleet

HALSEY'S RIGHT HAND. Rear Admiral Robert B. Carney, as Chief of Staff to the Commander of the Third Fleet, participated in some of the most important of the Pacific naval engagements. Earlier, while Chief of Staff to the Commander of the South Pacific Force, he saw action in the Solomons. He is pictured here on Bougainville talking to wounded war correspondent Rembert James (right).

A GENERAL JUMPS. Major Gen. James ("Slim Jim") Gavin led the famous 82nd Airborne Division from Sicily, Salerno, Anzio, to Normandy, Nijmegen, the Belgian Bulge. The young Brooklyn-born general would take a parachute jump as readily as his men. He is shown here, left, as he is strapped into his gear to make a jump to test wind drifts. Capt. John Thompson assists him.

Admiral Spruance of the Fifth Fleet

MIDWAY TO OKINAWA. Admiral Raymond Spruance was the skipper of a string of victories in the Pacific from his first great battle command at Midway to the final assault on Okinawa. Here, Spruance right, talks to his chief, Admiral King, at Saipan in the Marianas. Spruance achieved a reputation for toughness in battle, a toughness which sometimes cost lives but won victories.

VICEROY OF INDIA. Lord Archibald Percival Wavell, Viceroy of India, first became famous when his Imperial Army of the Nile drove the Italians out of Cyrenaica early in the war when the general outlook was dark for the Allies. In 1943 he became Viceroy of India. Wavell lost his left eye in the Ypres offensive of World War I. An Egyptian servant attends him here as he reads his morning newspaper during the African campaign. Lord Wavell also served in the Near East before the war.

Geiger of the Marines

A VETERAN CAMPAIGNER. Major Gen. Roy S. Geiger was Commander of the Marine's Third Amphibious Corps on Okinawa and was leader of the Allied Air Command in the Solomon Island campaign. He is shown here getting his bearings on Peleliu, stepping stone to Japan. When General Buckner was killed on Okinawa, Admiral Nimitz made General Geiger Commander-in-Chief of the Ryukyus forces.

OFF THE NORMANDY BEACHES. Admiral Alan G. Kirk, center, was Commander of the United States Navy Task Forces in the invasion of France. Aboard his flagship he is shown talking to one of his 20mm gun crews as H-Hour approaches. Anglo-American naval forces coordinated in the biggest and most complex invasion operation of the war.

A general at Anzio

MAPPING A WAY OUT. This picture of Major Gen. (later Lieut. Gen.) Lucian Truscott of the Fifth Arm
was censored during the touch-and-go stage of the Anzio beachhead, but when the beachhead finall
became a rear area the picture was released. Anzio was one of the hottest beaches of the war; Ital
one of the toughest theaters. General Truscott served valiantly and with distinction, later being pr
moted and shifted to the Western Front in Europe.

OOTBALL STAR COMES HOME. Lieut. Tom Harmon, former Michigan football star, survived after ailing out of a plane over the French Guiana jungles and after being missing in China for over a month. ere he is happily united with his wife, screen actress Elyse Knox, and daughter, Sharon Kristan Harmon.

GREAT
BATTLE SCENES
OF THE
SECOND WORLD WAR

"THIS IS IT." A dramatic close-up of a battle formation, this photograph takes you into the front lines along the Verde Trail in the Philippines. At the right is a machine gun position, backed by a tommygunner

and to the left, riflemen are deployed in their shallow foxholes. Members of the 32nd Division, they are exchanging fire with Japs on the next ridge. Note shattered foliage and battle smoke.

Unearthing a sniper

HIDDEN IN THE RUBBLE. In the ruins of every devastated German town, snipers lay in wait and took pot shots at the occupying forces. Here, in the rubble of Prum, Germany, riflemen of the Fourth Division scramble after a die-hard Nazi sniper.

The U.S.S. Lindsey is decapitated

REFUSES TO SINK. When the U.S.S. Lindsey was struck by two Japanese suicide planes her forward magazine exploded, shearing away the bow and leaving only twisted and jagged steel, above. Even this blow was not fatal, however, and the Lindsey was brought to port. The action took place off Okinawa on April 12, 1945, but the photograph was not released until after V-J Day.

THE LIVING PRAY. Troops stand with bowed heads as services are held for those who died in the invasion of Okinawa. Although the Okinawan campaign was unusually bitter, only about 7,000 Tenth

Army soldiers were killed, compared to some 87,000 Japanese. About 30,000 men of the Tenth Army were wounded. These figures do not include naval and air casualties of the Ryukus campaign.

IN THE BELGIAN BULGE. A Yank's gun is silhouetted against the snow as he places another clip of cartridges in position during the advance in the Houffalize sector. Two German soldiers, wearing camouflage snow suits, lie dead in the drifts. The bitter fight against von Rundstedt's sudden onslaught was made even more gruelling by the hardships of winter weather.

MOROTAI INVASION. Guns held clear of the water, infantrymen of the 31st Division wade from ships to shore during the invasion of Morotai Island, of the Palau group, in September, 1944. The small island was an easier nut to crack than its neighbor, Peleliu Island.

Casualties on Normandy beachhead

THEY SURVIVE ORDEAL. These American assault troops passed through withering fire on a Normandy beachhead and, although wounded, reached the comparative safety of the chalk cliff at their backs. Smokes and food were available for their comfort. Note the cards attached to their jackets, containing information for disposition of their cases in rear areas.

IN THE WAR'S WAY. Japanese children who were found hiding in the caves of Shuri, Okinawa, are led through the mud of the battlelines to safety behind the American lines. A marine lieutenant, attached to the 77th Division, carries the frightened baby, the other two walk demurely at his side. The Yanks gained a reputation for kindness to children in all theaters of war.

Kwajalein cafeteria

TIME OUT FOR LUNCH. One must eat, and so this infantryman on Kwajalein settles himself among the dead of the battlefield and partakes of his "C" rations. His comrade checks the action of his rifle

and both keep their heads low behind the shelter of a knocked out pillbox. The smoke of battle hangs like a pall over the shattered trees and debris.

A Liberator goes down in flames

SKY SACRIFICE. A B-24 Liberator of the U.S. Army 8th Air Force plummets to its death during an attack on the railway marshalling yards at Munster, Germany. The port wing is tearing loose as the blazing fuel tanks leave a trail of fire. Even in its death throes the German war machine was still capable of knocking out some of the heavy bombers that daily hammered Germany.

BOOBY TRAPS TOOK TOLL. A Third Army infantry man cautiously approaches a dead German soldier in the depths of the snow-covered Luxembourg forest. One of the war's most treacherous devices was the booby trap, an explosive which would be hidden in the least expected place and then detonated by any unsuspecting soldier who might run afoul of it.

2319

The blitz through France

DRIVE TOWARDS THE SEINE. When General Patton's men broke out of the Normandy pocket, infantry and armor coordinated in the lightning drive to Paris, as graphically shown here. On the approaches to

the Seine River bridge, north of Fontainebleau, France, this column is under heavy enemy fire but manages to give back better than it receives from the Nazis.

Strike three—but not out

THE BIRMINGHAM FIGHTS ON. Having survived two earlier attacks in the war, the light cruiser U.S.S. Birmingham was struck for a third time on May 4, 1945, when a Jap suicide plane plunged straight out of the sun to rip through the deck, above. This picture was not released until the end of the war. Crewmen are struggling to remove a shipmate who was killed while others fight fire with hose.

AWAY FROM WAR. His face drawn with pain, an infantryman of the 94th Division, Third Army, makes his way to an aid station in Holzerath, Germany, after being wounded in the front lines. His clothes are in shreds, probably from the impact of a shell explosion.

Infantrymen roll into Born

AN ARMY ON WHEELS. Rifles alert, 30th Division infantrymen enter Born, Germany, atop a reconnaissance car. The burning town was soon captured and the Ninth Army continued its final drive of the war to the River Elbe, last barrier before Berlin.

HOMES ARE RUINED. A white surrender flag is displayed on the shell-pocked, tightly shuttered house, above, but GIs approach warily, in fear of possible snipers or treachery. The home in the lower picture is under bombardment as two Yank infantrymen seek its shelter. Both houses are in German towns.

Little soldiers

THE BOTTOM OF THE BARREL. Towards the end of the war, Hitler's plight was made manifest by such captives as these, both under 14 years of age. The Nazis, having suffered millions of casualties, were desperate for manpower. Little more than children, these Nazis are searched by a Third Army Yank.

SNIPER HUNT. Bullets rattle in the streets of St. Malo, France, as one Yank crouches low and dashes across the road while his buddies draw a bead on a Nazi sniper. Occupation of the town was delayed several hours by German rearguard units.

Sniper hunt

IN THE FORESTS OF FRANCE. The grim business of hunting down human beings and shooting them in the wooded battlefields of the Western Front is dramatically pictured here. As two Yanks bend low and

run forward, a companion crouches by a tree and covers them with a tommygun. One Nazi has already been slain. There are two alternatives only—kill or be killed.

Scorched earth

HEAT WAVE. During the bitter struggle for "Big Apple" ridge on Okinawa, the Japanese burrowed into the earth and rocks and could only be dislodged by "heat treatments." The Japs were holed in along both sides of the sunken road, shown here. A flame-throwing tank of the 96th Division rolls through the mud, spouting flame and smoke, as an infantryman brings up the rear. In the lower picture, two marines blast their way towards Mount Suribachi on Iwo Jima.

SAIPAN SCRAMBLE. Marines in the first wave to hit the Saipan beach fall to their knees and crawl as withering enemy fire sings over their heads. One marine glances fearfully inland as they get set to take up pre-assigned positions which they must hold until additional troops are landed.

Bunker Hill casualties

TRAGEDY AT SEA. This pictrue, released weeks after the heroic fight of the U.S.S. Bunker Hill, shows only a few of the casualties suffered in the encounter with two Kamikaze planes in the Ryukyus on May

11, 1945. Total casualties were 392 dead or missing, 264 wounded. Here, the decks are still soaked with part of the millions of gallons of water used to combat flames caused by the Kamikazes.

Crash landing

MISSION COMPLETED. This B-29 Superfort made a successful strike at Tokyo but was crippled and forced to make an emergency landing on Iwo Jima. Brakes on the huge plane locked and she careened

into the flight line, plowed through four Mustang fighters and burst into flame. Two members of the crew were hospitalized for burns, two treated for minor burns, and the remainder escaped unhurt.

The drive through ruined Germany

DESOLATION. As the Allied armored columns ground deeper and deeper into Germany, scenes of desolation such as the one shown here were common. Debris litters the road, a dead German lies in the foreground. However, the victorious Yanks were frequently "softies" as attested by the wounded Nazi being given a lift on the front of the tank.

A TOUGH TARGET. Crouching behind a tree trunk, this marine on Tarawa tries to slam a bullet into one of the narrow apertures through which the Japs are sighting him. The usual debris litters the battle ground and the trees are chewed up by gunfire.

The siege of Stalingrad

BATTLE PANORAMA. One of the great epics of the war was the heroic defense of Stalingrad which marked the turning point in the German struggle with Russia. Begun in the summer of 1942, the siege lasted into February of 1943 and cost the German Sixth Army some 330,000 men. The picture here (top) shows the dogged Soviet soldiers grimly fighting amidst the wreckage of their great city. A huge force of Nazi planes battered the city on a 24-hour schedule. But the Russians held, and in October of 1942 launched a counteroffensive which by February, 1943, had hacked the Nazi forces to bits. It was Hitler's Waterloo in Russia. The lower picture shows Soviet soldiers charging under fire.

The Hornet's flight deck folds

RIPPED BY TYPHOON. Although the Japs were stung by the U.S.S. Hornet over a period of 18 months a sea, not once was the Hornet so much as hit by a single enemy bullet. It took a typhoon on June 5, 1945 to button down the lip of the carrier, above. She had already knocked out some 1,400 Jap planes and 1,270,000 tons of Jap shipping. Picture was released at end of conflict.

WASHED UP. The body of a Japanese soldier floats in the water of Tanapag Harbor, Saipan, after a futile counter-attack against American positions. The helmet is still in place, and fingers of right hand are crossed.

The British drive through Holland

ATTEMPT TO TURN SIEGFRIED LINE. British airborne troops are shown in the upper picture as they prepare to repulse the enemy which is a bare 100 yards distant. In the battle at Arnheim the British fought bravely but with initial failures. In the lower picture, the Tommies are shown advancing on Hertogen-bosch, key communication center for German troops in western Holland.

HOUSE CLEANING. An alert team of American soldiers methodically clears out the Germans from buildings in the suburbs of Duren, Germany. The bodies in the foreground attest the efficiency of the clean-up party. House in background has been sprayed with gunfire.

Last rites for Saipan heroes

SILENT SORROW. The tragedy of war is expressed in the faces of these Saipan marines as they listen to their Chaplain read last rites for their buddies who died the hard way—in battle.

ON THE DOUBLE. A soldier of the 88th Division, United States Fifth Army, dashes past burning German vehicles in a battle-scarred street of Vicenza, Italy. Although this picture was taken in April of 1945, the devastation indicates that the fighting was bitter to the very end of the Italian campaign.

A captured German photograph

TWO SHOTS FROM BEHIND. This picture, found on a German officer taken prisoner, bore no descriptive note and needs none. It is eloquent of Nazi ruthlessness and brutality.

-17s DROP EGGS. When the Russians finally drove into the heart of Berlin in the closing days of the war, they found the once great city a pile of rubble from repeated Allied air attacks such as the one shown here. B-17 Flying Fortresses of the United States Army 8th Air Force reach the smoke markers over the target area and release a cascade of bombs in unison.

Death of a tanker

FUNERAL PALL. A vast umbrella of black smoke goes up over a Pacific Fleet Train as one of its members, the oil tanker U.S.S. Mississinewa, is set aflame by enemy action. Duty aboard this type of ship was exceptionally hazardous since a single hit could turn the vessel into a raging inferno within seconds. Other ships of the Fleet Train stand helplessly by.

Yank kindness

CANDY FOR A CHILD. A bearded marine reaches through the barbed wire of an internment camp on Tinian to pass a piece of candy to a native child. GI candy won the hearts of enemy children in both the Pacific and European battle zones where American candy was a rare treat.

UNDER FIRE. The war in the Pacific was a series of beach stormings from Tarawa to Okinawa. Here, marines are shown piling ashore on Guam, above, and infantrymen are creeping up the beach of Cebu in the Philippines, below. Both beaches are under heavy enemy fire.

READY FOR DUTY. This smiling Navy flight nurse is one of the many who performed the great service of ministering to the wounded as they were borne from the battle areas by plane to rear area hospitals. She stands by the sign which designates the field from which Naval Air Transportation Service planes take off from Okinawa to hospitals in the Marianas.

ROUND-UP. In the top picture, infantrymen of the 94th Division march German prisoners through the shattered streets of Nening, Germany. The lower picture is a scene in the front lines in Belgium. Members of the 82nd Airborne Division have just clashed with a Nazi patrol, killing several of the enemy and bringing one back alive. The closeness of combat is evident in the attitudes and expressions of the men as they bend low and bring in their captive at gun-point.

Death comes close

U.S.S. LANGLEY HAS NARROW ESCAPE. Crewmen of the light carrier Langley hit the deck as a Japanese suicide plane swerves near and then is caught in the vessel's gun fire and heads harmlessly out to

sea (upper center of photo). But the crew had a hair-raising moment and one member raises his hands aloft in a mingled expression of thanksgiving and malediction on the foe.

American columns run into trouble

NAZIS FIGHT BACK IN FRANCE. The American tank and infantryman in the upper picture are seeking out an enemy machine gun nest which has opened up on them along a road near Coudray, France. Below, an American infantry column is attacked outside Brest, France. Although the German collapse in France was sudden and fast, the Nazis fought back ferociously as shown in these combat pictures.

COLUMN GOES UP IN SMOKE. As this German convoy, carrying ammunition and gasoline, retreated through France, a United States 9th Air Force P-47 Thunderbolt swooped in at deck level and sprayed the Nazis with incendiary caliber .50 bullets. One vehicle burst into flame, then another, and another, until the entire convoy is ablaze and 90 percent destroyed.

A Kamikaze strikes the U.S.S. Intrepid

INFERNO AT SEA. Although the U.S.S. Intrepid was attacked and hit four times by the Japanese, she was still in action at the end of the war. This picture, taken in November, 1944, but released months later, shows the blazing result of a strike by a Japanese suicide plane. The carrier was also struck by a torpedo during the American assault on Truk, caught a Kamikaze on its deck in October, 1944, and was again hit while operating off the Japanese homeland toward the end of the war.

LIBERATORS BOMB IWO JIMA. Phosphorus bombs, dropped by Jap Zekes, end in harmless puffs of smoke as the enemy makes a series of unsuccessful attacks on United States Army 7th Air Force Liberators. The American planes had already delivered a load of bombs to Iwo Jima, then occupied by the enemy.

Journey's end

A CEMETERY IN BOUGAINVILLE. The Second World War put American military cemeteries in the most remote corners of the earth. Here, in the jungles of Bougainville, a Navy Chaplain reads services over a

fresh grave as marines listen in grim sorrow. In this brief battle interlude the men do not bother to don shirts but the grief in their faces is no less sincere.

Phosphorus grenades sear Japs

ROUT FROM HIDING. Stubborn Japanese soldiers, hiding in a culvert near Aritao, Luzon, are showered with stinging phosphorus grenades by troops of the American 129th Regiment. Above, an infantryman fires a grenade from rifle attachment, and, below, troops wait for Japs to emerge, if still alive.

DEFENSE AGAINST ARTILLERY. Under mortar and artillery fire, infantrymen of the 94th Division, United States Third Army, dig foxholes near Kell, Germany, above. The Yanks in the lower picture are digging in on the beach after landing in southern France in the St. Tropez area.

The Russian juggernaut in Germany

SOVIET HAMMER HITS NEIDENBURG. The great miracle of the war was the Russian recovery from the German onslaught and then her own mighty counter-offensive which swept from Warsaw to Berlin in the

early months of 1945. Here, a Soviet armored column grinds into the broken town of Neidenburg in East Prussia. Fires arise from the shattered houses and the dead litter the streets.

A Jap machine gun nest is wiped out

DEATH VALLEY. Jap machine gunners sprawl dead in a ditch near Tanapag Harbor, Saipan, after a counterattack against American positions there. Guns and other equipment are scattered among the grotesque and badly mauled bodies.

AN AWKWARD MOMENT. Looking decidedly uncomfortable and frightened, a Japanese soldier comes out of hiding to give up to a GI of the Seventh Division on Okinawa. Another Jap is following right at his heels (lower left of picture). Note watch collection on Yank's wrists.

The tragedy of the U.S.S. Franklin

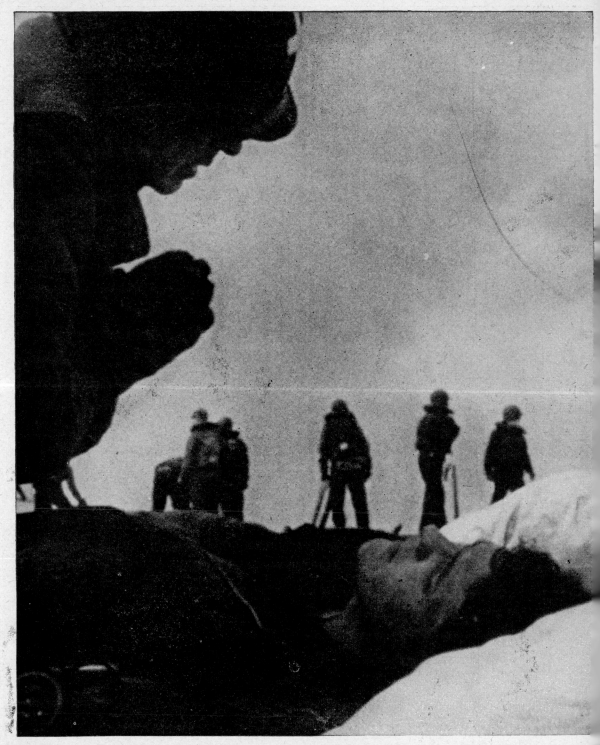

PRAYER FOR A HERO. His gloved hands pressed together, Navy Chaplain Joseph O'Callahan, Lieutenan[t] Commander (ChC), administers last rites to an injured crewman aboard the ill-fated Franklin. A Japanes[e] dive-bomber dropped two heavy bombs on the Franklin when she was operating 60 miles off the Japa[a]nese mainland on March 19, 1945. Although 832 of the crew gave their lives and 270 were wounded, th[e] ship survived and was brought 12,000 miles to the Brooklyn Navy Yard for repairs.

SIEGFRIED BASTION FALLS. British tanks move up to support infantry clearing snipers from the devastated German town of Cleve, above, strongpoint in the northern sector of the Western Wall. Lower picture shows Cleve after its capture. Formerly a picturesque medieval town with a pre-war population of nearly 25,000, Cleve was completely destroyed by the fighting and the preceding air bombardment. More than 700 R.A.F. Lancasters and Halifaxes joined the attack on the fortress town.

The U.S.S. Hazelwood limps home

HIT BY TWO KAMIKAZES. Her fires under control and her engineering plant again in operation, the destroyer U.S.S. Hazelwood begins the first leg of her journey to the States. She was hit while escorting a fast carrier striking force off Okinawa late in the evening of April 29, 1945, but the above picture was

held back by the censors until a later date. The first Kamikaze to strike succeeded in merely grazing the aftermount, but the second plunged into the superstructure creating the havoc shown here. Ten officers and 67 enlisted men were killed or missing.

Marauders smash German communications

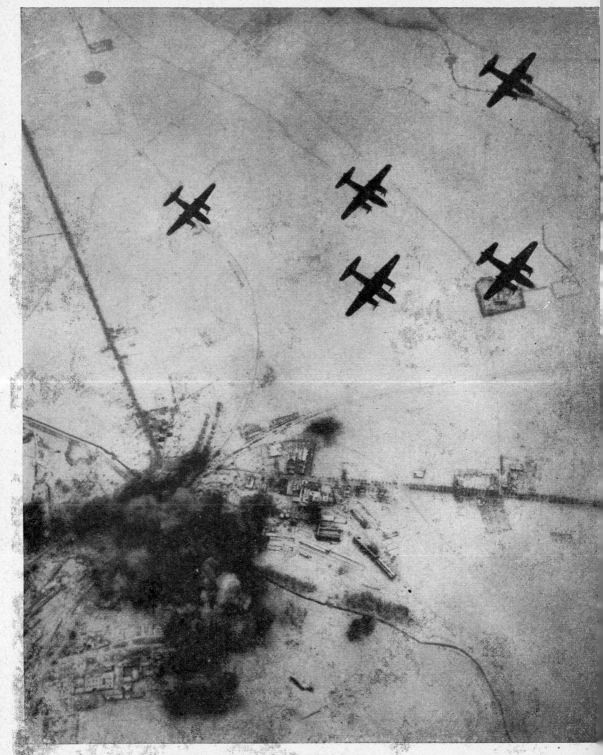

POUND MARSHALLING YARDS. The Allied round-the-clock bombing of German communications playe[d] a decisive part in the collapse of the Nazi war machine. Here, Ninth Air Force B-26 Marauders, flying i[n] precise formation, dump their eggs accurately on the important railroad bridge and marshalling yard a[t] Enskirchen, Germany. The last rail line over the Erft River was cut.

GIVE AND TAKE. Signal Corpsmen of the 100th Division, 7th Army, above, have been spotted by Nazi forward observers and are pinned to the ground by shell fire. Below, American infantrymen go into action fast, the GI at the left launching a fragmentation grenade from his rifle while his buddies lay down rifle fire against a nest of Nazis at close range.

The siege of Leningrad

RUSSIA STRIKES BACK. The seventeen months' siege of Leningrad and its subsequent breaking by the Russians was one of the great epics of the war. Soviet infantrymen are shown, top picture, as they take a German strongpoint on the Leningrad front. In the lower picture, Red soldiers appear as in a nightmare as they charge through the eerie murk of a burning battleground.

U.S.S. NEWCOMB SURVIVES FOUR HITS. Attacked by seven suicide planes and struck by four, the U.S.S. Newcomb was badly crippled while operating in the Ryukus. One Kamikaze caught the vessel amidships, tearing the gaping hole pictured here, and knocking out the steam and electric power, leaving her dead in the water. Temporary repairs by the crew enabled her to reach an advance base anchorage.

2375

A grim journey

MEDICS REMOVE WOUNDED. A victim of a handgrenade is brought back in a stretcher from the front lines on Kwajalein. The medics, members of the 7th Division, trudge through a recent battle area, still shrouded with smoke, and scarred by gunfire.

"MARCHING ALONG TOGETHER." The Second Marine Division met little opposition in its occupation of Iheya Shima, small island in the Okinawan group. In the scene above, a native girl and her baby brother watch the invaders much as they would watch a peace-time parade.

Battling in Burma

14TH ARMY ADVANCES ON RANGOON. Sikh troops go into the familiar infantry crawl as they advance cautiously on Japanese forces in a village near Pyawbwe, 22 miles southeast of Meiktila, Burma. This

drive culminated in the capture of Rangoon and the virtual end of the Burma campaign. In this picture a protective smoke screen mingles with the pall of battle.

Evicting a Jap

A TROUBLESOME TENANT.
Scouts of the 32nd Infantry Division in Northern Luzon crouch in a moment of indecision as they are fired upon from a nipa shack (picture on left hand page). Quickly organizing, they commence to sneak up on the shack through the deep weeds (picture at right). In the lower picture, the trigger-happy Jap decides to come out with his hands up.

Waiting their turn

SO FAR SO GOOD. The Yanks have made the beach and now they await the next step—inland. The marines in the upper picture are shown digging in just before the attack on Saipan. An amphibious tractor burning in the background indicates what they have already been through. The lower picture shows 3rd Division medics shortly after landing in the St. Tropez area, southern France.

BEGINNING AND END. Crouching low against a storm of enemy missiles, marines go over the top from their beachhead positions on Iwo, above. In the lower picture, a bandaged marine paces through the rows of crosses in Iwo Jima cemetery, looking for the graves of buddies who fell in battle.

Ducking shells on the Western Front

YANKS HIT THE DIRT. The GI at the extreme left, above, burrows into a pile of fertilizer, and his buddy runs for the cover of their tank as enemy shells scream over Schillingen, Germany. The lads in the lower picture are not resting—they're hoping the shells overhead do not bear their numbers.

BATTLEGROUND IS CEMETERY. Against the somber background of front-line battle, Coast Guardsmen and soldiers attend rites for their fallen comrades on Ie Shima. A Chaplain leads a service over the graves even as the smoke of battle still hangs low and threatening about them. The altar is crudely made, the grim-faced men wear battle garb and will return to the fighting after the services.

2385

Saipan beach

SUICIDE CHARGE. Dead Japanese litter the beach after a last desperate charge against American forces on July 6, 1944. While these final frenzied efforts to oust the Yanks only resulted in wholesale

slaughter, American forces also paid dearly, suffering an estimated 10,000 casualties which was considerably more than the enemy's toll of an estimated 1,500 troops killed.

The Red Army in Austria

ATTACK NAZI SATELLITE. The German-Russo front extended from the Baltic to the Balkans and an important part of the Red counter-offensive was the drive into Austria. Here, Soviet infantrymen supported by mammoth tanks, attack German positions in an Austrian farming district.

The war's path through France

TOWNS CRUMBLE AND BURN.
France not only suffered occupation by the enemy, but saw the course of battle pass through many of her towns, sometimes more than once. A small town on the Western Front is practically obliterated, above. A soldier lies dead in the street, a baby carriage is knocked over (right, background). The little Alsatian village, below, burns furiously from an artillery hit. The French First Army eventually had the satisfaction of helping to chase the Germans off French soil.

DEMOLITION CHARGES USED. Besides using handgrenades and flame-throwers to coax the Japs out of their caves and dugouts, the Yanks also used demolition charges as shown here on Saipan, above, and Guam, below. In the upper picture, note marine crouched in foxhole, extreme lower left of picture.

A Japanese tomb

JAPS RETURN TO ANCESTORS. This rugged concrete tomb served as a pillbox as well as last resting place for die-hard Japs on Okinawa. GI at extreme left sneaks cautiously upon the entrance from a side

angle while another crouches directly before the entrance with his sights leveled and ready for signs of the enemy. Men at upper right stand ready to cover the action. Note bodies in center of picture.

Moving up

TARAWA AIRSTRIP IS RINGED. Crouching and crawling in the sand, marines take shelter behind enemy pillboxes before advancing in the smoke and fire of battle toward the Jap airfield on Tarawa.

Medics save the wounded

ADMINISTER FIRST AID IN THE FIELD. An infantryman who fell in the Huertgen Forest, Germany, is treated by medics of the 4th Infantry Division, above, and in the picture below, medics of the 94th Division aid a soldier whose leg was cut off by shrapnel during the advance on Kell, Germany.

The U.S.S. Hancock survives "one-two punch"

VICTIM OF FREAK HIT. Crewmen of the U.S.S. Hancock pour water on the blazing deck after the carrier was crippled in a novel manner off Okinawa on April 7, 1945. A Japanese plane dropped a bomb on the Hancock, was then caught in the blast of its own bomb, and cartwheeled into a group of Navy planes on the after deck. One of the ruined planes is shown, below, and the furiously blazing Hancock is pictured, above. Since the carrier was miraculously back in action within four hours, these pictures were not released until the war's end. The toll of the Hancock was 29 killed, 35 missing, and 76 wounded.

Foxhole finish

A BITTER END. Foxholes often furnished a safe refuge in World War II but they were far from invulnerable. Both Japanese and American soldiers lie sprawled in the slit-trench on Guam, shown in the picture

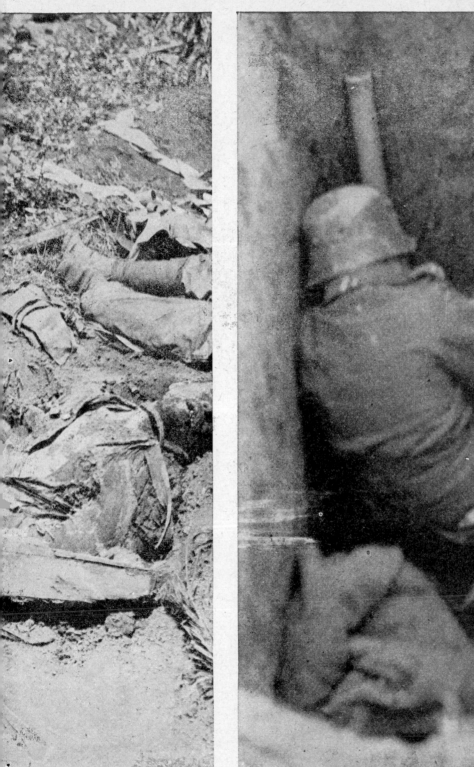

at the left. At the right, a Nazi bazookaman was killed in his foxhole near Windischleuba, Germany, by 6th Armored Division infantrymen.

The U.S.S. Maryland is hit

SILHOUETTE OF DISTRESS. A billow of smoke and a shower of fire are disgorged from the U.S.S Maryland as she takes a blow from a Kamikaze off Okinawa on April 7, 1945. Eleven men were killed six missing, and 36 wounded—but the ship continued to fight. Picture was held up by censors.

IT'S A STRIKE. Like a huge bird, a 12th Air Force B-25 swoops low in the Brenner Pass to drop its eggs flush on a railroad bridge near Dogna, Italy. Although the Allies continuously pounded the Nazi supply arteries in the north of Italy, the German armies held out for many bitter months, and the Allied progress up the Italian boot was slow and costly.

Cheating Davy Jones

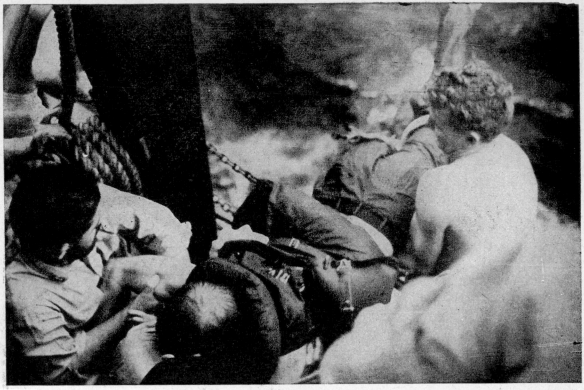

OUT OF THE DEEP. In the upper picture, one of twenty men, who were blown off the deck of the U.S.S. Houston, is hoisted aboard the destroyer Stephen Potter. The Houston, struck by two aerial torpedoes off Formosa in October, 1944, nevertheless made anchorage. The oil-smeared men, below, head for shore in a landing boat after being rescued from the U.S.S. Coolidge.

PHILIPPINE SEA CASUALTY. The United States Navy won a great victory in the Second Battle of the Philippine Sea in October, 1944. One of our few losses was the escort carrier U.S.S. St. Lo which burst into flames, above, and sunk after an attack by enemy planes.

An American column is shelled in Germany

THE NAZIS STRIKE BACK. American vehicles burn furiously on the road to Dusseldorf, Germany, after running into a German counter attack near Krefeld. Note the trench systems in the foreground and upper center. Although the Allied blitz into Germany was spectacularly successful, the Nazis were still capable of dealing out punishment as shown by this picture.

Putting the handcuffs on German U-boats

SUBS COME UP FOR AIR. At the end of the war in May, 1945, the first German submarine to surrender to the British Navy was the U.249, above, shown as its captured crew boards a British ship at Portland Harbor. Below, a German submarine surrenders to the U.S. Navy. During the rest of the month the greatest U-boat roundup of the war was carried out by both the Royal and the United States Navy.

Kamikazes catch carriers

CAUSE HAVOC. The disastrous effects of Jap suicide strikes are shown by these photographs of the U.S.S. Essex, above, and the U.S.S. Enterprise, below, each shown just after receiving hits amidships. Although separate incidents, the pictures are remarkably similar since both are carriers, both took Kamikaze blows. Pictures were held back until the end of the war, although the Essex action occurred in November, 1944, the Enterprise action in May of 1945, during the Okinawa campaign.

HEROES OF SALERNO. The battle of Salerno was one of the bloodiest engagements of the war. Fifth Army men who paid the price of victory are shown in the upper picture as a burial detail prepares graves which will be marked by crosses, placed temporarily on bodies. American casualties in the lower picture were caused when German bombers knocked out a half-track in which the men were riding.

British and American troops cross the Rhine

OPERATION IS ON A VAST SCALE. The combined airborne and amphibious crossings of the Rhine River in the vicinity of Wesel on March 24, 1945, was the greatest military operation since D-Day. British, Canadian, and American troops of the 21st Army Group under Field Marshal Montgomery combined in the vast push across the last natural barrier in the west. The upper picture shows paratroopers just after landing East of the Rhine and a huge glider nosing down for a landing. Lower picture shows a British regiment after crossing the river in "Buffaloes."

GERMANS ARE HALTED. The great German counter-offensive in Belgium came to a halt at the end of December, 1944, when the weather cleared and the Allies were able to throw in huge air forces against von Rundstedt's men. Above, U.S. Army engineers hit the road as they blow up a German pillbox. Below, dead German in a wood near Liesneux. Note vehicles in background.

Across the steppes of Russia

RETURN TRIP. Red soldiers pursue the Nazis back across the vast steppes which the Germans invaded early in the war. But in the winter of 1944 the Russians had the upper hand and they are shown here attacking in open terrain, above, and during a night operation, below. In the upper picture, bodies in the ditch are German soldiers.

AIRDROME IS BLASTED. B-24 Liberator bombers of Major Gen. Nathan F. Twining's 15th Air Force leave the Budapest-Tokal airdrome in Hungary a cloud of smoke after dropping their bombs on the Nazi-held base. Bombings of central Europe were an important part of the Allied overall strategy.

The assault on Iwo

DIGGING IN. As enemy fire sweeps the beach from Mt. Suribachi in the background, marines burrow into the volcanic sand of Iwo Jima. Equipment and supplies are being unloaded from landing craft which are under heavy enemy fire.

A mortar squad harasses the enemy

LAYS DOWN RAPID FIRE. A United States Army mortar squad ducks as it lets go a heavy shell at the Nazis in France. Entire pile of ammunition shown in foreground was fired within a few minutes after picture was taken. Note rifles stacked near at hand for instant use. In the lower picture, an infantryman dashes through a shattered orchard, still under fire, in Tittingen, Germany.

EVERYTHING GOES. Infantrymen of the 77th Division, above, use a Browning Automatic rifle, mortar fire and a rifle grenade against Japs along an escarpment on southern Okinawa. In the lower picture, marines on the beach of Tarawa start out on a patrol while buddies in background wait their turn.

Battling for the Marne

WORLD WAR II VERSION. Camouflaged tanks, upper picture, move into position to protect a bridge across the Marne River in France while infantrymen dash for cover from German sniper fire which rings about them from the other side of the river. But in World War II the Marne was quickly left behind and troops raced on to Germany where they fought the enemy in his own towns, lower picture.

ITALIAN PORT CAUGHT BY SURPRISE. American cargo vessels in the Italian port of Bari, on the Adriatic Sea, blaze fiercely after a surprise German bombing attack on the dawn of December 2, 1943. Secretary of War Stimson disclosed that the raid cost the Allies 17 cargo vessels, including five American ships, and 1,000 casualties. Losses were ascribed to lack of fighter protection.

The Nazis are routed from Brest

U-BOAT BASE FALLS. The Germans in the French town of Brest held out for 46 days before the siege was broken on September 19, 1944. In the upper picture, a United States tank destroyer fires point-blank range to clear a side street. Bottom picture shows German women among prisoner haul.

BRITISH TOMMY CARES FOR DEAD BUDDY. A British soldier shovels dirt on the body of his dead comrade to put out a fire which started when a sniper's bullet hit a phosphorus grenade he was carrying. In the lower picture, German snipers are caught by United States combat engineers, after the snipers had fired upon them in a wood near the Roer River where the Yanks had been repairing a bridge.

Opposition is fierce on Peleliu

LAST BARRIER TO PHILIP-
PINES. Peleliu, in the Angaur
group of islands, put up stiff
opposition since it was the last
obstacle to the return to the Philippines, only 300 miles away.
Die-hard Japs, in the upper picture, have holed up in a dugout
and refuse to come out. The marines later had to blast them
with phosphorus grenades. In
the lower picture, an American
soldier has been wounded and
is given a drink of scarce water
from a buddy's canteen.

The Infantry attacks a German town

ADVANCES ON LINDFORT. Troops of the 35th Division, United States Ninth Army, crouch low along the road to Lindfort, Germany (above), in preparation for an assault on the town. Other troops of the same outfit, below, move across an open field towards the same objective. These forces have just captured Rhineberg, Germany, and Lindfort is next on their timetable.

STORMING THE NORMANDY BEACH. This is what the German-held coast of France looked like to Allied soldiers as they swarmed from their landing barges in the face of fierce enemy fire on June 6, 1944.

Heavily loaded with their combat and field equipment, the men wade waist-deep through the water toward the smoke-shrouded, battle-strewn shore.

All quiet on this front

A JAP RESTS IN PEACE. A United States Army captain peers into the jungle lair of a Japanese soldier who has been killed during the fighting in the northern part of Luzon in the Philippines. Note the clips of cartridges scattered in the lower right corner of picture.

WINTER WAR. The long, severe Russian winters were a hardship to the Nazis, whereas the Soviet Army prepared especially for that condition. Here, Russian guardsmen are shown in the winter of 1942, operating against the Nazis on the Ukrainian front. Above, they wear snow-suits as they battle for a key height. Below, a patrol has killed a Nazi sentry and is firing on other opposition.

Injured survivors of the U.S.S. Indianapolis

MERCY SHIP. A landing craft takes injured survivors of the U.S.S. Indianapolis to Peleliu for hospitalization. The cruiser was sunk by enemy action in the Philippine Sea after delivering atomic bomb materials to Guam from the United States. There were 1,196 casualties.

A COUPLE OF TOUGH GUYS. These Yanks mean business. One prepares to toss a handgrenade at the Japs while the other holds his carbine alert as he gets set to take forward a bandoleer of ammunition.

2427

A Coast Guardsman sacrifices his life

KILLED AT BATTLE STATION. The bitter price of victory is epitomized in the twisted body of this Coast Guardsman, killed at his post when his ship was smashed by enemy action.

CASUALTIES LEAVE THE BATTLE. A Tarawa marine, who went over the top to get the enemy, is pulled back to the protection of the sea-wall after being wounded, top picture. A stretcher case, below, is taken along the Tarawa beach to a landing craft to be evacuated to a hospital. In the lower right corner of picture, note the legs of another casualty.

Fighting in the villages of Russia

DISLODGING THE NAZI INVADERS. Red infantrymen are shown in these pictures as they battle from house to house to clear the Germans from two of the many villages which were overrun early in the war. In the lower picture, a Soviet nurse dresses the wound of a Red infantryman.

A JAP AND A NAZI GIVE UP. The wounded Japanese soldier in the upper picture had to be blasted from the Agriculture Building in Manila and then carried bodily from the ruins by tanks of the First Cavalry Division. The Nazi, in the lower picture, comes out of a Maginot fort with his hands behind his head as a GI menaces him with his rifle. Combat engineers closed passages from one Maginot fort to another by setting off explosives.

WEAPONS
OF THE
SECOND WORLD WAR

PAPER BALLOONS WERE IN-EFFECTUAL. In a fantastic and futile effort to retaliate for the bombing of Tokyo, the Japanese released against the United States 9,000 free-flying paper balloons bearing incendiaries and bombs and costing approximately $18,000,000. Only a small portion of these reached our shores, killing six people, and starting small grass fires. One of the balloons which didn't explode is shown in the air, left. It has an inflated diameter of 33 feet. Since the balloons were not directed at specific targets but simply set adrift at the general area of North America, many of them came to roost harmlessly in trees, above. Below are shown an anti-personnel bomb, left, and an incendiary, right, which were carried by a paper balloon which fell in Western Canada. A number of the balloons were found in the ocean.

The "world's biggest bomb"

ALREADY OBSOLETE. This huge 45,000-pound bomb dwarfs the 500-pounder and the man standing beside it. Described as the "world's biggest bomb," its use was made unnecessary by the terrible force of the atom bomb, described by some as "small as a baseball." However large the atom bomb may be, its destructive force makes even this 45,000-pounder seem puny indeed.

RADAR PLOTS THE BATTLE. This dramatic photograph was taken in the radar plot room of an Essex class aircraft carrier during operations in the China Sea in December, 1944. Radar, an electronic device which throws out beams which locate objects, was a major weapon of World War II. It provided detection of airborne and surface objects, through fog and darkness, and greatly increased the accuracy of fire control and the safety of navigation.

The Navy unveils its deadly "bat" bomb

UNCANNY BOMB TOOK TOLL OF JAPS. Three months after V-J Day the Navy revealed a weird bomb which was directed to its objectives by radar and in the last year of the war took an immense toll of Japanese shipping. The 12-foot radar-guided bomb would follow its target despite evasive maneuvers, operating on much the same principle as a live bat which emits a short pulse of sound and directs itself by the echoes. The flying bombs were carried by large Privateer patrol bombers, one under each wing, above. Below, the bomb is shown as it is hoisted into position under the wing of the patrol plane.

THE JAP BID TO TURN THE TIDE. Kamikaze or suicide planes were the most desperate weapons the Japanese resorted to in their frenzied effort to stop the American advance toward Tokyo. The Kamikazes, first used on a big scale during the Second Battle of the Philippine Sea, would crash into their targets, pilot and all. Their use reached a peak during the Okinawa campaign. Here a Jap plane is shown as it misses its suicide plunge toward the U.S.S. Sangamon.

A Jap acts as direction finder for Marines

GUIDES STRIKE AGAINST HIS OWN COMMAND. In warfare, expediency often determines the weapon, and when Japanese Lieutenant Wada volunteered to lead marine fliers to secret Japanese headquarters in the Mindanao jungles, the Marines quickly accepted. Here, Wada scans terrain and gives directions for locating the long-sought 100th Japanese Army Division Headquarters. Wada was captured after living an animal existence on the island of Mindanao in the Philippines.

OPERATES ON NEW PRINCIPLE. A new type navigator, operating on a principle radically different from radar, was used for the first time on D-Day, guiding the flotillas of minesweepers and then directing the first landing craft to their exact destinations on the Normandy coast. This simplified navigator, weighing only 30 pounds, was developed by the British. It is a complete radio navigational system operating on the low frequency continuous wave carriers of synchronized transmitting stations, rather than on the high frequency carriers used by radar systems and subject to inaccuracies and complications. In the top picture, the pilot simply consults two dials which are easily interpreted by a grid map. The use of this navigator can be learned in a few minutes. Below, its use is shown in a small boat. A long 1,100-mile flight was made from England to Gibraltar, bringing the plane directly over the rock, so accurate is this simplified new system.

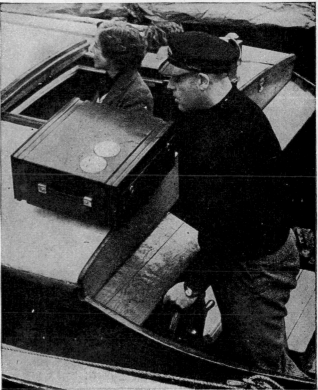

Rubber decoys hoaxed Hitler

"GHOST ARMY" HAUNTED NAZIS. Rubber landing craft, guns, tanks, planes and even men were set up at night by specially trained units to resemble real armies and fool the Nazis, the War Department revealed. These simulated forces would cover weak spots while real divisions would move forward against the enemy. The phony weapons shown here are made of inflated pneumatic tubes and painted fabrics. The enemy could not tell them from the real thing from the air or ground even at a few hundred yards' distance.

A Bofors gun blasts Nazi ground targets

ANTI-AIRCRAFT GUN IS GROUNDED. Towards the end of the war the Luftwaffe became so scarce that many anti-aircraft units turned their artillery from the sky to the ground. The versatile 40mm Bofors gun, shown here, kicks up a cloud of smoke as it strikes at a Nazi ground unit.

TERROR WEAPON. The famous German secret weapon, the V-2 rocket, was directed against England and the channel ports of northern Europe late in the war. Erratic in aim, it was still the most amazing innovation to come out of Germany's experimentation with new weapons. It is pictured here as it leaves Cuxhaven, Germany, bound for a target 150 miles away in the North Sea. For American experiments with the weapon after the war, see the chronological section of this volume.

A handgrenade is tossed to the Japs

CLOSE COMBAT WEAPON. A marine winds up to sling a handgrenade at an enemy pillbox on Tarawa. The handgrenade, a weapon of World War I, more than held its own in World War II. The Japanese liked to hide in caves and crannies where they could be dislodged only by grenades or flame-throwers. The weapon was also used against German pillboxes and in ferreting out snipers.

The war developed super bomber and fighter

THE PEAK OF AIR POWER. By the end of the war American industry had developed the ultra modern planes pictured here. The Northrop Flying Wing XB-35 long range flier, upper picture, is pushed along at high speeds by four eight-bladed co-axial pusher propellers, driven by four Pratt and Whitney Wasp Major engines. The ship weighs in at 209,000 pounds under gross overload conditions. The lower picture shows the new Boeing single seat fighter, said to be more versatile than any previous fighter, and capable of a speed of 450 miles per hour with twin contra-propellers.

Enemy guns are made use of by Allies

YANK INGENUITY. The huge German railroad gun, above, was used by the Yanks in France to mend a bombed out bridge near Aix. By dismantling the gun, men of the 343rd Engineer Regiment found they could use the remaining carriage to perfectly replace the bombed out section of the bridge. The gun in the lower picture was designed and manufactured by the Japanese to blast our shipping. A dejected Jap sits by the gun which never left the factory but has been marked "good" by the United States Navy and was later transferred to America.

DOUBLE POWER. The top picture shows one of the war's most carefully kept secrets, the Navy's FR-1 Fireball plane which uses both jet and conventional engines with propeller. The plane's tail structure is separated from the rest of the ship to reveal the jet engine. Note the tricycle landing gear, the first to be accepted for aircraft carrier use. The picture below illustrates the "Brodie" system, used late in the war. The plane, equipped with an overhead hook, engages a loop suspended on a cable and the loop and the plane slide along the cable until stopped by a friction brake. The value of such a system would be invaluable in, for example, a jungle region where landing fields could not be readily prepared.

The Navy's big guns roar

THUNDER OFF OKINAWA. Heavy guns of a Navy battleship belch fire and smoke as they bombard land targets on Okinawa. However, the real fire power of the Navy lay not in the big guns of the warships but in the planes such as the one pictured below taking off from a carrier to bomb Tokyo. Guns which were more frequently used than those above were the anti-aircraft batteries.

The Navy develops airborne television

BATTLES CAN BE WATCHED FROM AFAR. During the war the United States Navy developed a new television system which enables a ship or shore-based commander to broaden his horizon by 150 to 200 miles. The above televized picture of the Potomac was seen by people sitting in a comfortable Washington auditorium. The new system clicks the pictures from a plane and transmits them to a given station. The lower picture shows the television equipment in a JM-1 Marauder reconnaissance plane. Radio Corporation of America worked on the project with the Navy.

German war birds

THE ARADO 234 AND MESSERSCHMITT 262A-1. The plane shown in profile, top, is the German Arado 234, a jet-propelled bomber capable of speeds up to 470 miles per hour. The lower plane is the Messerschmitt 262A-1, German jet-propelled fighter. It has a wingspan of 41 feet, an overall length of 35.5 feet and an estimated speed in level flight of about 515 to 530 miles per hour. The lower picture shows the Walter engine, a jet-propulsion type used in Germany's fastest interceptors.

MANY LIVES WERE SAVED. The miracle of blood plasma saved the lives of many thousands of wounded soldiers in World War II. The blood donated by civilians at home often ended in dramas such as those depicted on this page. Above, plasma is administered to a wounded Yank in Sicily. The tragedy of war to women in a battle zone is mirrored in the faces watching the grim fight for life. Below, a Navy hospital corpsman is giving plasma to a casualty just behind the front lines in Okinawa.

The Navy's pilotless aircraft

"BUZZ BOMBS." The "Gargoyle," above, is the Navy's version of pilotless aircraft. Jet-propelled, it carries a 1000-pound armor-piercing bomb, controlled visually by radio after release. The "Jato" (jet assisted takeoff unit in the tail) thrusts the missile forward so that it attains a top speed of 700 miles per hour in a dive on a target. The two-ton GB-4 glide bomb, pictured below, was one of the Army Air Force's secret weapons. Launched from a plane, it has a range of 20 miles.

The bayonet was a much-feared weapon

COLD STEEL HELPED BEAT THE ENEMY. The bayonet, with the Garand rifle (or piece), was familiar to every soldier. Although bayonets may not have often killed the enemy, still bayonets were frequently "fixed" as in the charges shown here and had a salutary effect on both the carrier and the enemy. Infantrymen advance in St. Malo, France (above), and Luzon (below).

"Tiny Tim" did a big job

ROCKED THE ENEMY WITH ROCKETS. Rocket warfare was being adapted at the end of the war to all types of launchers including tanks, jeeps, ships, and planes. Above, an Army P-47 lets loose with a load of five-inch rockets and, below, a P-47 fires a pair of 11.75-inch, 1,300-pound rockets at a ground target. The lower plane is diving at 450 miles per hour. The rockets, which have the punch of a 12-inch artillery piece, are the largest developed for aircraft during the war.

SKY WATCH. In World War II blimps again proved their worth, ranging up and down the coast lines and sometimes as close as 60 miles to the front lines of ground battles. Blimp patrol duty was exceedingly hazardous since blimps lacked the speed, armor, and fire power of planes. The blimp's very slowness made possible a thorough scrutiny of any area. Here, a Navy blimp emerges from its hangar to take up its daily patrol duties from a base in the European theater.

A field piece rakes Japs on Iwo

LIGHT ARTILLERY. After the heavy bombardment of the beaches and after the taking of the beaches with small arms at close quarters, the field artillery took up the task of battering the Japs on Iwo. Here, the Fourth Marine Division is well entrenched as a field piece fires over the lines at the Japs.

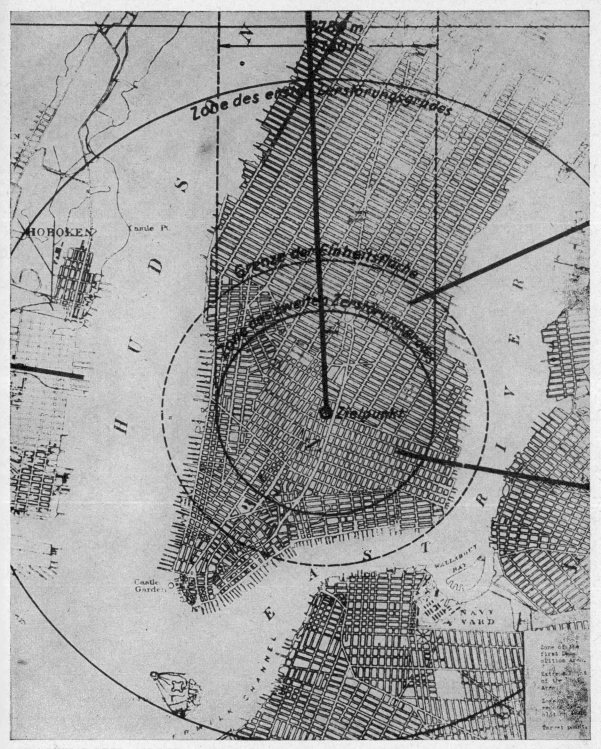

HE DREW A BEAD ON THE BOWERY. This map of New York City, taken from the files of Herman Goering, indicates target areas which the Germans planned to attack with rockets. The bull's-eye of the map is located in the vicinity of Delancey Street and the Bowery. Radiating from this point are zones of primary and secondary damage. The rockets were to be successors of the famous V-2 rockets.

The "winged wind tunnel"

"THUNDERJET." The Army's Republic XP-84 is unique with an air scoop in its nose, above. Bottom picture shows jet exhaust in tail. The blanket of secrecy was only partially lifted from this jet-propelled fighter after its successful flight tests at the Army Air Force testing base at Muroc Field, California. The Thunderjet was named from the Thunderbolt of which 15,329 were made for the Army during the war.

SHELLS FOLLOW RETREATING NAZIS. Part of the armored power of the modern army are these 155-mm. self-propelled guns, top, shown as they blast a path for the Third Army near Budesheim, Germany. In the lower picture, the muzzle blast from a 76-mm. gun swirls dust around an M-18 tank destroyer after it fires in support of infantry attacking Wiesloch, Germany.

Sulpha drugs reach the battle lines

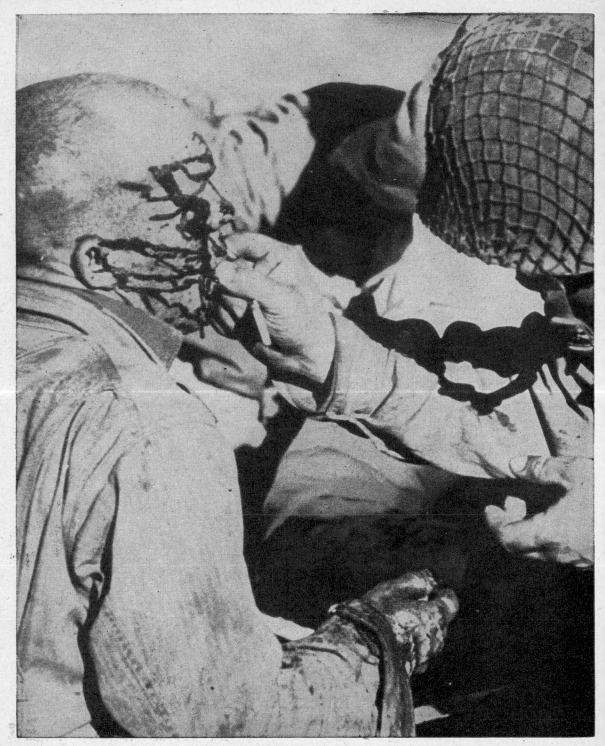

FIGHT INFECTION. A wounded gunner in Tunisia is given a sulpha tablet as an infection preventitive. Three companions in a half-track combat car were killed, but the lives of countless wounded soldiers were saved by the use of sulpha compounds. In addition to fighting infection, sulpha drugs were also used successfully to combat venereal disease, pneumonia, meningitis and other maladies.

"THE LILY" IS DEMONSTRATED. A tin-can carpet for landing planes at sea was invented during the war years by R. M. Hamilton of the English Navy but was not revealed until after V-J Day. The experimental seadrome shown in the picture is constructed of hundreds of buoyancy cans with hexagonal surfaces, each can six feet across and thirty inches deep. The "carpet" gives to the motion of the sea from any direction but remains sufficiently rigid to bear the weight of heavy aircraft. Floating fields like this can be assembled in one hour by a crew of forty men and the experiment proved the technical feasibility of larger seadromes in mid-ocean or bridges across such bodies of water as the English Canal, the British Admiralty claimed. Lily is a development of the Swiss Roll, a floating pier which was used successfully during the Normandy invasion. The Swiss Roll was unrolled from ships to beaches and could carry war vehicles. This invention, like the Lily, was dependent upon the principle of tension.

Tanks sear Germans

FLAME THROWERS ROUT THE ENEMY. Flame-throwing devices, attached to armor or carried by individuals, frequently played a decisive role in wiping out strong points of the enemy in World War II. On the left-hand page, flame-throwing tanks belch their fury on German resistance, while a marine flame-throwing tank, above, blasts a Japanese pillbox on Saipan.

Science snoops out Japs

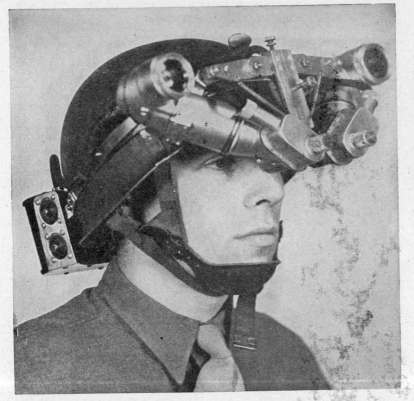

BULLETS FIND ENEMY IN DARKNESS. The snooperscope, above, and the sniperscope, below, both using the infra-red ray principle, ferreted out the enemy on the blackest of nights and enabled American soldiers to train their guns on the unsuspecting victims and shoot them like targets in a gallery. The enemy cannot detect the infra-red light of these devices but he himself is visible when he thinks himself safe in the dark. About 30 percent of the Japanese casualties in the Okinawa campaign are attributed to these weapons.

LOB SHELLS OVER HILLS. The mortar was particularly deadly because its trajectory was an arc and could reach into defiladed enemy positions. Above, a Yank crew fires a 4.2 mortar at enemy positions on Bougainville and, below, members of the 81-mm. mortar crew, Third Division, fire on Germans in the Rigney area, southern France.

An anti-tank crew goes into action

READY FOR THE KNOCKOUT. An American anti-tank crew unlimbers its gun to take care of troublesome Nazi tanks in Aachen, Germany. The town was devastated as a small German garrison held up the American advance for many days. In addition to the anti-tank gun which the GIs are readying for action, note also the heavy caliber machine gun mounted on the half-track.

EMPTIED ON JAPS. This mountain of clover-leaf containers was filled with 81-mm. mortar shells before the contents were transferred to the Japanese on Bougainville. Ammunition was, of course, the common denominator of most weapons of war.

A D-Day secret is revealed

CREDITED WITH SAVING LIVES ON NORMANDY BEACH. Sherman tanks took to the water and hit the Normandy Beaches on D-Day, saving an estimated minimum of 10,000 lives, it was revealed on September 18 after V-J Day. The tanks were disguised, above, but when they rolled ashore, below, they pulled down their canvas camouflage and blasted away at the enemy. They were kept afloat by means of air cells and their canvas-rubber aprons.

"SEEING EYE." The use of radar was especially valuable to the PT boat, above, since many of its missions were accomplished under cover of darkness which radar enabled it to penetrate. The antenna was housed in the "radome" bulb shown at top of the mast-like structure in center of boat. Another small craft which rendered great service was the coast guard cutter, one of a flea fleet of air-sea rescue boats, shown below keeping a rendezvous in the icy north Atlantic.

Night bombers could see targets

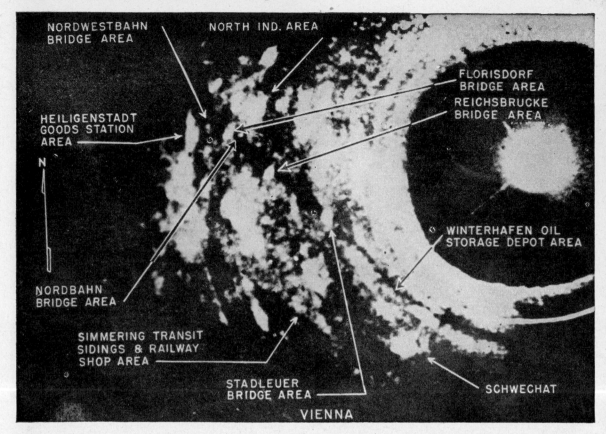

NORDWESTBAHN
BRIDGE AREA

NORTH IND. AREA

FLORISDORF
BRIDGE AREA

REICHSBRUCKE
BRIDGE AREA

HEILIGENSTADT
GOODS STATION
AREA

N

WINTERHAFEN OIL
STORAGE DEPOT AREA

NORDBAHN
BRIDGE AREA

SIMMERING TRANSIT
SIDINGS & RAILWAY
SHOP AREA

STADLEUER
BRIDGE AREA

SCHWECHAT

VIENNA

RADAR PIERCED DARKNESS. Still another use of widely used radar was to furnish eyes for night bombers. The radar photo of Vienna, Austria (above), snatched away the protective cover of darkness from bridges, shops and warehouses which bore the full brunt of Allied bombing fury. The lower radar photo shows the familiar outlines of Manhattan as seen by radar at night.

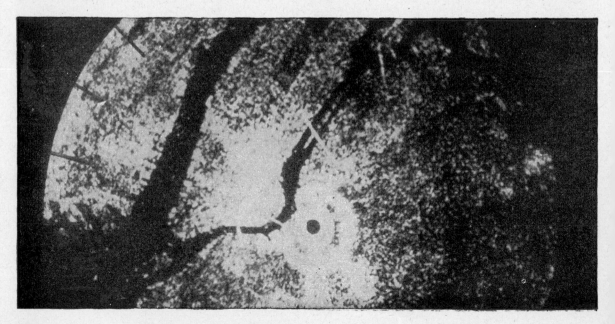

INFANTRYMEN STOP JAP ARMOR. Lying directly in the path of a Japanese tank on Luzon, above, infantrymen fire point blank with a bazooka to knock out the tank which is concealed by smoke. This weapon was also used against gun emplacements as in the picture below, where a GI (at right) lets go with his bazooka at a Nazi position on the French front.

Rockets on land and sea

NEW WEAPON PUMMELS FOE. One of the great innovations of World War II was the development of rocket warfare. Above, a hit-and-run mobile unit launches its rockets at Japs on Iwo Jima and, below, an LST bristles with rocket equipment. British officers stand on the bridge.

NOBEL PRIZE AWARDED TO DISCOVERERS. Many thousands of wounded soldiers were helped to recovery by the miracle drug, penicillin. The Nobel prize was awarded to three men whose scientific work was largely responsible for the development of the discovery: Sir Alexander Fleming, Dr. Ernst B. Chain, and Sir Howard W. Florey. In this picture, Fleming is shown, left, with one of the wounded soldiers who benefited from penicillin.

Radio shell fuze helped win the war

RATED SECOND TO ATOMIC BOMB. The "radio proximity fuze" which is no larger than a pint milk bottle and fits into the nose of a shell (above), was a major secret weapon of the war. The device consists of a tiny radio sending and receiving set which explodes the shell or bomb within an effective distance of a target. The fuze was a potent factor in the accuracy of anti-aircraft guns used to combat the Nazi buzz blitz of London, helped mightily in knocking out Japanese suicide planes, and was used by artillery in stopping von Rundstedt's counter-offensive in Belgium. The lower picture shows the size of one of the experimental fuzes held in a man's hand. The handle is a radio antenna. The radio set was powered by a generator driven by the wind of the shell's flight. About 80,000 persons worked on the highly secret project; an estimated 800,000,000 dollars were spent.

COORDINATE WITH INFANTRY. The tank played a major role in the highly developed blitz tactics of World War II. Above, tanks of the Third Armored Division proclaim the beginning of an assault as they open fire on Breining, Germany. Below, a United States tank fires point blank at an enemy target in Aachen, Germany, as infantrymen peer warily from doorways on either side of the battle scarred street.

Japanese aircraft were carried under water

LAUNCHED FROM SUBMARINES. These giant submarines, taken from the Japanese at the end of the war, carried two planes each in a compact hangar situated just forward of the conning tower. A portion of the dome-like entrance to the hangar can be seen below the rail of the conning tower. The long catapult leading forward was used for launching the planes. Along the port side of the sub is a gun with specially constructed carriage which allows the gun to lie flush with the deck when not in use.

A machine gunner gets a well earned rest

AFTER NINETEEN DAYS OF IT. The nightmare of nineteen days of jungle fighting shows in the weary features of this marine as he lugs his heavy machine gun to a rear rest area on Cape Gloucester. The heavy machine gun was a powerful weapon and its operation was especially hazardous since the enemy would concentrate all its efforts on knocking out a machine gun nest.

Yanks take shelter behind a tank

UNDER FIRE. Enemy shells screaming overhead, these grim GIs huddle beneath a tank in the ruins of Geich, Germany. The tommygun, held by the Yank at the left, was a common weapon of World War II and was a favorite in particular with the Soviet soldier.

IT ALSO PROWLED THE PACIFIC. This tiny submarine, its story told only after V-J Day, struck powerful blows at the mighty German battlewagon Tirpitz and, late in the Japanese war, was active in delivering stinging blows to Japanese vessels. Serving in the Royal Navy, it is shown speeding on the surface of Sydney Harbor, Australia, base of the British Pacific Fleet. Thirty to fifty feet long, it was manned by three or four crewmen and traveled ten or twelve feet beneath the surface of the water.

Radar fights unseen foe

LOCATES AIRCRAFT AT NIGHT. Radar was an invaluable aid in knocking the enemy out of the night skies over England. Here, a predictor detachment of British servicewomen of the A.T.S. (Army Auxiliary Territorial Service) guides a gun battery (background) onto invisible enemy planes coming over Britain in a night raid. The "on target-fire" order has just been given.

DISPLAY "PUSH-BUTTON" BOMBS. In a spectacular Army Air Forces "fair" at Wright Field, the public had a chance to view for the first time some of the scientific marvels developed by the air technical service command. The "roc," a strange contraption (above) with a television set in its head, is a high angle bomb that can be guided to its target by a control plane. Radio controlled bombs were used in the war in Italy and Burma, but the invention of the atom bomb makes their future use dubious. However, the extraordinarily compact and powerful engines on display could well be the motors of the future. The engine shown below is capable of 5,000 horsepower and weighs 5,500 pounds.

A reminder of the war's most powerful weapon

ATOM RUBBLE. Months after the world conflict, two Australian soldiers, above, view the ruins of Hiroshima, target of one of the two atom bombs which precipitated the end of the war. Although the atom bomb was cloaked in secrecy, some of its implications were revealed in the spectacular tests at Bikini atoll in the Pacific Ocean almost a year after V-J Day. See the chronological section of this volume for a full report on this sensational post-war development.

TWO IN ONE. A tiny Navy cub hospital plane is lifted from the belly of a huge Curtiss Commando transport at the airstrip on Peleliu Island. Two of these 1,200-pounders were part of the cargo on a routine flight from Guam. Planes were shipped in sections and reassembled at destination.

Water was no obstacle

AMPHIBIOUS CRAFT WERE MANY AND VARIED. In the top picture, riflemen fire on Japs from an amphibious tractor which brought the Yanks ashore on Peleliu. In the lower picture, "alligators" transport men of the 351st Infantry Regiment across the Po River in Italy.

AN ARMY TRAVELS ON GAS. This pipeline in Manila Harbor carried fuel oil inland to tank farms which in turn supplied the armies. In Europe similar operations carried oil from the Normandy beachhead to Germany. The lightning drive of Patton was closely followed and made possible by oil lines.

A warship fights off Jap planes

ANTI-AIRCRAFT GOES INTO ACTION. Helmeted crews of bristling anti-aircraft batteries reload to fight off Jap planes attacking off Saipan in the Marianas. These protective guns frequently saw more action than a warship's big guns, since the attack was usually carried out at long range by aircraft.

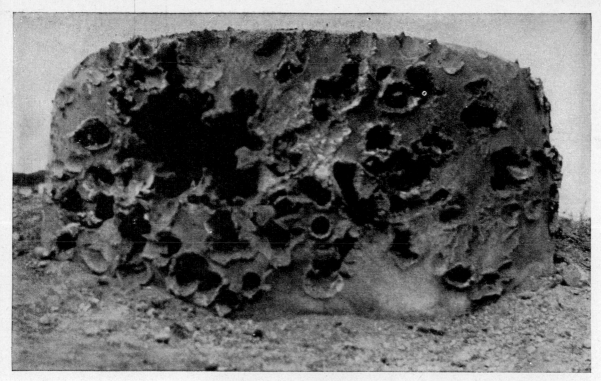

LIKE CHEESE BEFORE YANK GUNS. The pillbox, considered impregnable early in the war, proved vulnerable as Allied weapons were developed. The pillbox, shown above, was punctured by tank fire in France. Flame-throwers were also a potent weapon against this type of defense. Below, a GI examines one of the four different air-changing machines found in a type 108D pillbox, captured from the Germans on the Siegfried Line near Aachen, Germany.

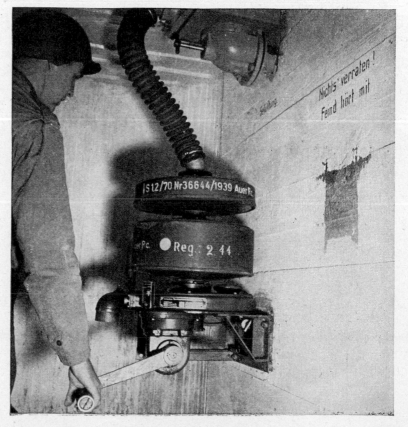

The "Viper" was secret Nazi weapon

CAPTURED PHOTOS REVEAL UNIQUE MISSILE. The "Viper," a piloted, rocket-propelled missile, was designed to attack Allied aircraft with cannon, rockets, or by ramming. The pilot automatically ejected himself before ramming. In the picture at the left, the contraption is prepared for launching, and at the right it zooms skyward. The Nazis were developing many new weapons at the war's end.

USED BY MARINES. Designed for beachhead use, this light-weight, portable radar unit can be dismantled and carried in four 100-pound cases. The "umbrella" antenna acts as a reflector in sending out radio pulses and as a receiver in catching the echoes reflected within its 80-mile range.

The "Weasel"

CONQUEROR OF MUD AND WATER. An M29-C, nicknamed the "Weasel," clambers up a mud embankment in Europe with the greatest of ease. The famous "Weasel" was equally at home on land or water and was highly maneuverable in mud and difficult terrain of all kinds.

MANILA AND BREST ARE HAMMERED. The giant gun above is an American 240mm. howitzer, pictured after hurling a shell at the walled city of south Manila in the Philippines. Below, an 8-inch gun of a field artillery unit just outside Brest, France, slams one of its massive shells into the city to soften it up for the final infantry assault.

"Long Toms" disrupt a Jap column

LONG DISTANCE DESTRUCTION. The murderous "Long Toms" in the upper picture are assaulting an advancing Japanese column ten miles away on Leyte Island in the Philippines. Below, an American gun crew fires a 155mm. self-propelled gun at an enemy pillbox near Gressenich, Germany.

NO MATCH FOR AMERICAN POWER. A Yank lieutenant inspects the turret of a Jap tankette knocked out in the battle for Shuri on Okinawa. The miniature tank measures only ten feet by four feet, is about five feet high, and carries a crew of two men.

Atomic storm

LETHAL CLOUDS FORM OVER BIKINI LAGOON. This striking photograph, taken from seaward, was made several minutes after the underwater burst and shows the formation of radioactive clouds settling over the target fleet and changing the entire appearance of the Bikini Lagoon. The small dark spots are some of the vessels about which vapor waves are forming.

Exploring the ionosphere

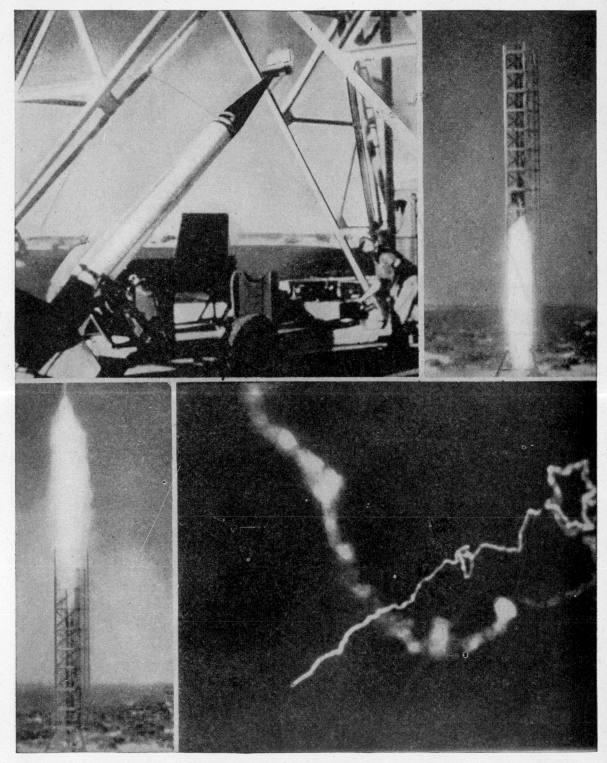

THE "WAC CORPORAL" TAKES OFF. The Army's ionosphere rocket, known as the "Wac Corporal," is loaded into its launching tower, upper left, soars upward, upper right and lower left, and leaves a windblown trail of exhaust against the sky, lower right. In quest of various secrets of the sky, the Army conducted a series of these tests in New Mexico, equipping the rockets with instruments.

A FIREBALL LIGHTS THE WATER. This spectacular picture shows an early stage of the Able burst taken from such height that the whole of the lagoon shows. The shape is still that of the fireball, and the shock wave has travelled a short distance from the center of the impact. The ships have been obscured for reasons of security.

A DIVER GOES OVERSIDE. One of the crew of divers which prepared the ships for Test Baker, this man wears a grotesque face mask and "long underwear" protective clothing. This outfit is much more comfortable than conventional diving suits, and all that is required to work in warm shallow water such as that of the Bikini lagoon.

DAMAGE AND METHOD. The upper picture shows the damage done to the U.S.S. *Skate* in the first test. A scientist is testing it for radioactivity. In the lower picture, the "Cinderella" ship waits her mission. The underwater bomb was suspended beneath this ship which was blown to fragments in the Baker burst.

Test Baker from overhead

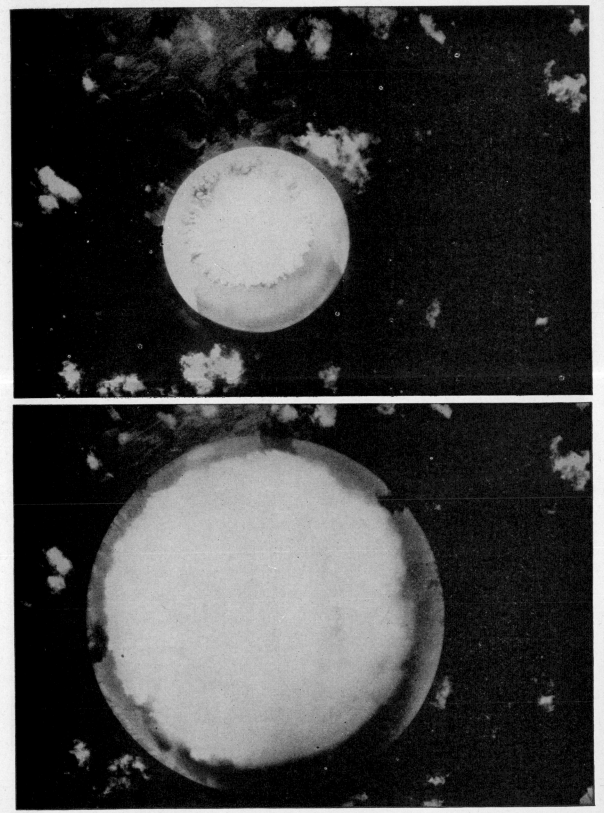

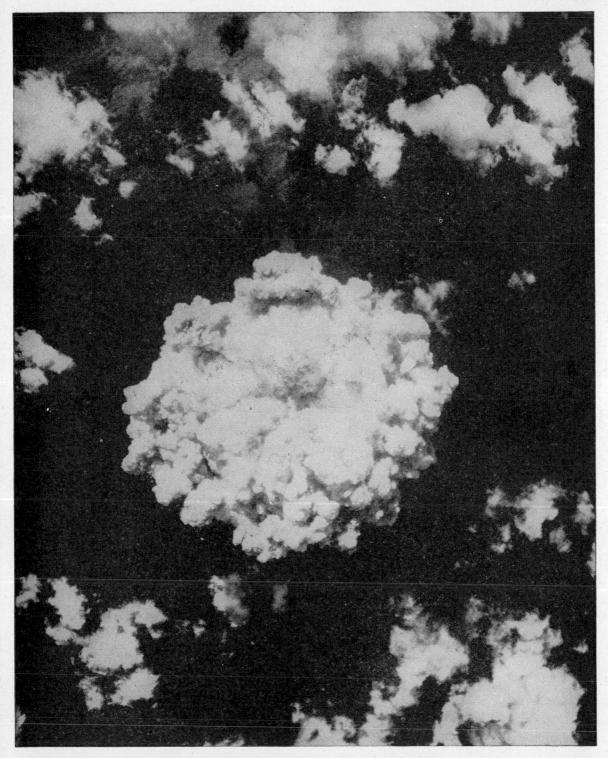

LOOKING STRAIGHT DOWN ON THE BURST. Robot planes, flying directly over the scene of the test, were able to make photographs from on top. On the opposite page two stages in the first development of the burst. On this page, what looks like a tree when seen from surface level becomes a cauliflower when seen from on top.

Spectacular beauty

THE TREE RISES. The "cauliflower" is rising from the center of the ring of vapor, formed when the moisture in the air was suddenly precipitated by the burst. A familiar phenomenon to physicists, it appeared with melodramatic effects in the underwater test. This photograph shows the typical cloud formations which attended the Bikini tests.

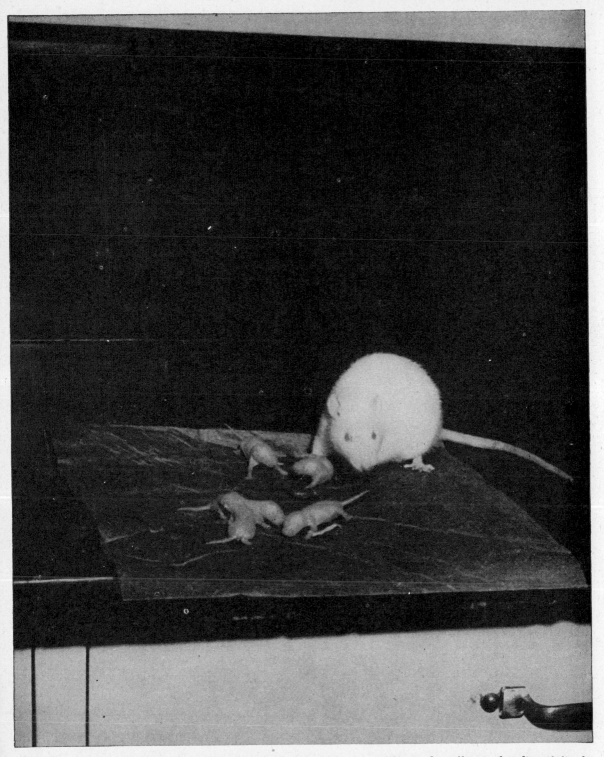

EFFECTS OF RADIOACTIVITY ON GENETICS. Scientists are studying the effects of radioactivity in many connections, and the lives of the test animals are being followed closely. Here a white rat which was exposed to the blast watches over her two-day old litter. It will take several generations of breeding before definite findings are made.

2505

INDEX

A.E.F., see American Expeditionary Forces

A.T.S., see British Army Auxiliary Territorial Service

Aachen, 1605-1607, 2468, 2477, 2489
—Surrenders, 1605

Aandalsnes, 8, 82, 88

Aarhus University, 1625

Abbeville, 119, 741

Abemama, 1031, 1089

Abetz, 455

Abrial, Adm. Jean, 143

Abruzzi Mountains, 1045

Abyssinia, 280, 304, 368, 416, 456, 541, 568-569
—Map, 457

Abyssinia-Sudan frontier, 312

Achkel, Lake, 909

Acquafondata, 1158

Acre, 488

Acroma, 691-692

Adak Island, 918

Adamson, Col. Hans C., 808

Addis Ababa, 260, 416

Aden Harbor, 171

"Admiral Graf Spee," 39, 41, 42, 52, 58

Admiralty Arch, 59

Admiralty Islands, 1032, 1203

Adolph Hitler Bridge, 1807

Adolf Hitler Line, 1268

Adolf Hitler tank division, 872

Adriatic Sea, 1265, 2417

Advanced base sectional dock, 1979

Aegean ports occupied, 424

Aegean Sea, 458-459

Afmadu, 380

Africa, East, 255, 304, 312, 456, 569
—Maps, 457

Africa, French North—Allied invasion, 814-815

Africa, Italian East, 8, 259

Africa, North, 8, 221, 223, 229, 232, (map) 257, 259, 269, (Italians invade Egypt) 272-273, 275, 280, 328, 338-339, 342-345, 358, 366, 371-375, 401-403, 412, 435, 456, 520, 562-569, 590, 592-593, 598-599, 602-603, 606-609, 612, 690-693, 700-703, 706-707, (Battle of Egypt begins) 712-713, 716-719, 771, 772, 810-811, (American landing) 814-819, 820-827, 834, 839-843, 847, 850-851, (Casablanca Conference) 856-861, 880-885, 890-893, 896-913, (Allied victory) 924-925, (Algiers Conference) 930-933, 939, 2299, 2462
—Allied landings, 814-819
—See also names of places

Africa, North—Maps
—British advance into Libya, 374-375
—British drive from Bengasi into Tripolitania, 812-813
—Cape Bon peninsula, 911
—Eighth Army breaks through Mareth Line, 897
—In 1940, 257
—July of 1942, 719
—Second British offensive in Libya, 598-599

Africa, South, see South Africa

African Rifles, King's, 569

Afrika Korps, 520, 612, 690-691, 693, 700, 768, 771, 807, 813, 842, 847, 851

Agat Beach, 1390

Agijosa, 1073

Agordat, 372

Agrigento, 964-965, 970, 971

Agropoli, 1038, 1043

Ailette Canal, 154

Ainsworth, Rear Adm. W. L., 1621

Air Battle over the Strait of Dover, 198-199

Air blitz on Sicily, 942

Air changing machines, 2489

Air Technical Service Command, 2483

Air war over Berlin, 1162, 1184-1185

Air war over Burma, 1596, 1787

Air war over Budapest, 2411

Air war over Denmark, 1625

Air war over Dresden, 2207

Air war over England, 178-184, 217, 230, 237, 259, 347-357, 1118, 1180, 1320, 1336, 1381, 1402, 1502, 1622, 1650, 2445, 2476, 2482
—Maps, 290-291
—See also Battle of Britain

Air war over Europe, 130-131, 277, 699, 1228-1229, 2472

Air war over France, 130-131, 148, 550, 631-633, 1068, 1229

Air war over Germany, 520, 1004, 1070, 1114, 1162, 1182-1183, 1184-1185, 1228-1229, 1341, 1788, 1832-1833, 1866, 2292, 2318, 2369, 2372

Air war over Holland, 493

Air war over Italy, 800-801, 1572-1573, 1641

Air war over Japan, 1180, 1322, 1544, 1652-1653, 1761, 1785, 1814, 1830, 1967, 1978, 1987, 2276

Airborne army, 1543, 1793
—lands in Holland, 1580

Airborne invasion of Southern France, 1442-1443

Airborne invasion on Western Front, 1832-1833

Airborne landing at Rangoon, 1931

Airborne television, 2451

Airborne troops, 1583
—at Arnhem, 1582
—in France, 1324

Aircraft carriers, 622-623, 1724, 1958-1961, 2003, 2450
—Aircraft carrying submarines, Japanese, 2478
—"Ark Royal" (Brit), 317, 323, 464, 558-559
—"Baby," 1406
—"Bunker Hill" (U.S.), 1958-1959, 2332-2333
—"Courageous" (Brit), 31
—"Eagle" (Brit), 315
—"Enterprise" (U.S.), 2406
—"Essex" (U.S.), 2406
—"Franklin" (U.S.), 1836-1837, 2368
—"Hancock" (U.S.), 2397
—"Hornet" (U.S.), 664-666, 2340
—"Illustrious" (Brit), 315
—"Intrepid" (U.S.) 2358
—"Langley" (U.S.), 2354-2355

Aircraft Carriers (cont'd)
—"Lexington" (U.S.), 520, 682-683
—"Princeton" (U.S.), 1616-1617
—"Ryukaku" (Jap), 683
—"St. Lo" (U.S.), 2403
—"Saratoga" (U.S.), 2227, 2233
—"Syukaku" (Jap), 683
—"Victorious" (Brit), 464
—"Wasp" (U.S.), 786
—"Yorktown" (U.S.), 520, 696
Aircraft industry, U. S., 2447
Aisne, 117
Ait Kebir, 1120
Aitape, 1180, 1241
Ajaccio 172
"Ajax," 41, 294
Akarit, 898-899
Aktinino, 1009
Akyab, 1232, 1714
Ala, Hussein, 2199
Alagir, 848
Alban Hills, 1179
Albanic, 259, 261, 300, 311, 322, 331-
　　332, 362, 431, 433
—Maps, 362
Albert Canal, 104
Aleutian Islands, 698, 705, 772, 918-
　　921, 1014-1019
Alexander, Gen. Sir Harold R. L. G.,
　　638, 925, 930, 1254, 2267
Alexandria, 153, 221, 512, 520, 712,
　　806
Algeria, 172, 192, 771, 814
"Algerie," 833
Algiers, 771, 818-819, 823, 827, 839,
　　930, 933
"Algonquin," 2182
Ali, Raschid, 444
Allard, Maj. Jacques, 1120
Allen, Maj. Gen. Terry, 2290
Allenstein, 1543, 1737
Allied advance through Tunisia—Map
　　911
Allied air attack on Rabaul, 654-655
Allied airborne army, 1845
Allied air forces, 814, 942
Allied air forces—North Africa, 804
Allied air supremacy in the desert, 840
Allied armored columns, 2336
Allied Civil Affairs Bureau, 1477
Allied Commission Camp at Ancona,
　　Italy, 2149
Allied conference at Casablanca, 857
Allied conquest of Abyssinia, 568-569
Allied engineers, 1879
Allied Fifth Army, 1144, 1258, 1273
—**See also** American Fifth Army; Fifth
　　Army
Allied fleets, 988, 996
Allied forces in Burma, 1939
Allied Fourteenth Army, 1838
—**See also** American Fourteenth
　　Army; British Fourteenth Army;
　　Fourteenth Army
Allied invasion armada at Lingayen
　　Gulf, 1704
Allied invasion of French North Africa,
　　814-815
Allied invasion of Sicily, 952-953
Allied invasion of the European con-
　　tinent, 1031
Allied landing in the Arctic Circle, 528
Allied landings in southern France,
　　1437-1444
Allied leaders confer in Algiers, 930,

Allied march through Tunisian capital,
　　924-925
Allied navies improve anti-submarine
　　measures, 878
Allied troops leave Crete, 468
Allied troops pour into Belgium, 96
Allies advance in Burma hills, 1620
Allies advance in the Pacific, 1014
Allies capture Pantelleria, 936-937
Allies dominate New Guinea, 1406
Allies go to Norway's aid, 76
Allies land men and stores on Sicilian
　　beaches, 956
Allies retake Stavelot, 1685
Allies take Catania, 991
Allies take Mandalay, 1838
"Alligators," 1611, 1267, 2486
Alola, 782
Alsace, 167, 1710, 1738
Altavilla, 1638
Altenfjord, 1223
"Altmark" incident, 54-55
Aluminum, 195
Amba Alagi, 456, 541
Amchitka Island, 918
American and British First Army, 772
American and Canadian sailors, 265
American arms released to the Allies,
　　32
American assault troops land on Nor-
　　mandy, 1284
American attack in France, 1469
American bombers blast Berlin for the
　　first time, 1182-1183
American built planes in North Africa,
　　566-567
American cemetery in Belgium, 1886-
　　1887
American column shelled in Germany,
　　2404
American cruiser, 622, 623
American Eighth Army, 1793, 1816-
　　1817
American engineers, 1549
American Expeditionary Forces, 620,
　　814-815, 818-819
American Fifth Army, 700, 1254, 1544,
　　1572, 1589, 1903
—**See also** Allied Fifth Army; Fifth
　　Army
American First Army, 1524, 1543, 1556-
　　1557, 1605, 1637, 1680, 1682, 1684,
　　1688, 1731, 1758, 1800-1804, 1831,
　　1853, 1861, 1886, 1893, 1905, 2286
—**See also** American and British First
　　Army; British First Army; First
　　Army
American heavy artillery, 1156
American infantrymen outside Paris,
　　1516
American invasion convoy headed for
　　Green Islands, 1237
American landing barge at Guadal-
　　canal, 868
American landing craft, 920, 921
—**See also** Landing Craft
American Negro troops, 1356
—Signal Corps, 1779
American Ninth Army, 1779, 1780,
　　1793, 1795, 1825-1827, 1862, 1879,
　　1889, 1893, 1897, 2262
—35th Division, 2421
—**See also** Ninth Army
American patrol enters Bizerte, 908-
　　909

American planes for Britain, 33
American planes help defeat the Africa Korps, 842
American reinforcements landing on Papua, 844-845
American Seventh Army, 772, 962, 996, 1560, 1647, 1649, 1793, 1835, 1888, 1921, 1927, 1937, 1957, 2275
—See also Seventh Army
American 75th Division, 1713
American Sixth Army, 1679, 2274
American 69th Division, 1906
American soldiers of Japanese descent, 1462
American tactical air forces, 1832-1833
American tank destroyer, 823
American tanks, 771, 822
American Tenth Army, 1857
American Third Army, 1543, 1545, 1644, 1793, 1829, 1841-1842, 1861
—87th Division, 1841
—See also Third Army
American troops land in northern Ireland, 620
American Twelfth Army, 1545
American 240mm howitzer, 2493
American Volunteer Group, 617, 626, 630, 679, 2264
American war production, 32, 267
Americans arrive in Iceland, 498
Americans close in on Cherbourg, 1338
Americans enter Belgium, 1546
Americans enter Cherbourg, 1346-1347
Americans land at Guam, 1390
Americans landing on Rendova, 944
Americans on the Champs Elysees, 1488-1489
Americans, repatriated, 1222
Americans return to Corregidor, 1762-1763
Americans return to Wake Island, 1060-1061
Americans seize Roer dams, 1750
America's Neutrality Law, 32
America's women soldiers in the Orient, 1700
Amerika, 1651
Amiens, 119, 151,
Amphibious craft, 2486
Amphibious tractors, 1576, 2486
Amphibious trucks, 958-959
Amplifier Units, 1359
Amsterdam, 93, 1208
Amur River, 2024
Anapa, 829
Ancona, 1179, 2149
Andaman Islands, 642-643
Andernach, 1811
Anderson, Gen., 821, 834, 930
Anderson, Brig. Gen. Lawson S., 2059
Anderson shelter, 180
Andoy, Rosalinda, 2109
"Andy," 1104
Angarita, Isaias Medina, 2099
Angaur, 1544, 1574, 1578, 2420
Angers, 1509
Anglo-Chinese forces, 673
Anglo-Egyptian Sudan, 260
Anglo-Greek forces, 436
Anglo-Indian forces, 372
Anglo-Polish alliance, 7
Anglo-Soviet twenty year pact, 689
Animals, 1651
Anshan, 1323
Ansirana, 681

Anti-aircraft batteries, 2488
Anti-aircraft guns, 2444, 2488
Anti-personnel bomb, 2434
Anti-submarine measures, 878
Anti-tank crew, 2468
Anti-tank gun, 2468
Anti-U-boat Warfare Committee, 803
"Antonescu," 1231
Antonescu, Gen., 264
Antwerp, 1547, 1627
Anzacs, 53, 174, 328
—Arrive in England, 174
—In the Near East, 53
Anzio, 1032, 1130, 1131, 1135, 1148-1149, 1152, 1179, 1189, 1206-1207, 1238, 1265, 2297, 2302
Anzio Army engineer shore regiment, 1149
Anzio beachhead, 1129, 1230
Anzio Harbor, 1148
Aosta, Duke of, 416, 456
Aparri, 584-585
Apennines, 1595, 1793, 1797
Apolonia, 592
Appian Way, 1135
Arab soldiers, 177
Arabs, 445, 474, 484, 835, 1984
"Arado," 234, 2452
Arakan, 1939
"Arandora Star," 189
Araki, Gen. Sadao, 2110
Arawe, 1032
Archangel, 797
Arctic Circle, 528-529, 1112
Arctic convoy route, 796-797
Ardennes salient, 1706
Arena, 1181
Argentan, 1447
Argentina, 2084
—Post-war elections, 2184
—rally for freedom, 2084
Argentina—Political leaders
—Farrell, Gen. Edelmiro J., 1187, 2184
—Peron, Juan D., 2184
—Tamborini, Jose P., 2184
—Ramirez, Pedro, 1197
Argirocastro, 259
"Arizona," 574
"Ark Royal," 317, 323, 464, 558-559
"Arkansas," 2227, 2229
Armavir, 725, 737
Army of the Nile, 440
Army Service Forces, 1453
Arnhem, 1580-1587
Arnim, Gen. von, 925
Arno River, 1426-1427
Arnold, Gen. Henry H., 1307, 2254, 2278
Arras, 119
Art collections, 1890
"Artigliere," 294, 295
Artillery, 2458
Ashida, 2093
Asmara, 372, 412
Asperg, 2196
Aspern Bridge, 1876
Assam, 676, 1227, 1733
Assam-Burma frontier, 923
Associated Press, 1778
"Astoria," 731
"Athenia," torpedoed, 11
Athens 439, 1544, 1602-1604, 1628, 1670
—Liberated, 1602-1604
Athlone, Earl of, 85

Atlantic Charter, 504-505, 689
Atlantic Fleet, 2259
Atlantic Wall, 1251, 1283
Atomic bomb, 1794, 2015-2023, 2075, 2171, 2483-2484
—Bikini atoll experiments, 2211, 2217, 2218-2225, 2227-2233, 2496-2497
—Hiroshima, 1794, 2015, 2016-2017, 2018, 2075, 2484
—May, Dr. Alan Nunn, 2189
—Meitner, Dr. Lise, 2171
—Nagasaki, 2021, 2070
—Post-war discussions, 2114
—Victims, 2070
—See also Baker Day; Operation Crossroads
Atomic research, Japanese, 2158
Atrocities, 446, 524, 660-661, 871, 876-877, 974-975, 1003, 1520, 1523 1588, 1880, 1904
—Films, 2123
—See also War guilt investigations
Atsugi airfield, 2038-2039
Attlee, Clement, 1794, 2010, 2114, 2242
Attu, 705, 772, 918-919, 1014
Auchinleck, Gen., 712, 718
Auckland, 61
"Augusta," 504, 1283 2008
Augusta, 963, 988
Aulock, Col. von, 1456
Australia, 168, 174, 269, 396, 484, 519, 650, 728, 867-868, 1047, 1235, 2481
Australia—Political leaders
—Menzies, 399
Australia threatened, 618
Australian air contingent, 45
Australian Air Force, 397, 563, 640-641
Australian and American soldiers building a road through the jungle, 778-779
Australian artillery, 226
Australian engineers, 780-781
Australian forces, 367, 1103, 1925
Australian gunners, 226
Australian Imperial Force, 226
Australian infantry, 845-847
Australian infantry in Syria, 473
Australian National Emergency Bill, 168
Australian Navy, Royal, 66, 731
Australian 9th Division, 1991
Australian Parliament, 168
Australian troops, 175, 358, 373, 401, 717, 738, 1794
Australian troops at Sanananda, 944
Australians invade Borneo, 1991
Australians storm Balikpapan, 2004
Austria, 7, 1794, 2472,
Austria—Political leaders
—Seyss-Inquart, Arthur, 2125, 2237
"Avenger," 1067, 1111, 1316
Aversa, 2144
Avola, 992-993
Avranches, 1331, 1404, 1416, 1468
AVRE tank, 1515
Axis, 385
—See also German, Italian, Japanese headings
Axis Powers, 520
Axis prisoners, 613
Axis retreat in Tunisia, 911
"Axis Sally," 2197
Axis ships detained in American ports, 415

Axis tanks, 690-691
Axis troops cleared from Libya, 861
Axter, Lt. Col., 1927
Azad, Dr., 662, 734
Azov, Sea of, 772, 1032

B

B.B.C., 744
"B-17 Flying Fortress," 699, 741, 1015, 1182-1183, 1186-1187, 1229, 1320, 1341, 1788
"B-24 Liberator," 1269, 1848, 2318, 2411
"B-25 Mitchell, 842, 1236-1237, 1720, 1867,
"B-26 Marauder," 1068, 1331, 1748-1749, 2372
"B-29" Superfortress," 1322, 1332, 1429, 1544, 1652, 1746, 1784, 1787, 1794, 1814, 1830, 1859, 1987, 2018, 2219, 2334-2335
—Bomb Tokyo, 1652-1653
—In action, 1323
—Over Honshu, 1967
Bad Mergentheim, 1863
Bad Weisse, 1976
Badoglio, Marshal, 173, 1031, 1035, 1041, 1195
Baedeker Raids, 669-671, 695
Bagdad, 260, 444
Baguio, 2058
Bailey bridge, 1595, 1660
Baka bomb, 1994
Baker Day, 2227-2233, 2496-2497
—Blandy, Adm. W. H. P., 2227
—Ships, 2227, 2229, 2233
Baky, 2203
Balearics, 1041
Balikpapan, 618, 2004
Balikpapan oil wells, 619
Balkans, 260, 404, 418, 422, 424, 766, 1478, 1543, 1601, 1671-1673, 1725, 2257
—German advance (map), 443
—Map, 1671
Balloon protection against robot bombs, 1502
Balloons, Japanese, 2434-2435
Balloons, Paper, 2434-2435
Baltic states, 260, 1179, 1194, 1368, 1396, 1671, 1744
—Baltic front, 1851, 1875
—Map, 1671
Bangkok-Rangoon railway, 1596
Banjalucka, 766
Barce airfield, 592
Bardia, 232, 259, 343-344, 358, 592, 602-603, 612, 707, 806
Bardossy, MM., 426
Barges land troops at Rangoon, 1933
Bari, 2417
"Barracudas," 1223
Barrage balloon, English, 235
Barrage balloons, 1402, 1502, 1661
Barrios, Dr. Gonzalo, 2099
Bartek, Pvt. John F., 808
Basseage, Maj. Gen., 907
Bastia, 1062-1063
Bastille Day, 197
Bastogne, 1682, 1687, 1691, 1701
Bastogne taken by the Allies, 1695
"Bat" bomb, 2438
Bataan, 519, 658-661, 2040

Bataan "Death March," 2081, 2175, 2176,
Bataan village, 659
Bataisk, 723
Batavia, 519
Bates, Jean, 2226
Bath, 669, 670-671
Batov, Col. Gen., 1571
Battle for Breslau, 1819
Battle for Stalingrad opens, 760-761
Battle of Akarit, 898-899
Battle of Berlin, 1006-1007, 1182-1183
Battle of Britain, 228, 234, 237, 259, 262, 278-279, 286-291, 297, 303, 309, 313, 319, 325, 347-357, 361, 394, 398, 408-409, 427-429, 448-451, 764
—See also Air war over England
Battle of Egypt begins, 712-713
Battle of Germany, 1543, 1581
Battle of Midway, 520, 696
Battle of Tarawa, 1088-1089
Battle of the Atlantic, 408
Battle of the Atlantic Committee, 803
Battle of the Bulge, 1543, 1680, 1690-1695, 1711, 1937, 2297, 2312, 2409
—Map, 1684
Battle of the Coral Sea, 520
Battle of the Java Sea, 519
Battle of the Mareth Line, 892-893
Battle of the Philippine Sea, Second, 1544, 1615, 1618, 1619, 1621, 2264, 2439
Battle of the Solomons, 783
Battle lull on the Western Front, 1698
Battleships
—"Admiral Graf Spee" (Ger), 39, 41, 42, 52, 58
—"Arizona" (U.S.), 574, 577
—"Arkansas" (U.S.), 2227, 2229
—"Bismarck" (Ger), 463
—"California" (U.S.), 578-579
—"Duke of York" (Brit), 112-113
—"Dunkerque" (Fr), 192, 833
—"Giulio Cesare (Ital), 1041
—"Jean Bart" (Fr), 818
—"King George V" (Brit), 369
—"Malaya" (Brit), 323
—"Maryland" (U.S.), 577, 2400
—"Massachusetts" (U.S.), 2006
—"Nagato" (Jap), 2227
—"Nelson" (Brit), 542, 1035, 1037
—"Nevada" (U.S.), 1283, 1290, 2219, 2225, 2227
—"New York" (U.S.), 1767, 2227
—"Oklahoma" (U.S.), 574, 577-578
—"Pennsylvania" (U.S.), 579, 2227
—"Prince of Wales" (Brit), 462-463, 582-583
—"Provence" (Fr), 833
—"Repulse" (Brit), 582-583
—"Rodney" (Brit), 1035, 1037
—"Roma" (Ital), 1041
—"Royal Oak" (Brit), 29
—"Scharnhorst" (Ger), 282, 1112
—"Schleswig-Holstein" (Ger), 15
—"South Dakota" (U.S.), 2039
—"Strasbourg" (Fr), 192, 833
—"Tennessee" (U.S.), 577
—"Texas" (U.S.), 1319
—"Tirpitz" (Ger), 1223, 1639
—"Vittorio Veneto" (Ital), 406
—"Warspite" (Brit), 1037, 1283
—"West Virginia" (U.S.), 577
—"Yamato" (Jap), 1615, 1870

Batum, 708
Bausnez, 1694
Bavaria, 1874, 1888, 2115
Bavarian Alps, 1927
Bay of Bengal, 630
Bayeux, 1180, 1325
Bayonet, 2455
Bayot, Eugene, 2112
Bazooka, 1198, 1342, 2473
Beachhead in Sicily 972-973
Bear Island, 1112
"Beast of Belsen," 2121
Beaton, Cecil, 756
Beatty, Capt. Frank E., 2251
Beaverbrook, Lord, 195
Beck, Col. Gen. Ludwig, 1394, 1395
Beckum, 1962
"Beetle," 1328
Beirut, 475
"Belfast," 1112, 1283
Belfort, 160, 1543
Belfort Gap, 1646-1647
Belgian Bulge, see Battle of the Bulge
Belgian civilians, 98-99
Belgian infantry, 125
Belgian refugees, 98-99
Belgian soldiers, 97, 1551
Belgian squadrons, 741
Belgium, 8, 96, 97, 104, 112-113, 123, 125-126, 132, 1569, 1684 2297, 2476
—German advance in 1940 (map), 132-133
—German invasion, 95
—Surrenders to Germany, 8
—Western Front, 1524, 1543, 1546, 1549, 1554, 1556-1558, 1680-1688, 1690, 1694, 1699, 1706, 1708, 1711, 1713, 1731, 1741, 1826, 1886-1887,
—See also Battle of the Bulge; under names of cities and towns
Belgium-Luxembourg salient, 1683
Belgium—Political leaders
—Leopold, King, 8, 125
Belgrade, 420, 998-999, 1543, 1671
Belgrade liberated, 1601
Belsen concentration camp, 1914-1915, 2121
Beltran, Luis, 2099
Benedictine Monastery at Cassino, 1164
Benes, Dr. Eduard, 216
Bengal railway, 1972
Ben Gardane, 861, 881
Bengasi, 259, 373, 414, 520, 563, 590, 592-593, 771, 810-813, 847
Benina, 592
Benina road, 563
Berchtesgaden, 1904, 1909
Berdiansk, 546
Beresina River, 486-487
Bergen, 8, 75
Bergeret, Gen., 165, 173
"Berkeley," 741
Berkey, Rear Adm. Russell, 1817
Berlin, 29, 193, 270, 425, 526, 1004-1007, 1114, 1182-1187, 1544, 1793, 1902, 1913, 1916, 1928, 1934, 1935, 1940, (1945) 2161
—Falls to the Russians, 1934
Berlin radio, 1045, 1078, 1430, 2197
Berlin Sportspalast, 1185
Berneval, 741
"Berwick," 324
Berthof, Col. Chaney L., 1281
Bessarabia, 260, 264, 480, 1194, 2235

Bettancourt, Dr., 2099
Bevin, Ernest, 1949, 2010, 2074, 2117, 2165
Biak Island, 1180, 1266-1267
Bialystock, 1179
Biddle, Francis, 1883, 2123, 2126
Bieldwius, Gen., 907
"Big Apple Ridge," 2330
Big Three meet in Potsdam, 2008
Bikini Atoll, 2484
—Atomic bomb experiments, 2211, 2217, 2218-2225, 2227-2229, 2496-2497
—Juda, King, 2210, 2211
—Natives move to Rongerik, 2211
Bilibid Prison, 1753, 2058
Bilin River, 626-627
Billancourt, 632-633
Binalonan, 1727
Bingham, Maj. Sidney V. Jr., 1386
Bir Hakeim, 691-692
Birdcage Walk, 1381
Birkett, Norman, 2126
"Birmingham," 2322
Bishop self-propelled gun tank combination, 993
"Bismarck," 463, 464, 559
Bismarck Archipelago, 736, 1032, 1235
Bizerte, 172, 772, 820-821, 834, 904-905, 909, 913, 964
Bjervik, 124
Bjornfjell, 124
Black Dragon Society, 2113
Black market in Italy, 2208
"Black Prince," 1283
Black Sheep Squadron, 2285
Black Shirts, 1279
Blamey, Gen. Sir Thomas, 2042
Blandy, Vice Adm., 2219, 2224, 2227
Blemont, 1414
"Blenheim," 130, 453, 493, 550
Blerick, 1664
Blimps, 2457
Blood plasma, 1153, 1171, 1303, 1345, 2453
Blue Beach, 1707
Bock, Gen. von, 536, 688, 760
Boeing, 2447
Boettiger, Mrs. John, 1375
Bofors gun, 2444
Boguchar, 714
Bologna, 1035, 1572, 1544, 1589, 1641, 1793, 1797, 1903
Bolzano, 1035
Bombay, 734
Bombers, night, 2472
Bombs, 2436
—Armor-piercing, 2454
—Atom, 2484
—Glide, 2454
—High angle, 2483
—Japanese, 2435
—Push button, 2483
—Radar directed, 2438
—Radio controlled, 2483
—White phosphorus, 1050-1051
—See also Atomic bomb
Bone, 1041
Bong, Maj. Richard I., 2260, 2295
Bong, Mrs. Marjorie, 2260
Boniface, 1062
Bonn, 1800, 1807, 1821
Booby traps, 1743, 2319
Boppard, 1842
Bordeaux, 197

Borneo, 168, 519, 642, 1794, 1925, 1991-1992, 2005
—Beaches and airstrips bombed, 1992
Borowletz, Maj. Gen., 907
Bose, Subhas Chandra, 2170
Bosnia, 998, 1108, 1110
Bosnian mountains, 766-767
"Bostons," 635
Bou Arada, 885
Bougainville, 1031, 1081, 1102, 1103, 1104-1105, 1154-1155, 1188, 1198, 2296, 2467, 2469
—Hill 700, 1188
Boulogne, 8, 133, 240, 527
Boyington, Lt. Col. Gregory, 2285
Bracken, Brenden, 100
Bradley, Gen. Omar N., 1284, 1294, 1399, 1484, 1531, 1545, 1600, 1861, 1893, 2258
Brauchitsch, Gen. Walther von, 165, 1395
Braun, Eva, 2119
Braun, Prof. Wernther von, 1927
Bray Dunes, 136
Brazil, 1389, 2174
Brazil—Political leaders
—Dutra, Gen. E. G., 1799, 2174
Brazilian Expeditionary Force, 1797, 1799
Brazilian troops in Italy, 1389
Brazilians on Italian Front, 1799
Breda, 1209
Breining, 2477
Bremen, 720, 1793
—Harbor, 1942
Bremervoerde, 1970
Bren gun, 177, 208
—Carriers, 328, 412, 484
—Detachment, 97
Brenner Pass, 65, 1035, 2401
Breslau, 1742, 1751, 1808, 1819
Brest, 169, 588-589, 1180, 1421, 1434, 1479, 1513, 2418, 2493
Brest-Litovsk, 7, 26, 480
Bridgehead over the Rhine, 1841
Bridging the Belfort Gap, 1646-1647
Briere, Francois, 2166
Brindisi, 1031
Britain and Russia become allies, 490
Britain, Australian troops in, 226
Britain is at war with Germany, 9
Britain prepares for war in the desert, 221
Britain strengthens her defenses in Malaya, 495
Britain's chief base in Norway, 80
Britain's offer to India rejected, 662
British advance in Abyssinia, 457
British advance into Libya (map), 374-375
British advanced front in Italy, 1132
British aid for Greece, 307, 323
British Air Force, see Royal Air Force
British air power in the desert, 840
British airborne troops, 379
British aircraft industry, 259
British amphibious forces invade Greece, 1593
British and American guns in action, 1512
British and Canadian assault troops in Sicily, 957
British and Free French forces enter Syria, 472
British and Free French in Cairo, 413

British and French forces at Caen, 1291
British and Imperial troops evacuated from Greece, 440
British and Russians enter Iran, 507
British and Russians join in Baltic area, 1926
British anti-aircraft gunners, 608-609
British anti-tank gun, 693
British anti-tank gunners, 611
British armored car, 96
British armored division in training, 852
British Army Auxiliary Territorial Service, 393, 2482
British Army court at Luneberg, 2121
British artillery, 312, 371
—In Libya, 701
British assault on the Rhine, 1945
British at Caen, 1364-1365
British at Menin Gate, 123
British bases leased to U. S., 386
British begin the liberation of Greece, 1593
British block Nazi attempt to gain control of Iraq, 444
British Blue Book, 7
British boarding the "Altmark," 54-55
British bombing planes, 233
British Bren carrier, 810-811
British Bren gunners in action in Tunis, 910
British Broadcasting Company, 744
British capture Nijmegen bridge, 1584
British coast, 276
British Coastal Command, 284
British Columbia, 864
British commandos raid coast of Norway, 601
British destroyer rams St. Nazaire dock gates, 648-649
British destroyers, 67, 241
British drive from Bengasi to Tripolitania, 812-813
British Eighth Army, 592, 598-599, 712-713, 771-772, 804-805, 810-813, 846-847, 850-851, 861, 900, 913, 940-941, (in Sicily), 962-965, 996, 1031, (in Italy), 1035, 1069, 1077, 1086, 1119, 1175, 1255, 1544, 1572, 1589, 1668, 1903, 1932
—See also Eighth Army; Maps and diagrams—African campaign
British Empire air scheme, 45
British enter Cancello, 1071
British evacuate Crete, 468-469
British evacuate Malaya, 621
British evacuation in Greece (map), 443
British Expeditionary Forces, 16, 46, 60, 112-113, 119, 123, 134, 136, 140, 158, 162, 260, 1799, 2284
British First Army, 820-822, 884-885, 909,
—moves on Tunis, 820
—See also American and British First Army; First Army
British 1st Corps, 1378
British 1st Division, 937
British Fleet, 8
British forces in Blerick, 1664
—In Burma, 1191, 1620, 1931
—In France, 8
—In Holland, 1598
—In Iceland, 497-498
—In Malaya, 495

British forces (cont'd)
—In Norway, 8, 124
British Fourteenth Army, 1191, 1939
British guerrilla expedition in Burma, 923
British gunners, 707
British heavy field gun, 602-603
British home front, 383
British Imperial Defense Staff, 2284
British infantry, 367, 606-607, 858
—Advancing behind tanks in Tripolitania, 850-851
British infantrymen in Anzio, 1159
British Intelligence, 847
British intervene in Indonesia, 2096
British land in Madagascar, 680
British landing craft near Dieppe, 740-741
British mechanized column, 307
British mechanized equipment, 1845
British Mediterranean fleet, 316
British medium guns, 1845
British medium howitzer, 367
British mine-laying destroyer, 67
British mortar platoon in France, 1377
British move up in Italy, 1144
British Museum, 449
British naval bases in the Pacific, 642-643
British Navy, 29, 50, 67, 88, 147, 169, 196, 219, 225, 232, 293-295, 315, 316, 324, 376, 406, 740, 741, 806, 814-815, 941, 1035-1037, 1112-1113, 1933, 2405, 2463, 2481
—Bombards Cherbourg, 293
British occupy the capital of Eritrea, 412
British offensive in Egypt begins, 804-805
British Pacific Fleet, 2481
British paratroops, 378
British patrol marches into Tunis, 908-909
British radio navigational system, 2441
British reach Antwerp, 1547
British retreat to Singapore, 621
British return to Singapore, 2078-2079
British route from Benghazi to Tripolitania, 812
British Royal Engineers, 896
British-Russian mutual assistance pact, 490
British seamen on raft for eighty-three days, 863
British Second Army, 1547, 1566, 1582-1584, 1587, 1651, 1654, 1698, 1716, 1726, 1739, 1850, 1914-1915, 1941, 1981, 2268
—See also Second Army
British second offensive in Libya (map), 598-599
British secret anti-invasion defense, 1974
British self-propelled guns in Italy, 1131
British signal corps detachment, 221
British 6-pounder anti-tank gun in action, 861
British 6th Airborne Division, 1926, 2117
British soldiers at Tobruk, 702
British Somaliland, 8, 222, 260
British take Mandalay, 1838
British tank crews, 275, 890-891
British tanks, 177, 712-713

British tanks (cont'd)
—In Libya, 562-563
British territories, 219
British troops, 123, 312, 681
—And tanks, 307
—at Catania, 1022-1023
—Coming ashore at Salerno, 1042-1043
—Enter Teheran, 540
—In Augusta, 988
—In Belgium, 1706
—Land in Norway, 76
—In Sicily, 964-965
British warships, 88, 171
British Woman's Land Army, 793
British wounded evacuated from Sicily,
961
Brittany, 1180, 1414-1416, 1420, 1434,
1531
"Brodie" system, 2449
Bromfield, A. B., 50
Brooketon, 1992
Brown House, 1929
Browning automatic rifle, 2415
Bruccoli, 962
Bruchsal Prison, 2111
Brunei, 1991-1992, 2004
Bruneval, 631
Brussels, 105-106, 115, 126, 1551
—liberated, 1551
Bryansk, 548-549, 1008-1009, 1032
Bryansk-Kharkov railway, 1009
Bryansk- Konotop railway, 1009
Bucharest, 264, 1478
Buchenwald concentration camp, 1880,
1904
Buckingham Palace, 84, 271
Buckner, Lt. Gen. Simon Bolivar Jr.,
1985, 2294, 2300
Budapest, 426, 1543, 1671-1673, 1725,
1808, 2186
Budapest-Tokal airdrome, 2411
Budenny, Marshal, 503, 508
Budesheim, 2461
Buenos Aires, 2084
Buerat-el-Hsun, 851
Buergerbraukeller, 34
"Buffaloes," 2408
Bukovina, 1179, 1216
—Northern, 264, 2235
Bulgaria, 260, 264, 384, 1132, 1473,
1543, 1671
—Post war border discussions, 2234-
2239
Bulgaria—Political leaders
—Filoff, Prof., 385
Buna, 772, 779, 782, 844-845, 854-855
"Bunker Hill," 1958-1961, 2263, 2332-
2333
—Honors its dead, 1961
Burgsteinfurt, 1973
Burma, 616-617, 626-627, 630, 636-637,
638, 642-643, 653, 673-674, 676-
679, 923, 1075, 1145, 1174, 1179,
1190-1192, 1205, 1215, 1226-1227,
1232, 1405, 1466, 1471, 1522, 1577,
1596, 1620, 1660-1661, 1689, 1787,
1823, 1838-1839, 1930-1931, 1933,
1939, 2289, 2378-2379, 2483
—Maps, 673, 1838
—North, 1405
—**See also** China-Burma-India Theater;
under names of cities and towns
Burma Oil Company, 636-637
Burma Road, 519, 673, 1145, 1179,
1577

Burrough, Adm. H. M., 1944-1945
Buzz bombs, 2454
Byelgorod, 687, 710, 976-977, 982, 1008
Byrnes, James F., 2008, 2027, 2074,
2114, 2198, 2199, 2234

C

"C-47," 1531, 1602, 1691
"C-48," 1442-1443
C Rations, 1163, 1712
Cabanatuan prison camp, 1745
Cadogan, Sir Alexander, 2198, 2199
Caen, 663, 1180, 1285, 1291, 1364-1365,
1369, 1377-1378, 1468, 1504, 2268
—Falls to the British, 1377
Cagayan Valley, 1794
Cairo, 176-177, 413, 1032
—Anti-British demonstrations, 2181
Cairo conference, 1097-1098
Cairo Declaration, 2008
Calabria, 379, 1031, 1035
Calabritto, 1144
Calais, 8, 131, 140, 240
Calcutta, 2157
"California," 578-579
Camels, 222
Cameras
—Automatic, 2230
—Radio-controlled, 2217, 2220
—Remote-control, see Cameras, Radio
controlled
—Used in Atomic bomb experiments,
2217, 2220, 2222-2223, 2230
Camerlle, 1248
Camouflage
—Rubber decoys, 2443
Camp Borden, 267
Camp No. 6, Formosa, 2068
Camp show in France, 1412
Camp Vassar for displaced persons,
1964
"Campbeltown," 648-649
Campoleone, 1159
Canada, 85, 188, 267
—Air Force, see Royal Canadian Air
Force
—Japanese balloons over western,
2434-2435
—Spy suspects, 2189
Canada—Military leaders
—Crerar, Lt. Gen. H. D. G., 2287
—Moore-Cosgrove, Col. L., 2042
Canada—Political leaders
—Athlone, Earl of, 85
—King, Mackenzie, 1568
Canada's airmen arrive in England,
48
Canadian Air Force, 48
Canadian armored vehicles, 1508
Canadian Army, 1285, 1463
—In Holland, 1941
Canadian artillerymen at Caen, 1369
Canadian assault troops in Sicily, 957
Canadian First Army, 1566, 1795-1796,
1800, 2287
—Takes Cleve, 2369
Canadian forces, 84, 158
Canadian, French, 1st Division, 84
Canadian hospital in England, 1372
Canadian infantry, 85
—In Ortona, 1134
Canadian mortar experts in Italy, 1246

Canadian officers and men, 265
Canadian Pacific fleet, 298
Canadian soldiers in France, 1447
Canadian tanks in France, 1504
—In Italy, 1268
Canadian troops, 85, 742, 1119
—In Italy, 1037
—In Sicily, 964-965
Canadian-U.S. highway agreement,
    864
Canadian-U. S. joint defense board,
    864
Canadians advance along the Seine,
    1470
Canadians at Caen, 1342
—At Dieppe, 741-742
—At Montreuil, 1519
Canadians enter Falaise, 1521
Canadians land and move on Caen,
    1285
Canadians land at Dieppe, 740-741
Canadians mount guard at Bucking-
    ham Palace, 84
Canadians return to Dieppe, 1533
Cancello, 1071, 1072
Canea, 467
Canine Marine, 747
Cannes, 1439
Canterbury, 695
Cap d'Antibes, 1439
Cape Bon peninsula, 772, 911, 913
Cape Gloucester, 1032, 2479
Cape Hoskins, 1235
Cape May, 1965
Cape Pasero, 959
Cape Serrat, 885
Capizzi, 991
Caproni bomber, 280, 313
Capuzzo, 564-565, 707
Carke, Col. Harry E., 2150-2151
Carentan, 1180, 1299, 1312, 1358
—Captured, 1312
Carantan-Periers road, 1414-1415
Carley float, 530
Carney, Rear Adm. R. B., 1621, 2296
Carol, King, 264
Carpathian Mountains, 1133, 1224,
    1396, 1590, 1640
Carretta, Donato, 1552
Carrier planes strike at Tokoyo, 1761
Carroceto, 1128, 1159
Carthage, 930
Caruso, Pietro, 1552-1553
Casablanca, 771, 818, 856
Casablanca Harbor, 818-819
Casale, 1158
"Cassin," 579
Cassino, 1032, 1150, 1164, 1179, 1189,
    1248, 1253, 1258-1259, 1263, 1268
—Falls to the Allies, 1263
Cassino, Mount, 1210-1211
Castel Benito, 840, 851
Castiglioncello, 1462
Castleforte, 1179
Casualties and losses—Allied
—Aircraft, 239, 263, 278, 291, 599,
    744, 1173
—Cargo vessels at Bari, 2417
—Corregidor (1945), 1763
—Dieppe, 743-745
—Eastern Front, 983
—Eniwetok, 1171
—Fifth Army in Italy, 2407
—Iwo Jima, 1770-1771, 1789
—Leyte, 1609

Casualties and losses (cont'd)
—Marianas, 1418
—Normandy beachheads, 1298, 1300-
    1304
—North Africa, 599
—Okinawa, 1966, 1997, 2310-2311
—Philippine Sea, 2403
—Philippines, 658
—Saipan, 2387
—Shipping, 405, 408, 622-623
—Southern France, 1444
—Tarawa, 1031, 2429
—U. S. total casualties, 2057
—Western Front, 1585, 1886
—See also Ships
Casualties and losses—Enemy
—African campaign, 925
—Aircraft, 130, 239, 263, 278, 291, 453,
    599, 837, 868 903, 915, 1031, 1173
—Berlin, 1934-1935
—Burma, 1939
—Corregidor (1945), 1763
—Eastern Front, 483, 553, 555, 830,
    837, 886, 983
—Guadalcanal, 868
—Iwo Jima, 1789
—Japanese shipping, 641, 683, 697
—Japanese ships sunk by Allied sub-
    marines, 2012
—Leyte, 1609
—Marianas, 1418
—Matapan engagement, 406-407
—North Africa, 564, 599, 807, 902-903,
    915
—Okinawa, 1966, 1999, 2310-2311
—Philippines, 659
—Rabaul, 1031
—Saipan, 2386-2387
—Shipping, 868, 915
—Ships in Rotterdam Harbor, 493
—Stalingrad, 2339
—Tarawa, Makin, Abemama, 1089
—Truk, 1168
—Western Front, 1585, 1793, 1893
Catania, 772, 942-943, 962, 964-965,
    989-991, 996, 1022-1023, 1037
Catholic Church, 2180
Catroux, Gen., 413, 472, 477, 489, 932
Caucasus, 520-521, 546, 724-725, 737,
    771, 828-829, 831, 848-849, 1032,
    1220
Cavagnari, Adm., 173
Cavite, 584-585, 595, 604-605, 1736
—Evacuated, 595
Cebu, 1570, 1677, 2083
Cebu Harbor, 1570
Cekhira, 898
Celebes, 519, 618, 642-643
Cemetery, American, in Belgium, 1886-
    1887
Cemetery Ridge, 1975
Central Pacific, 1201, 1316
Central Pacific force, U. S. Pacific fleet,
    1193
Centuripe, 991
Cernauti, 1179, 1216
Ceylon, 1953
Chad, Lake, 860, 1496
Chadwick, Sir James, 2020
Chain, Dr. Ernest B., 2475
Chalbaud, Carlos Delgado, 2099
Chalmers, Rev. Dr. Allan Knight, 1184
Chamarro, 1520
Chamberlain, Neville, 9, 60, 100
Chamberlain, Maj. Gen. S. J., 2035

Changsha, 1337
Changteh, 1106
Channel Islands, 188
Chapelle, Bonnier de la, 839
Charter of the United Nations, 2000
Chartres, 1474-1475
Chateau-Thierry, 154, 1180, 1524
Chatou, 1517
Chaumont, 155
Chaunggyi River, 679
Chelsea Hospital, 303
Cheng Chow, 794-795
Chennault, Maj. Gen. Claire, 1098,
    1226, 2264
Cherbourg, 162, 1180, 1344, 1346-1347,
    1349, 1350, 1351, 1353-1354, 1355,
    1361, 1376, 1403, 1468, 1485
Cherbourg Harbor, 1355, 1380
Cherbourg peninsula, 1282-1283, 1302,
    1414-1415
Chermiaeff, Lt. Gen. Ivan, 1944-1945,
    1946
Chernigov, 531, 536
Cherry, Capt. William T., 808
Chiang Kai-shek, Generalissimo, 888,
    1032, 1097-1098, 1340, 2001, 2156,
    2247
Chiang Kai-shek, Mme., 1097-1098,
    1340, 2156, 2247
Chicagof Harbor, 918-919
Chickunan, 1978
Chihkiang, 1968
Children, Dutch, 1631
Children, refugee, 2149
Children, Yugoslav, 2183
Chile
—Labor demonstrations, 2173
Chin Hills, 1620
China, 672, 888-889, 926-929, 1097,
    1108, 1145, 1227, 1233, 1340, 1357,
    1527, 1544, 1634, 1636, 1689, 1732-
    1733, 1794, 1968, 2001, (1945)
    2154-2155, 2198, 2247, 2264, 2303
—American occupation, 2090-2091,
    2116
—Post war, 2066
—Post-war relations with U. S., 2156
China—Military leaders
—Ho Yin-chen, Gen., 2281
—Hseuh Yeuk, Gen., 1106
—Hu, Gen., 1233
China—Political leaders
—Chiang Kai-shek, Generalissimo,
    888, 1032, 1097-1098, 1340, 2001,
    2247
—Fu Ping-sheung, 1084
—Quo Tai-chi, Dr., 2198
—United Nations Security Council,
    2198
—See also China-Burma-India Theater
China-Burma-India Theater
—General, 630, 642-643, 676-679, 1075,
    1145, 1179, 1190-1192, 1217, 1226-
    1227, 1232, 1577, 1620, 1689, 1787,
    1939, 2265
—Burma, 616-617, 626-627, 638-639,
    653, 673-674, 676-679, 923, 1174,
    1205, 1215, 1226, 1232, 1405, 1466,
    1471, 1522, 1596, 1660-1661, 1823,
    1837-1839, 1930-1931, 1933, 2289,
    2378-2379
—China, 888, 1233, 1250, 1357, 1544,
    1634, 1636, 1689, 1732-1733, 1794,
    1898-1899, 2001, 2002, 2247, 2264-
    2265

China-Burma-India Theater (cont'd)
—India, 519, 627, 735, 923, 1075, 1179,
    1195, 1217, 1227, 1382, 1620, 1787,
    1931, 1972, 2001
China-Burma-India Theater—Maps
—Allies take Mandalay, 1838
—Burma, 673, 1838
—May of 1944, 1232
China Incident, 576-577
China Sea, 1867, 1898-1899
China Sea, East, 1870
Chinchow, 2155
Chindwin River, 677, 1191, 1660
Chinese Air Force, 673
Chinese Army, 888, 1145, 1233
Chinese capture Tengchung, 1577
Chinese Communist Forces, 2155
Chinese Expeditionary Forces, 1250
Chinese famine victims, 794-795
Chinese Fifth Army, 676
Chinese 57th Division, 1106
Chinese forces, 639, 653
—On Burma Front, 1838
Chinese guerillas, 794
Chinese gunners in hills above Teng-
    chung, 1577
Chinese High Command, 888
Chinese infantryman, 639
Chinese on the march, 928-929
Chinese recapture Liuchow, 2001
Chinese refugees in Tengchung, 1527
Chinese Sixth Army, 676, 2066
Chinese sniper, 639
Chinese troops, 928-929
—American trained, 1190-1191, 1233
—In Burma, 1174, 1215
—In the India-Burma theatre, 1217
Chinese war production, 888
Chinese with U. S. forces, 2265
Chittagong, 630
Choiseul, 1083
Christian, King, 8
Christmas in the Belgian Bulge, 1688
Chuguyev, 686, 1008
Chungking, 928-929, 1340
Churchill, Winston, 29, 100, 142, 206,
    231, 386, 399, 449, 792, 803, 814,
    975, 991, 1024, 1057, 1067, 1180,
    1195, 1439, 1443, 1462, 1638, 1794,
    1949, 1984, 2010, 2016, 2242, 2245
— Algiers Conference, 930
—Atlantic Charter meeting, 504-505
—Cairo Conference, 1032, 1097
—Casablanca Conference, 856-857
—July 14, 1940 broadcast, 201
—Offers France Union of Nations, 160
—Post-war visit to U. S., 2191
—Potsdam Conference, 2008
—Quebec Conference, 1568
—Sets up Greek Regency, 1544
—Signs treaty with Russia, 689
—Teheran Conference, 1032, 1101
—Visits Moscow and the Middle East,
    755
—Visits Roosevelt, 914-915
—Yalta Conference, 1754-1755
Churchill, Mrs., 2191
Churchill tanks, 745, 882, 885
Ciano, Count, 173, 285, 385, 1121
Ciechanow, 1722
Cincar-Markovich, 404, 426
Cireno, 592
Citadel in St. Malo, 1457
Civilian casualties in France, 1362
Civilian defenders of Britain, 184

Civilians, French, 1378
Civilians welcome British troops at Pachino, 963
Clacton, Essex, 86
"Clare," The, 220
Clark, Lt. Gen. Mark, 818, 826-827, 1031, 1033, 1038, 1179, 1254, 1258, 1265, 1272, 1277, 1281, 1388, 1422, 1793, 1799, 2267, 2270
—Submarine mission to Africa, 2270
Clark Field, 1544, 1720
Clement, Brig. Gen. William T., 2294
Cleve, 2369
Clydeside, 394
Coblenz, 1800, 1829
Codreanu, 264
Coentin peninsula, 1180
Coggins, Lt. Clarence E., 1501
"Colbert," 833
Collins, Maj. Gen. J. Sawton, 1348, 1351
Colmar, 1543
Cologne, 501, 520, 694, 1800, 1807
Colosseum in Rome, 1274-1275
"Columbus," 44
Combat engineers span the Roer River, 1780
Coming ashore at Tarawa, 1094
Comiso, 942, 959
Commandos, 528, 648-649, 741-742, 975, 1533, 1738
—Allied, 1246
—At Spitzbergen, 528
—British, 601, 1626-1627, 2281
—In southern France, 1450
Commanster, 1713
Como, Lake, 1922-1923
Compiegne, 151, 164
Concentration camp near Brest, 1424
Concentration camps, see Atrocities; War crimes investigations; under names of specific camps
Conference at Pearl Harbor, 1411
Conferences, Allied
—Algiers, 930
—Atlantic Charter, 504-505
—British-Free French in Cairo, 413
—British-Russian mutual assistance pact, 490
—Cairo, 1032, 1097
—Casablanca, 856-857
—Churchill visits Roosevelt, 915
—Churchill visits Moscow and the Middle East, 755
—Paris Peace Conference, 2234-2235
—Potsdam, 2008
—Quebec, 1568
—Teheran, 1032, 1101
—Yalta, 1754-1756
Connally, Tom, 1891, 2165
Constanta, 1179
Constantine, 823
"Conte Biancamano," 415
Cosmic bomb, 2020
Convoy battle, 862
Convoy routes to Britain, 408-409
Convoy survivors rescued after battle with U-boats, 862
Convoys, 198-199, 241, 796-797, 816-817, 862, 878, 966-967, 1056-1057,
—Enemy, 470
"Coolidge," 2402
Copenhagen, 68
Coral Sea, 682-683, 786
Corinth, 436, 1593
Corlett, Maj. Gen. Charles H., 1139

Corregidor, 519, 594, 605, 651, 658, 675, 1762-1763
"Corsair," 1993
Corsica, 934-935, 1041, 1062-1063
Corsican patriots, 1062
"Cossack," 54, 56, 1283
Cossack cavalry, 572-573, 754, 980-981
Cossack Guards, 848-849, 1224
Cossack Guards Division, 875
Cossack troops, 604
Cossack village, 1058
Cossacks in the Ukraine, 1264
Costa dell Ambra, 957
Costa Rica, 415
Cotabato, 1895
Cottbus, 1808, 1854
Councill, Col. William H., 2172
"Courageous," 18
—Officers and men, 19
Courier Bay, 680
Coutances, 1461
Coventry, 318-321
Cox, Oscar, 1891
Cracow, 7, 1543, 1715
—Liberated, 1717
Crailsheim, 1874
Cranborne, Lord, 386
Crerar, Lt. Gen. H. D. G., 2287
Cretan bishop, 307
Crete, 260, 307, 434, 458-459, 466-469, 974-975
—Maps, 468-469
Crewmen fight to save the "Bunker Hill," 1960
Crimea, 546, 556, 580, 685-686, 829, 1032, 1065, 1256, 1754
Crimean peninsula, 1032
Cripps, Sir Stafford, 490, 662, 734
Croat Fascist troops, 766
Crocker, Gen. J. T., 1378
Crocodile flame-thrower, 1739
Cross-channel gun, 1514
Crowley, Leo, 1891
Croydon Airport, 247
Cruisers
—"Achilles" (Brit), 61
—"Ajax" (Brit), 41, 294
—"Algerie" (Fr), 833
—"Astoria" (U.S.), 731
—"Augusta" (U.S.), 504-505, 1283
—"Belfast" (Brit), 1112, 1283
—"Berwick" (Brit), 324
—"Birmingham" (U.S.), 2322
—"Black Prince" (Brit) 1283
—"Canberra" (Austral), 731
—"Colbert" (Fr), 833
—"Dorsetshire" (Brit), 464
—"Dupleix" (Fr), 833
—"Edinburgh" (Brit), 31
—"Eugenio Di Savoia" (Ital), 1195
—"Exeter" (Brit), 41, 52
—"Fiume" (Ital), 406
—"Foch" (Fr), 833
—"Gloucester" (Brit), 406
—"Gneisenau" (Ger), 588-589
—"Hood" (Brit), 462-463
—"Houston" (U.S.), 2402
—"Indianapolis" (U.S.), 2426
—"Jamaica" (Brit), 112-113
—"Jean de Vienne" (Fr), 833
—"La Galissonaire" (Fr), 833
—"La Marseillaise" (Fr), 833
—"Lutzow" (Ger), 283
—"Mauritius" (Brit), 1283
—"Norfolk" (Brit), 112, 462

Cruisers (cont'd)
—"Orion" (Brit), 1283
—"Pensacola" (U.S.), 2227
—"Perth" (Austral), 66
—"Pola" (Ital), 406
—"Prinz Eugen" (Ger), 463, 588, 2227
—"Quincy" (U.S.), 731
—"Renown" (Brit), 323, 376
—"Salt Lake City" (U.S.), 2227
—"San Giorgio" (Ital), 365
—"Santa Fe" (U.S.), 1837
—"Sheffield" (Brit), 1112
—"Southampton" (Brit), 31
—"Tuscaloosa" (U.S.), 1283
—"Vincennes" (U.S.), 731
—"Wilkes-Barre" (U.S.), 1959
—"York" (Brit), 294-295
—"Zara" (Ital), 406
Cunard White Star Line, 214
Cundell, Charles, 832-833
Cunningham, Lt. Gen. Sir Alan, 563
Cunningham, Adm. Sir Andrew, 316, 914, 956, 1041
Curtiss "Helldiver," 1614-1615
Curtiss "Commando" transport planes, 2485
Cuxhaven, 2445
Cyclotron, 2020
Cyclotrons, Japanese, 2158
Cyrenaica, 259, 414, 520, 562-563, 592-593, 613, 2299
—Falls to the British, 592-593
Cypriots, 46
Czechoslovakia, 7, 1543, 1590, 1737, 1793
—Government in London, 216
—Post war border discussions, 2234-2235
Czechoslovakia—Political leaders
—Benes, Dr. Eduard, 216
Czechoslovakian Air Force, 253
Czechoslovakian troops, 216, 741
Czestochowa, 7, 1717

D

D.N.B., 1121
DUKWS, see Landing Craft, "ducks"
"D" Day, 1180, 1282-1285, 2422-2423, 2470
—Operations, 2441
Daber, 1854
Dabrowa, 1734, 1783
Dabrowa coal fields, 1543
Daftari, Akbar, 2199
Dakar, 281
Daladier, M., 2011
Dalmatia, 998
Damascus, 260, 475, 477, 1984
—Occupied, 477
Danube River, 1476, 1672, 1673
Danzig, 7, 15, 26, 720-721, 1851
—Corridor, 1793
—Bay of, 1751
Dardanelles, 2266
Darlan, Adm. Jean, 455, 771, 818, 839
Darwin, 650
"Dauntless," 1060-1061, 1204
Dauser, Capt. Sue S., 2279
Davao, 591, 1406, 1429, 1983
"Dave's Dream," 2219
Davies, Lt., 289

Davis, Brig. Gen. Benjamin O., 1409, 2293
Daylight raid on Rumanian oilfields, 986-987
Death-Alley, 1105
Death's Head Division, 629
de Bono, Marshal Emilio, 1121
Decoys, 2442, 2443
Dedeagach, 424
Deffeccia, 569
De Gaulle, Gen. Charles, 186, 197, 268, 281, 292, 413, 857, 930, 932, 941, 1325, 1374, 1474-1475, 1484, 1487, 1497, 1498, 1638, 1951, 1984, 2011, 2246
de Laborde, Adm., 832
Delft, 90
Delvino, 332
Demolition charges, 2391
Dempsey, Lt. Gen. Sir Miles, 1598, 1739, 2268
Denmark, 8, 68, 128, 1625, 1793, 1941
—German invasion of, 8, 68
Denmark—Political leaders
—Christian, King, 8
Denmark and Norway invaded, 68
Dentz, Gen. Henry, 260, 477, 488
Denys, Gen., 125
Derevyanko, Lt. Gen. Kuzma Nicolaevich, 2042
Derna, 232, 371, 590
Desert sandstorm, 810-811
Destroyers
—"Artigliere" (Ital), 295
—"Berkeley" (Brit), 741
—"Campbeltown" (Brit), 648
—"Cassin" (U.S.), 579
—"Charles S. Sperry" (U.S.), 1959
—"Cossack" (Brit), 1283
—"Downes" (U.S.), 579
—"English" (U.S.), 1959
—"Exmoor" (Brit), 962
—"Glowworm" (Brit), 67
—"Grenville" (Brit), 50
—"Hammon" (U.S.), 696
—"Hardy" (Brit), 69
—"Hasty" (Brit), 406
—"Hazelwood" (U.S.), 2370
—"Kanaris" (Gk), 988
—"Mohawk" (Brit), 31
—"Renshaw" (U.S.), 2102-2103
—"Newcomb" (U.S.), 2375
—"Saumarez" (Brit), 1113
—"Savage" (Brit), 1113
—"Scorpion" (Brit), 1113
—"Sims" (U.S.), 683
—"Stembel" (U.S.), 1959
—"Stephen Potter" (U.S.), 2402
—"Stord" (Nor), 1113
De Tassigny, Gen. de Latre, 1647, 2277
Detection of airborne and surface objects, 2437
Deutsche Werke yard, 283
Deutz, 694
Devers, Lt. Gen. Jacob L., 1453, 2292
Dewey, Thomas E., 2198
DeWitt, Lt. Col. J. H., 2169
Diego Suarez, 680
Dieppe, 740-745, 1504, 1533
Dijon, 155, 160, 1566-1567
Dinant, 1556-1557
Dinard, 1455
"Diomede," 336
Displaced persons center in Germany, 1964

Divinsk, 1179
Djebel Chemse, 898
Djebel Fatnassa, 898
Djebel Houmana, 898
Djedeida, 821, 834
Dmitriev, 886
Dnieper Dam, 1074
Dnieper River, 503, 506, 508, 1032, 1070, 1143, 1194
Dniepropetrovsk, 509, 1032, 1074, 1078-1079
Dobruja, southern, 264, 2235
Dodecanese Islands, 2235
Doe, Maj. Gen. Jans A., 1817
Doenitz, Grand Adm. Karl, 1395, 1928-1929, 2124-2125, 2237
Dogna, 2401
Dogs, 747, 1096, 1104, 1154-1155, 1466, 1651
Domei, 2025, 2030
Don River, 710-711, 722, 754
Donets Basin, 555, 689
Donets River, 686, 688, 704, 872
Doolittle, Lt. Gen. James H., 664, 2276
Doolittle raid, 1180
Doolittle Squadron, 666, 2159, 2276
"Doric Star," 39
Dorn, Lt. Col. Frank, 676
Dornberger, Maj. Gen. Walter, 1927
Dornier, 237, 279
—"Flying Pencil," 236
Dorogobuzh, 628
"Dorsetshire," 465
Dortmund-Ems Canal, 213
Dostler, Gen. Anton, 2144
Douglas "C-48," 1442-1443
Douglas "Dauntless," 1060-1061
Dover, 217, 242-243, 262, 499
Dover Harbor, 217
"Downes," 579
Downing Street, No. 10, 9, 100
Dresden, 2207
Drive on Paris, 154
Drury Lane Theatre, 327
Duala, 292
"Ducks," 959, 970-971, 1130-1131, 1492
Duisburg, 720
"Duke of York," 1112
"Dunkerque," 833
Dunkirk, 8, 123, 131-147, 192, 277
—Evacuation, 131, 2267
"Dupleix," 833
Durazzo, 259
Dusseldorf, 720, 2404
Dutch children evacuated, 1631
Dutch civilians, 1598
Dutch Fleet, 519
Dutch Harbor, 698, 705
Dutra, Gen. E. G., 1799, 2174
Dvina River, 1368

E

Eagle, 315
Eaker, Lt. Gen. Ira, 2292
East Africa, see Africa, East
East Anglia, 122
East Indies, 1794, 1991-1992, 2004
Eastern Front
—(1941) 478-483, 485-487, 500, 502-503, 506, 508-511, 519, 520, 521-523, 531-539, 544-549, 551-557, 570-573, 580-581, 586-587, 604

Eastern Front (cont'd)
—(1942) 614-615, 628-629, 634, 646-647, 668, 684-688, 704, 708-711, 714-715, 722-725, 737, 754, 760-763, 769, 771-772, 774-777, 828-831, 836-837, 848-849
—(1943) 872-877, 886-887, 976-983, 1008-1013, 1032, 1052-1053, 1070, 1074, 1085, 1099
—(1944) 1117, 1133, 1143, 1179, 1194, 1200, 1202, 1216, 1218-1220, 1224, 1231, 1256, 1264, 1310, 1343, 1366-1368, 1379, 1396, 1413, 1425, 1430, 1435, 1473, 1476, 1478, 1528, 1543, 1571, 1588, 1590, 1640, 1669, 1671
—(1945) 1715, 1717-1719, 1721-1722, 1725, 1734, 1737, 1740, 1742, 1744, 1751, 1781, 1783, 1793, 1808, 1818-1821, 1824, 1851, 1854-1855, 1875-1876, 1885, 1902, 1916, 1934-1936, 2286, 2291, 2374, 2410, 2425, 2430
—See also under names of cities, towns, etc.
Eastern Front—Maps
—After eight weeks, 506
—Allied junction in Germany, 1910-1911
—April of 1945, 1885, 1910-1911
—As the third year ended, 769
—As the third year opened, 521
—Finland, 506
—German retreat in the Caucasus, 830
—Germany invades Russia, 478-479
—March of 1944, 1220
—Russian drive on Baltic and Balkan states, 1671
—Russian drive to the Oder, 1747
—Russian winter advance (1941-1942), 684
—September of 1943, 1010
—Stalingrad, 799
Eastern Mediterranean, 47
Faton, Charles A., 1891
E-boats, 1056-1057
Eboli, 1087
Echt, 1779
Eckernforde, 1956
Eden, Anthony, 53, 204, 689, 930, 1084, 1100-1101
Eder Dam, 916
Eder River, 916
"Edinburgh," 31
Egypt, 53, 176, 221, 229, 259, 269, 272-275, 328, 340, 440, 520, 563, 712-713, 716, 718, 768, 771, 804-805, 807, 1756
—Anti-British demonstrations 2181
—Battle of Egypt begins, 712-713
Egypt—Political leaders
—Farouk, King, 1756, 2212
Egyptian soldiers, 177, 229
Eichelberger, Lt. Gen. Robert L., 1817, 2060
Eiffel Tower, 1492
8 inch guns, 2493
8 inch rifle, 1735
8th Air Force, 2278, 2292
Eighth Army, 712-713, 716, 804-805, 807, 810-813, 846-847, 850-851, 858-859, 861, 881, 890-893, 896-901, 924-925, 940-941, 959, (in Sicily) 962, 965, 988, 991, 992, 996, 1033, (in Italy) 1035, 1042, 1043, 1069, 1076, 1077, 1086, 1135, 1119, 1150, 1175, 1210, 1211, 1246, 1255, 1257,

Eighth Army (cont'd)
　　1258, 1427, 1595, 1628, 1793, 1924,
　　2267
—Advances towards Tripoli 850-851
—Attacks Mareth defenses 892-893
—Breaks through Mareth line, 897
—Clears "Hell Fire" Pass, 807
—Enters Florence, 1426-1427
—5th Regiment, 1257
—In Sicily, 959
—Signallers, 1086
—Takes Catania, 989
—**See also** British Army; Maps and
　　diagrams—African campaign
18th Airborne Corps, 1893
80th Division, 1880
81st Infantry, 1574
82nd Airborne Division, 2297
84th Infantry Division, 1964
85th Division, 1728
80 mm mortar section, 749
31 mm mortar, 2467
—Shells, 2469
Eindhoven, 699, 1543, 1582
—Liberated, 1583
"Eisenach," 415
Eisenhower, Gen. Dwight D., 773, 814,
　　839, 902, 925, 941, 1041, 1284,
　　1307, 1398, 1399, 1600, 1781, 1861,
　　1904, 1946, 2164, 2253
—Algiers Conference, 930
—Awarded Legion of Merit by Presi-
　　dent Roosevelt, 1107
—In Paris, 1484
—Returns to the United States, 1998
El Adem, 691, 692, 707
El Agheila, 402, 598-599, 812, 840, 847
El Alamein, 520, 700, 712-713, 771,
　　804, 859
El Aqqaqir, 804
El Duda, 566, 691, 707
El Gatrun, 860
El Guetter, 826-827
El Musaid, 275
El Sollum, 272-273, 275
Elas forces, 1670
Elbe River, 1793, 1905-1906, 2324
Electronic "eye," 2437
11th Airborne Division, 1760, 2038
Elizabeth, Princess, 1951
Elizabeth, Queen, 175, 271, 1372, 1409,
　　1951
Elkhalidi, Awyn, 2166-2167
Emden, 1114
Emirau, 1204
"Empress of Britain," 298-299
Ems River, 213
Endre, Laszlo, 2203
**Enemy guns are made use of by
　　Allies,** 2448
Enfidaville, 900, 913
Engels, 1889
England, (1940) 86, 174, 178, 187-
　　188, 195, 201-202, 207, 216, 220,
　　234, 237, 239, 242, 244, 263, 271,
　　286-289, 297, 303, 319, 325, 347-
　　349, 351-353, (1941) 361, 382, 427-
　　429, 448-451, (1942) 669-671, 744,
　　764, 793, (1943) 1000-1001, (1944)
　　1118, 1320-1321 1336, 1339, 1354,
　　1372, 1381, 1339, 1402, 1502-1503,
　　1622-1623, 1650, (1945) 1794, 2010
—Auxiliary Fire Service, 184
—Defense, 202, 204-206, 208, 231

England (cont'd)
—Foreign troops in, 216
—Home Guard Navy, 205
—Home Guard of Local Defense
　　Volunteers, 204, 237
—Newfoundland troops in, 228
—North-east, 231
—Polish troops in, 220
—Southeast, 245, 252
—Southern, 181, 202, 216
—Volunteer Observer Corps, 184
—**See also** under Air war over Eng-
　　land; Battle of Britain; Britain;
　　British; Great Britain
**England's first taste of death from the
　　sky,** 86
England's shipping lanes, 1503
"English," 1959
English aircraft factories, 195
English anti-aircraft defense, 182-183
English balloon barrage 183
English Channel, 185, 198-199, 240-
　　242, 276, 410, 1282-1283, 1311,
　　1331, 1503, 1974
English coast, 499
English county regiment, 177
English light tanks, 209
English warships, 1376
Eniwetok Atoll, 1146, 1169, 1171
Enna, 964-965
Enskirchen, 2372
"Enterprise," 2406
Enybor, 623
Epirus, 432, 434
Erft River, 2372
Eritrea, 260, 280, 304, 372, 403, 1121
Ernst Ludwig Bridge, 1835
Esperia, 1179
Espionage, 1250, 1337, 1996, 2071,
　　2189, 2197, 2202, 2440
Espiritu Santo, 1525
Essen, 1879
"Essex," 2406
Essex, 122, 262, 290
Estonia, 260, 511, 522,1032, 1142-1143,
　　1379, 1413, 1425, 1543, 1588
Ethiopia, 260, 368, 1121
Euboea, 437
"Eugenio Di Savoia," 1195
Eupen, 1566
Europe, 256, 1020
—Post war border discussions, 2234
　　2235
—Western, 233
Evans Signal Laboratories, 2169
"Exeter," 41, 52, 669-671
"Exmoor," 962

F

FR-1 Fireball, 2449
Faenza, 1544, 1665
Faid Pass, 882
Fairey "Battle" planes, 131
Falaise, 1433, 1447, 1454
Far East, 495
Farben, I. G., 2115
Fabrik Kaufbeuren Gunpowder Works,
　　2115
Farouk, King, 1756, 2212
Farrell, Gen. Edelmiro J., 1197, 2184
Fascist Grand Council, 984
Fascist Iron Guard, 264

Fascist trials in Rome, 1552
Fascist Tribunal, 1121
Federal Bureau of Investigation, 2202
Feisal II, 260
"Fella," 415
Fenton, Col. Francis I., 1997
Fenton, Pvt. Michael, 1997
Feodosia, 556, 580
Ferebee, Maj. Thomas W., 2018
Fernandez, Dr. Eduardo, 2099
Ferrara, 1903
Ferris, Brig. Gen. Benjamin, 1340
Ferryville, 904-905, 909
Fezzan oasis, 860
Fiat "C. R. 42," 313
Fiedler, Gen. Maj. Erich, 2140-2141
Field artillery, 2458
Fields, Benjamin F., 2226
15 mm howitzer, 1403
15th Air Force, 1269, 2411
Fifteenth Army, 1893
5th Air Force, 1748, 1898, 1978
Fifth Army, 1033, 1038-1039, 1043,
　　(enters Naples) 1054-1055, 1069,
　　1072, 1120, 1122-1123, 1129, 1144,
　　1151, 1158, (Cassino) 1164, 1179,
　　1246, 1254, 1258, 1270, (Rome)
　　1271, 1276, 1277, 1278, 1387, (Leg-
　　horn falls) 1388, 1422, 1462, 1550,
　　1595, 1624, 1790, 1793, 1797, (vic-
　　tory in Italy) 1932, 2267, 2302, 2407
—100th infantry battalion, 1422
—**See also** Allied Fifth Army; Ameri-
　　can Fifth Army
Fifth Fleet, 1761, 1794, 1858-1859, 2243
5th Marine Division, 1764
51st Highland Division, 924-925
Fighting French, 860, 913, 932
—**See also** Free French
"Fighting 69th," 1069, 1163
Filipino children, 1812
Filipino guerillas, 1712, 1757
Filipino troops, 519, 652
Filipino underground forces, 1712
Filoff, Prof., 385
Finland, 8, 37, 62-63, 260, 523, 645,
　　1220, 1310, 1473, 1543, 1671
—Central, 62
—Gulf of, 8, 1143
—Invaded by Russia, 8
—Karelian Isthmus, 8
—Kuusamo, 8
—Maps, 506
—Peace treaty with Russia, 8
—Post war border discussions, 2234-
　　2235
—Salla, 8
—Viipuri, 8
Finland—Political leaders
—Kallio, President, 62
Finnish Air Force, 8
Finnish family, 37
Finnish northern front, 49
Finnish ski detachments, 49
Finnish ski troops, 8
Finns and Russians meet at Hangoe, 63
Finns evacuate Hangoe peninsula, 63
Finschhafen, 1031
"Fireball" plane, 2449
1st Airborne Division, 1586
First Allied Airborne Army, 1580, 1582,
　　1846-1847
1st Allied Airborne troops, 1585
1st Armored Division, Rifle Brigade,
　　902-903

First Army, 820-821, 822, 834, 911,
　　1399, 1605, 1690, 1805, 1840, 1843,
　　1853
—Captures Cologne, 1800
—104th Division, 1840
—**See also** American First Army; Brit-
　　ish First Army
First bombs drop on England, 122
1st Cavalry Division, 2431
1st Division, 1821
1st Division, U. S. Marines, 1574-1575,
　　1871
First Far Eastern Front, 2037
First French town falls to the Allies,
　　1312
1st Special Task Force, 1459
First Ukrainian Army, 1715, 1717, 1916
First week of Sicilian invasion, 959
First White Russian Army, 1544, 1740,
　　1747, 1916
Firth of Forth, 30
Fismes, 1506
Fitzroy, Captain, 792
"Fiume," 406
Flame-throwers, 1198, 1881, 2005, 2464,
　　2489
—German, 431
—In action, 1419
—Used by British Armies in France,
　　1510
Flame-throwing devices, 2465
Flame-throwing tanks, 1969, 2330, 2464
Flanders, 8, 123
Fleming, Sir Alexander, 2475
Flensburg, 720, 1981
Flight nurse, 1869
Floating airfields, 2463
Floating drydock, 1746, 1979
Floating pier, 2463
Florence, 1426-1428, 1445-1449
Florentines returning to their homes,
　　1428
Florey, Sir Howard W., 2475
Florida Island, 520, 727, 728, 758-759,
　　788-789
Floyd Bennet Field, 1111
Flushing, 1626-1627
Flying bombs, 1118, 1320-1321, 1336,
　　1354, 1381, 1502, 1622, 1696, 1927
—Factory, 1547
"Flying Fortress," 699, 741, 1015, 1182-
　　1183, 1186-1187, 1229, 1320, 1341,
　　1788
Flying Tiger, 679
—**See also** American Volunteer Group
"Flying Wing," 2447
"Foch," 833
Foch, Marshal, 116
Foggia, 1031
Folkestone, 252, 262
Food problems, post war, 2212
Foot soldier's view of war on
　　Okinawa, 1990
Ford, Henry II, 2082
Foreign Ministers' Council, 2074
Foreign Ministers' deputies, 2192
Forli, 1544
Formia, 1179
Formosa, 1978, 2068
Forrestal, James V., 1422, 1439, 1441,
　　2248
Fort Bragg, 1123
Fort Capuzzo, 343
Fort Dinant falls to the Allies, 1556-
　　1557

Fort Driant, 1648
Fort Lamy, 860
Fort Mears, 698
Fort Sill, 1123
Fort William McKinley, 584, 597
"Fortress Europe," 1020, 1229
40 mm Bofors gun, 2444
41st Division, 1260, 1267, 1816-1817
42nd Division, 1863
Fosdick, Rev. Dr. Harry Emerson, 1184
Foss, Cheryl June, 2295
Foss, Maj. Joe, 2295
Foss, Mrs., 2295
4.2 mortar, 2467
4.5 inch rockets, 1645
14 inch London range German gun, 1514
14th Air Force, 1636, 2264
Fourteenth Army, 1596, 1620, 1930, 1931
—Advances on Rangoon, 2378-2379
—See also Allied Fourteenth Army; American Fourteenth Army; British Fourteenth Army
4th Division, 2308
4th Infantry Division, 2396
4th Marine Division, 2458
4th Marine Wing, 2059
Fowkes, Maj. Gen. C. C., 569
Foxholes on Bougainville, 1188
France
—(1939) 8, 16-17, 46
—(1940) 60, 94, 116-121, 130-131, (Dunkirk) 134-137, 148, 150-151, 154-158, 162-167, 172-173, 186, 194, 197, 243, 296, 307, 309,
—(1941) 377, 499, 550
—(1942) 631-633, 635, 648-649, 663, 740-744, 771, 832-833
—(1943) 963, 1068, 1101
—(1944) 1196, 1199, 1229, 1251, 1344-1356, 1373, 1472, 1474-1475, 1477, 1479-1501, 1504-1517, 1523-1524, 1529, 1531-1533, 1543, 1545, 1548, 1679
—(1945) 1793, 1794, 1944, 1945, 2011, 2246, 2271, 2373, 2390, 2414, 2416, 2418, 2422-2423, 2467
—Allied invasion of southern, 1437-1444
—Allied landings in, 1282-1309
—Accepts Italian armistice terms, 172
—Allied battle for France (maps), 1414-1415, 1468
—Declares war on Germany, 7
—FFI Alpine Regiment, 2277
—German advance in 1940 (maps), 132-133, 154-155
—Germany ocupies half France (map), 166
—Northern, 105, 110, 118, 120, 132, 491
—Post war border discussions, 2234-2235
—Postwar elections, 2101
—Ships, see Ships
—France, Southern, 1436-1437, 1446, 1448, 1450, 1453, 1458-1459, 1480, 1482-1483, 1543, 1663, 2382
—Surrenders to Germany, 8, 160-161, 163-166
—War crimes investigations, 2092, 2098
—Western Front, 1180, 1282-1309, 1311-1315, 1324-1325, 1327, 1329-

France (cont'd)
1331, 1338, 1342, 1358-1365, 1369-1371, 1377-1378, 1380, 1386, 1398-1401, 1403-1404, 1407, 1414-1417, 1420-1421, 1423-1424, 1431, 1437-1444, 1446-1461, 1467-1470, 1519, 1521, 1526, 1555, 1559, 1561, 1565-1567, 1645, 1662-1663, 1666, 1702, 2327-2329, 2455, 2493
—See also under names of cities and towns
France, Vichy, 260
France—Military leaders
—Abrial, Adm. Jean, 143
—Allard, Maj. Jacques, 1120
—Bergeret, Gen., 165, 173
—Catroux, Gen., 413, 472, 477, 489, 932
—Darlan, Adm. Jean, 455, 771, 818, 839
—De Gaulle, Gen. Charles, 186, 197, 268, 281, 292, 413, 857, 930, 932, 941, 1325, 1374, 1474-1475, 1484, 1487, 1497, 1498, 1638, 1951, 1984, 2011, 2246
—De Laborde, Adm., 832
—Dentz, Gen. Henry, 260, 477, 488
—De Tassigney, Gen. de Latre, 1647, 2277
—Gamelin, Gen. Maurice Gustave, 16, 116
—Gensoul, Adm., 192
—Giraud, Gen. Henri Honore, 119, 839, 857, 925, 930, 932, 941, 1062
—Juin Gen. Alphonse Pierre, 1254-1255
—Koenig, Gen. Joseph, 1484
—Le Clerc, Gen. Jacques, 860, 1291, 1452, 1484, 1496, 2042, 2271
—Legentilhomme, Gen., 477
—Le Luc, Adm., 165, 173
—Muselier, Adm., 186
—Parisot, Gen., 173
—Sevez, Gen. Francois, 1944-1945
—Weygand, Gen. Maxime, 116
France—Political leaders
—Daladier, M., 2011
—Laval, Pierre, 194, 663, 1431, 1505, 2011, 2092, 2098
—Petain, Marshal Phillipe, 160, 161, 190, 296, 455, 663, 1446, 2011, 2246
—Reynaud, Paul, 160, 2011
Franco Gen. Francisco, 161, 296, 2187
—Franco regime, 2187
Franco-German agreement, 455
Franco-German Armistice, 160-161, 163-166
Frank, Hans, 2125, 2237
Frankfort, 150, 1544, 1747, 1808, 1843, 1854, 1902
"Franklin," 1836-1837
Fraser, Adm. Sir Bruce, 2042
Frederick, Maj. Gen. Robert T., 1459
Free French, 186, 191, 260, 281, 292, 413, 472, 477, 488, 691, 741, 857, 860, 913, 932, 1474, 2246, 2271, 2277
—See also Fighting French
Free French and British meet in Cairo, 413
Free French forces, 612, 1255, 1325, 1417
Free French Navy, 186
Free French troops, 484
French Air Force, 860

French airports, 172
French and Arabs clash, 1984
French Army, 1062, 1291
French artillery, 149
French battleships, 192
French Cameroon, 292
French citizen soldiers, 1500
French civilians, 1329, 1378, 1404
French coast, 499
French coastal town, 276
French collaborationists, 1373, 1486-1487, 1505, 1517, 1548, 1560
French Colonial infantry, 268
French Colonials, 681
French Colonies, 292, 680
French commemorate Armistice Day, 1638
French Committee of National Liberation, 933
French Equatorial Africa, 1496
French First Army, 1566-1567, 1646-1647, 2275, 2277, 2390
French Fleet, 172, 190-192, 771, 832-833
—Scuttled at Toulon, 771, 832-833
French forces, 1180
French forces cross the Sahara, 860
French forces in Norway, 124
French Forces of the Interior, 1180, 1460, 1475, 1495, 1498, 1523, 1560
—Alpine Regiment, 2277
French Foreign Legion, 216
French, Free, see Free French
French freed from a German prison camp, 1862
French Indo-China, 519, 520
French infantrymen and tanks, 1710
French-Italian armistice, 172
French Mediterranean Fleet, 832-833
French Morocco, 843, 856-857, 1120
French National Assembly, 194
French National Committee, 932
French Ninth Army, 119
French North Africa, 814-815
French North African government, 839
French 130 mm guns, 843
French Partisians Franc Tireus, 1500
French patriotic youth organization, 839
French patriots, 1373, 1424, 1431, 1532, 2270
French patrol, 28
French ration cards, 1359
French refugees, 1477
French regiment in Italy, 1120
French sabotage, 1199
French 2nd Division, 1491
French 2nd Armored Division, 2271
French 75mm guns, 149
French soldiers, 147, 167, 1158, 1444
—With the fifth army, 1158
French tanks, 96, 114
French troops, 124, 823
French underground, 1199, 1424, 1431
French women, 1373, 1505, 1517
French workers, 663
Fresnes prison, 2098
Freyberg, Gen., 847
Frick, Wilhelm, 2125, 2237
Friedeburg, Gen. Adm. Hans Georg, 1941, 1944-1945, 1946, 1948, 1971
Fritzsche, Hans, 2125, 2237
Fu Ping-sheung, 1084
Funk, Walther, 2125, 2237
Futa Pass, 1544, 1572, 1589

G

GB-4 glide bomb, 2454
G. I. Joe, 1308
Gabes, 898, 900
Gabr Saleh, 564
Gaeta, 1258
Gafsa Oasis, 881
Gailani, Raaschid Ali Beg, 260
Gale, Col. Guy, 1281
Galicia oilfields, 26
"Galileo Galilei," 170
Gallabat, Fort, 312
Gallipoli, 1033
Galway, 159
Gambut, 566
Gamelin, Gen. Maurice Gustave, 16, 116
Gandhi, 662, 734
"Gargoyle," 2454
Garand rifle, 2455
Garigliano River, 1126-1127
Garsson, Henry, 2226
Gasmata, 1235
Gasoline, 100 octane, 1269
Gavatu, 727
Gavin, Maj. Gen. James, 2297
Gavrilovitch, Stoyan, 2166-2167
Gavut Island, 730
Gavutu, 727, 759
Gazala, 691
Gdynia, 7
Gehres, Capt. Leslie E., 1837
Geiger, Maj. Gen. Roy, 1859, 2300
Geilenkirchen, 1716, 1739
Gela, 959, 962, 966
"General A. W. Greely," 2148
General Grant tank, 719
General Sherman tank, 1119
Geneva Convention, 127, 907, 1080, 1201
Genoa, 800-801, 1793, 1932
Gensoul, Adm., 192
George, VI King, 271, 325, 386, 916, 925, 940-941, 1041, 1306, 1439, 1600, 1951, 2268
George, Lloyd, 792
Georgian military highway, 829
Georgievsk, 737, 772
Gerbini, 942
German advance from May 10 to June 1 of 1940 (map), 132-133
German advance in Belgium (map), 132-133
German advance in France (map), 132-133, 154-155
German advance in North Africa (map), 719
German advance in the East, 506
German advance in white Russia, 486-487
German advance in Poland, 21
German advance in Russia, 769
German advance in the Ukraine, 508-509
German advance through Balkans (map), 443
German air-changing machines, 2489
German Air Force, 23, 107, 108, 178, 199, 239, 245, 262, 278-279, 319, 325, 347, 500, 669, 670-671, 760, 834, 937, 943, 1038-1039, 1183, 1185, 2417
—Over southern France, 1458

German Air Force (cont'd)
—Over Italy, 1148, 1206-1207
—See also Air war over England
German air war on French civilians, 120
German airborne attack on Crete, 458-459
German Alpine troops, 829
German-American Bund, 2196
German animal transport column, 157
German anti-aircraft guns, 150
German antipersonnel mine, 1362
German anti-tank gunners, 424
German armed motorcyclists, 94
German armies join forces with Italians in Albania, 432
German Armistice Commission, 813
German armored division, 690-691
German Army, 829, 1038, 1219, 1607, 1862, 1945
German artillery, 12, 22, 423
German assault on Thala, 882
German blitzkrieg, 7
German bombers tackled by the R.A.F., 279
German campaign in Greece (map), 443
German civilians, 1006-1007, 1633, 1847, 1962
—see horror films, 1973
German coastal guns, 276, 1311
German columns advance in Greece, 422
German concentration camps, 1880, 1973
German counter-attack in Tunisia, 834
German counter-offensive at Nettuno, 1129
German counter-offensive in Belgium, 2409
German cruiser, 72
German cyclists, 126
German dams and power plants wrecked by R.A.F., 916-917
German "Death's Head" Division, 629
German defeat in France, 1468
German drive threatens Stalingrad and Rostov, 714-715
German E-Boats, 741
German Elite Guard, 1395
German "flak-train," 699
German flame-throwers, 431
German Fleet, 462, 1956
German forced labor battalions, 1314
German forces in Greece, 1602
—in Italy, 1793-1794
—in North Africa, 402
—on the Western Front, 1680
German generals at prisoner of war camp in North Africa, 907
German gun in action, 51
German gun train, 1519
German heavy motorized unit, 156
German hide-out in Cherbourg, 1352
German High Command, 771
German high-velocity guns, 240
German horse and mechanized units in Russia, 581
German infantry, 22, 73, 151, 523
German infantry and tanks in Mariupol, 547
German infantry in retreat, 978-979
German infantry in Rostov, 723
German invasion of Russia, 478-479

German-Japanese-Italian treaty, 285, 1121
German jet propelled bomber, 2452
German jet propelled fighter, 2452
German jet propelled pilotless plane, 1118
German light tank, 105
German long-range guns, 276, 499
German machine gunners, 687
German Mark VI tank, 1512
German military band, 71
German mines, 1292
German motorized column, 118
German motorized units in Simferopol, 557
German Navy, 8, 72, 1112, 1944
German Ninth Army, 1934
German nurses, 1363
German offensive in Libya, 690-691
German one-man submarine, 1152
German Panzer troops, 1285
German Panzer division, 418
German Panzer vehicles, 551
German "People's Army," 1667
German paratroops, 91
German patrol, 28
German pillbox, 2489
German pillbox in Normandy, 1369
German plan to attack New York City with rockets, 2459
German planes, 181, 236
German planes raid the Firth of Forth, 30
German pontoon bridges, 117
German prison camp, 1862
German prisoner of war camp, 1679
German prisoners, 836-837, 1844, 1850, 1853
—in the Piazza del popolo, 1278
German propaganda, 663
German railroad gun, 2448
German retreat before Moscow, 586-587
German retreat from France, 1555
German retreat in Libya, 590
German retreat in the Caucasus, 830
German reverse in the Crimea, 604
German rocket bomb, 1622
German-Russian agreement on Poland, 26
German-Russian pact, 1528
German S. S. guards, 193
German Safety Service, 270
German seaplanes, 75
German secret weapon, 1118, 2445
German Seventh Army, 1447, 1454, 1504
German shock-troops, 128
—in Russia, 511
German Sixteenth Army, 628, 647, 668
German soldiers, 104, 668, 2326
—Firing a Russian village, 978-979
—in Russia, 572-573
German staff officers, 163
German storage cave in France, 1470
German "Stork" plane, 402
German storm troopers, 193
German submarines, 36, 802-803, 2405
German tank crew surrendering to British infantrymen, 810
German tank and motorcycle reinforcements, 688
German tanks, 22, 70, 73, 104, 532-533
—enter Bulgaria, 385

German tanks (cont'd)
—Mark VI tank, 1512
—Tiger tank, 1512
German transports and supply ships, 83
German troops, 71, 73, 79, 103
—enter Stalino, 552-553
—firing homes of Russian peasants, 872
—in Bosnia, 1110
—in Sicily, 964-965
—occupy Corinth and Greek Islands, 436
—prepare for the invasion of Britain, 308
German U-boat surrenders to U. S. Navy, 1965
German V-1, 1696, 1703
German V-2 rocket, 2445
German V-2 scientists surrender to Americans, 1927
German victory parade in Greece, 438
German war crimes investigations. See War crimes investigations—Europe
German war production, 632-633, 635, 720
German warships, 558
German warfare on Britain-bound convoys, 408-409
German Westphalia, 916-917
German winter line in southern Italy, 1122-1123
German winter retreat in Russia, 872-873
Germans break through in the Ukraine, 502
Germans capture Tobruk and Mersa Matruh, 706-707
Germans cross the Aisne, 117
Germans cross the Don River, 710-711
Germans cut off in the Ukraine, 1194
Germans enter burning Kiev, 537
Germans flee from Tilsit, 1730
Germans flood Holland, 1208
Germans fortify Crete, 974-975
Germans in Norway, 73
Germans launch offensive in the Crimea, 685
Germans launch summer offensive in Russia, 976-977
Germans on the Pripet Marshes, 1099
Germans open drive for the Caucasus oil fields, 724-725
Germans recapture Rostov, 722-723
Germans trapped in Estonia, 1425
Germany
—(1939) 7
—(1940) 68, 212, 260, 283, 285, 296,
—(1941) 425, 520
—(1942) 644-645, 694, 772,
—(1943) 916-917, 1004-1007, 1114
—(1944) 1182-1187, 1341, 1394, 1524, 1543, 1633, 1667, 1669
—(1945) 1788, 1793, 1819-1821, 1856, 1868, 1885-1890, 1904-1906, 1909, 1913-1916, 1918-1919, 1926-1929, 1934-1937, 1940-1942, 1962, 1964, 1970, 1973, 1976, 2009, 2207, 2318, 2372, 2396, 2384, 2399, 2404, 2414, 2416, 2421, 2445, 2477
—Air War, 772
—Allied prison camp for German officers, 2140-2141
—American occupation, 2115

Germany (cont'd)
—Bruchsal Prison, 2111
—Declares war on Russia, 260
—Declares war on the U. S., 578
—Demands on Poland, 7
—Eastern Front, 1544
—Foreign laborers, 1856
—Invades Belgium, 8, 95
—Invades Denmark, 8
—Invades Holland, 8, 90
—Invades Luxemburg, 8
—Invades Norway, 8
—Invades Poland, 7
—Non-aggression pact with Russia, 7
—North, 150
—Nuremberg trials, 2122-2129, 2135, 2139, 2194, 2236-2237, 2238-2239
—Occupies half France (map), 166
—Post-war, 2073
—Russian occupation, 1918, 2161
—Ships, see Ships
—Surrender, 1793, 1944-1949
—Surrender in Italy, 1924
—Surrender in northern Italy, 1793-1794
—Surrender of North German forces, 1941
—Surrender ratified in Berlin, 1947
—Surrenders unconditionally at Reims, 1944-1945
—U. S. Clergy protests Allied air raids, 1184
—U. S. post-war destruction of war plants, 2115
—Western Front, 1564, 1581, 1592, 1605-1607, 1644, 1648-1649, 1659, 1750, 1758, 1779, 1780, 1782-1783, 1800-1808, 1810-1811, 1813, 1815, 1829, 1831-1833, 1840-1848, 1861-1866, 1879-1880, 1897, 1900-1902, 1921, 2323-2326, 2336, 2461, 2468, 2489, 2494
—See also Africa, North; Air war; Battle of Britain; Battle of the Bulge; Eastern Front; Italian Front; under names of cities and towns; War crimes investigations —Europe
Germany—Military leaders
—Basseage, Maj. Gen., 907
—Beck, Col. Gen. Ludwig, 1394, 1395
—Bieldwius, Gen., 907
—Beck, Col. Gen. Ludwig, 1394-1395
—Bock, Gen. von, 536, 688, 760
—Borowletz, Maj. Gen., 907
—Doenitz, Grand Adm. Karl, 1395, 1928-1929, 2124-2125, 2237
—Dostler, Gen. Anton, 2144
—Fiedler, Gen. Maj. Erich, 2140
—Friedeburg, Gen. Adm. Hans Georg, 1941, 1944-1945, 1946, 1948, 1971
—Goering, Reichsmarshal Herman, 163, 165, 309, 1394, 1957, 2124-2125, 2127, 2128-2129, 2139, 2194, 2236-2237, 2239, 2459
—Jeschonnek, Gen., 309
—Jodl, Col. Gen. Alfred Gustav, 1944-1945, 1946, 2124-2125, 2237
—Keitel, Field Marshal Wilhelm, 1395, 1947-1948, 2124-2125, 2128, 2237
—Kesselring, Field Marshal Albert, 1129, 1263, 1955
—Kirchenpauer, Gen. Maj. Wilhelm, 2141
—Kluge, Field Marshal von, 1447

Germany—Military leaders (con'td)
—Krause, Maj. Gen., 907
—Kretschmer, Commander Otto, 411
—Kunzel, Gen., 1941
—Loerzer, Gen., 309
—Manstein, Gen. von, 685
—Meendsen-Bohlken, Adm. Wilhelm, 1956
—Milch, Field Marshal, 1395
—Neuffer, Maj. Gen., 907
—Oxenius, Maj. Gen. Wilhelm, 1944
—Quast, Gen. von, 907
—Raeder, Grand Adm. Erich, 165, 2124-2125, 2237
—Theissen, Gen. Karl, 2140
—Vaerst, Maj. Gen. von, 907
Germany—Political leaders
—Frank, Hans, 2125, 2237
—Frick, Wilhelm, 2125, 2237
—Fritzsche, Hans, 2125, 2237
—Funk, Walther, 2125, 2237
—Goebbels, Joseph Paul, 193, 270
—Hess, Rudolph, 165, 454, 2124-2125, 2127, 2128-2129, 2139, 2236
—Himmler, Heinrich, 1394-1395, 1971
—Hitler, Adolf, 7, 34, 65, 160-161, 163-165, 193, 259, 296, 983, 984, 1045, 1181, 1194, 1248, 1394-1395, 1494, 1659, 1794, 1909, 1928-1929, 2118-2119
—Ley, Dr. Robert, 1970
—Neurath, Constantin von, 2125, 2237
—Papen, Franz von, 1877, 2125, 2129, 2237
—Ribbentrop, Joachim von, 7, 8, 26, 165, 285, 385, 404, 2125, 2129, 2139, 2237
—Rommel, Field Marshal Erwin, 520, 563, 567, 691, 700, 702, 768, 813, 851, 1109, 1209
—Rosenberg, Alfred, 2125, 2127, 2237
—Rundstedt, Field Marshal Karl von, 536, 1543, 1680, 1684, 1695, 1741, 1937, 2312
—Schacht, Hjalmar, 2125, 2237
—Shirach, Baldur von, 2125, 2237
—Speer, Albert, 2125, 2237
—Streicher, Julius, 2125, 2237
Geromont, 1711
Gestapo, 1199, 1394-1395, 1971
Ghadames, 860
Ghent, 1543
Ghetto in Warsaw, 2130-2131
Gibraltar, 153, 2266
Gibson, Wing-Commander G. P., 916
Giessen, 1843
Gilbert Islands, 622-623, 1031, 1032, 1088-1089, 1102-1103, 1137, 1163, 1252
Gilchrist, Huntington, 2166-2167
Gillars, Mildred, 2197
Giraud, Gen. Henri Honore, 119, 839, 857, 925, 930, 932, 941, 1062
—and De Gaulle at Algiers, 932
Giropa Creek, 854
"Giulio Cesare," 1041
Glasgow, 454
Gleiwitz, 1783
Glennon, Cardinal John J., 2180
Glide bomb, 2454
Glider troops, 1846
Gliders, 952, 1324
"Gloucester," 406
"Glowworn," 67
"Gneisenau," 588-589

Goebbels, Joseph Paul, 193, 270
Goering, Reichsmarshal Herman, 163, 165, 309, 1394, 1957, 2124-2125, 2127, 2128-2129, 2139, 2194, 2236, 2237, 2459
Gojjam, 368
Gold Coast troops, 380
Golikov, Gen., 490
Golubov, Gen., 634
Gomel, 508-509, 531
Gondar, 541, 568-569
Gordon Highlanders, 858
Gort, Gen., 16, 60, 143, 2284
Gothic Line, 1179, 1544, 1572, 1589, 1624, 1641
"Graf Spee," see **"Admiral Graf Spee"**
Gran Sasso Hotel, 1044-1045
Grand Fascist Council, 1121
Great Bitter Lake, 1756
Great Britain, 218, 269, 519, 689, 2010
—Air Force, see Royal Air Force
—British Blue Book, 7
—Casualties and losses, see Casualties and losses—Allied
—Declares war on Germany, 7
—Navy, see British Navy
—Ships, see Ships
—**See also** Africa, North; under Air war over England; Battle of Britain; Britain; British; China-Burma-India Theater; England; Italian Front; Pacific Theater; Western Front
Great Britain—Military leaders
—Alexander, Gen. Sir Harold R. L. G., 638, 925, 930, 1254, 2267
—Anderson, Gen., 821, 834, 930
—Auchinleck, Gen., 712, 718
—Cunningham, Lt. Gen. Sir Alan, 563
—Cunningham, Adm. Sir Andrew, 316, 914, 956, 1041
—Dempsey, Lt. Gen. Sir Miles, 1598, 1739, 2268
—Fraser, Adm. Sir Bruce, 2042
—Gort, Gen., 16, 60, 143, 2284
—Harwood, Rear Adm. Henry, 41, 42-43, 58
—Ironside, Gen. Sir Edmund, 2284
—Leese, Gen. Sir Oliver, 1255, 1258, 1629, 2267
—Longmire, Air Marshal, 413
—McCreery, Lt. Gen. Sir Richard, 1629
—Montgomery, Field Marshal Sir Bernard L., 700, 804, 813, 847, 859, 892, 900, 930, 960, 962, 991, 1033, 1035, 1037, 1135, 1255, 1283, 1294, 1325, 1398, 1531, 1545, 1600, 1793, 1926, 1941, 2253
—Mountbatten Adm. Lord Louis, 1192, 1382, 1939, 2078, 2281
—Percival, Lt. Gen. A. E., 2045
—Phillips, Adm. Sir Thomas, 583
—Ramsay, Adm. Sir Bertram, 2287
—Spears, Gen., 413
—Sturges, Maj. Gen., 681
—Syfret, Rear Adm., 681
—Wavell, Gen. Sir Archibald, 307, 338, 371, 413, 2299
—Wilson, Gen. Sir Henry Maitland, 2266
—Wingate, Maj. Gen. Orde Charles, 2289
Great Britain—Political leaders
—Attlee, Clement, 1794, 2010, 2114, 2242

Great Britain—Political leaders (cont'd)
—Beaverbrook, Lord, 195
—Bevin, Ernest, 1949, 2010, 2117, 2165
—Bracken, Brenden, 100
—Cadogan, Sir Alexander, 2198, 2199
—Chamberlain, Neville, 9, 60, 100
—Churchill, Winston, see under Churchill
—Cranborne, Lord, 386
—Cripps, Sir Stafford, 490, 662, 734
—Eden, Anthony, 53, 204, 689, 930, 1084, 1100-1101
—George, Lloyd 792
—George VI, King, 271, 325, 386, 916, 925, 940-941, 1041, 1306, 1439, 1600, 1951, 2268
—Halifax, Lord, 64, 369, 447
—Henderson, Sir Neville, 7
—O'Brian, John Lord, 2199
—United Nations General Assembly, 2165
—United Nations Security Council, 2198, 2199
—Wavell, Gen. Sir Archibald, 307, 338, 371, 413, 2299
Greater Germany, 1876
Greece, 259, 260, 300-301, 305-307, 310-311, 322-323, 330-331, 333, 362, 422-424, 431, 434-439, 1544, 1593, 1602-1604, 1628, 1670
—Italian invasion of, 259
—Italian ultimatum, 301
—Map, 362
—Post war border discussions, 2234-2235
—Regency, 1544
—Ships, see Ships
Greece—Political leaders
—Metaxas, Gen., 301
Greek Air Force, 333
Greek airmen, 332
Greek Army, 332, 433
—Surrenders, 434
Greek civil war, 1544, 1628, 1670
Greek concentration camp, 331
Greek infantry, 305
Greek islands, 437
Greek mule transport, 322
Greek patriots, 1603
Greek soldiers of the Epirot, 434
Greek troops, 301, 322
Greek warships, 301
Green Islands, 1203, 1237
Grenades, 2446
Grenadier Guards, 231
Grenoble, 1501, 1507
—Treason trial, 1548
"Grenville," 50
Grese, Irma, 2121
Gressenich, 2494
Griffin, Col. T. N., 2152
"Gripsholm," 1222
Gromyko, Andrei, 2198, 2199, 2200-2201
Groves, Maj. Gen. Leslie R., 2020
Grozny oilfields, 737, 829, 830, 848-849
Gruenther, Maj. Gen. Alfred M., 1272
Grumman "Avenger," 1067, 1111, 1316
Guadalcanal, 520, 727, 728, 730, 732, 746, 748-749, 753, 758-759, 772, 783, 788-789, 790-791, 866-869, 944, 1031, 1102-1103, 1406, 2256
—Final offensive, 866

Guam, 642-643, 1180, 1390-1392, 1418-1419, 1429, 1432, 1520, 1530, 2030-2031, 2391, 2398, 2426
—returns to the United States, 1432
Guards' Chapel, London, 1381
Guerrilla warfare, 260, 2257
Guerrillas
—Allied, 923
—Filipino, 1834
—Yugoslav, 998-999
Guiana, French, 2303
Gulf of Finland, 63, 1143
Gulf of Sirte, 592
Gummersbach, 1893
Guns, mobile, 2461
Gurkhas, 1257
—over Rangoon, 1931
Gustav line, 1189, 1253, 1257, 1259
Guyon-Witzschel, Louise, 2135

H

"H"-Hour, 2301
Habania airport, 260
Habbaniyah, 444
Hague, The, 90
Haguenau, 1666
Haile Selassie, 260, 368
Hailar, 2024
Halfaya (Helafaya), 563, 592, 598-599, 612, 707, 807
"Halifax," 526, 588-589, 800
Halifax, Lord, 64, 369, 447
Hall, Leonard, 1904
Halmahera, 1530, 1544
Halsey, Adm. William F., 1544, 1562, 1615, 1621, 2038, 2264
Hamamoto, 2151
Hamburg, 720-721, 1941
"Hamilcar" gliders, 1580
Hamilton, R. M., 2463
Hamm, 1879
"Hammon," 696
Hampden, 130
"Hancock," 2397
Handgrenade, 2446
Hangman's Hill, 1211
Hangoe Peninsula, 8
Hangoe, 63
Hannover, 1793
Hardanger Fjord, 78
"Hardy," 69
Harmon, Lt. Tom, 2303
Harmon, Sharon Kristan, 2303
Harmon, Mrs. Tom, 2303
Harriman, Averill, 755
Harwood, Rear Adm. Henry, 41, 42-43, 58
"Hasty," 406
Hata, Field Marshal Shunroku, 2037, 2146
Hawaii, 1410
"Haw Haw, Lord," 1981
"Hazelwood," 2370-2371
Heavy artillery, 2493
Heavy machine gun, 2479
Heinkel, 131, 1889
—"III," 278-279
—jet planes, 1889
Helfrich, 2042
"Hellfire Pass," 275
Helmond-Venlo railway, 1651
Helsinki, 37-38

Henderson Field, 520, 732, 788, 868
Henderson, Sir Neville, 7
Hennecke, Adm. Walter, 1348
Henri Chapelle, 1886
Hensel, M/Sgt. Frederic, 2204-2205
Heraklion, 458-459
Hersfeld, 2140-2141
Hertogenbosch, 1598
Hess, Rudolph, 165, 454, 2124-2125, 2127, 2128-2129, 2139, 2236
Hesselbach, 1866
Hewitt, Adm. H. K., 818, 1038, 1441
Hickam Field, 575, 577
High angle bomb, 2483
Highland regiments, 621
Hill 604, 2306-2307
Hill 700, 1188
Hill, Rear Adm. Harry W., 1092
Himara, 362
Himmler, Gudron, 2135
Himmler, Heinrich, 1394-1395, 1971
Himmler, Mrs. Margaret, 2135
Hiranuma, Baron Kiichiro, 2146
Hirohito, Emperor, 577, 2085, 2137, 2185
Hiroshima, 1794, 2015, 2016-2017, 2018, 2075, 2484
Hirota, Koki, 2146
Hitler, Adolf, 7, 34, 160-161, 163-165, 193, 259, 296, 983, 984, 1045, 1181, 1194, 1394-1395, 1494, 1659, 1794, 1909, 1928-1929, 2118-2119
—and Mussolini meet, 65
—Cartoon, 1248
—reported dead, 1929
Hitler, Adolf, Bridge, 1807
Hitler Line, 1268
Hitler-Stalin pact, 1528
Hitler tank division, 872
Hitler Youth, 1318-1319, 1996
Ho Yin-chen, Gen., 2281
Hobby, Col. Oveta Culp, 2273
Hodge, Maj. Gen. John R., 1859
Hodges, Gen. Courtney H., 1524, 1600, 1861, 1905, 2286
Hoenzollern Bridge, 1807
Hokkaido, 2006
Holden, Tech. Sgt., 1272
Holland, 8, 90, 92, 102, 103, 108, 130, 133, 493, 699, 1208, 1543, 1580, 1582-1587, 1779, 1941, 2297
—German invasion of, 8, 90
—Surrenders to Germany, 8
—Underground, 1208
—Welcomes British Bombers, 493
—See also Netherlands; Pacific Theater; Western Front
Holland—Military leaders
—Helfrich, Adm., 2042
Holland House, 303
Hollandia, 1180, 1225, 1239-1245,
Holmes, John Haynes, 1184
Holtz Bay, 918-919
Holzerath, 2323
Home Guard of Local Defense Volunteers, 204, 237
Homma, Lt. Gen. Masaharu, 2081, 2175-2177
Homs, 851
Honan, 794-795
Hong-Kong, 519, 600
Honolulu, 577, 1809
Honshu, 1967, 2006
"Hood," 462-463
Hoover, Herbert, 2212

Hopkins, Harry, 1100-1101
"Hornet," 664-665, 666
"Horsa" gliders, 1580
Horse Guards Parade, 58
Hospital plane, 1869
Hotel de Ville, 1351
Houffalize, 1708, 2312
"Houston," 2402
Houx, 1549
Howie, Maj. Thomas D., 1386
Howitzers, 226, 228
Ho Yin-chen, Gen., 2281
Hseuh Yeuk, Gen., 1106
Hsipaw, 673, 1838
Hu, Gen., 1233
Hudson, R. S., 793
Huertgen Forest, 1637, 2396
Hukawng Valley, 1174, 1191
Hull, Cordell, 1084, 1375, 2027, 2134
Hulrich, 1874
Hunan Province, 1968
Hungarian divisions on the Eastern Front, 552
Hungarian motorized troops, 426
Hungarians break treaty of friendship with Yugoslavia, 426
Hungary, 260, 426, 1543, 1671-1673, 1725, 1808, 2411
—Post war border discussions, 2234-2235
—War crimes investigations, 2186, 2203
Hungary—Political leaders
—Baky, 2203
—Bardossy, M. M., 426
—Endre, Laszlo, 2203
—Imredy, Bela, 2186
Huntziger, Gen., 165, 173
Hupeh, 888
Hupeh-Honan border, 929
Hurley, Patrick J., 2138
"Hurricane," 236, 278, 589, 453, 550
Hutton, Gen., 638
Hyde Park, 2209

I

I. G. Farben, 2115
Iceland, 496-498
"Idarwald," 336
Ie Jima, 1871
Ie Shima, 2032, 2034, 2385
Iheya Shima, 2377
Ilchester, Lord, 303
"Illustrious," 315
Ilmen, Lake, 629
Imperial airborne Commando forces in Burma, 1205, 2289
Imperial Army of the Nile, 2299
Imphal, 676, 1179, 1226, 1232
Imredy, Bela, 2186
Incendiary bomb, 2435
Inch Garvie Island, 30
Indaw, 1544
"Independence," 2225, 2227
India, 255, 269, 340, 519, 630, 677, 734-735, 923, 1179, 1382, 1787, 1227, 1972
—Air Force, 626-627
—Congress, 662, 734
—Independence movement, 2157, 2170
—Supply route for China, 1145
—See also China-Burma-India Theater

India—Political leaders
—Bose, Subhas Chandra, 2170
—Gandhi, 662, 734
—Nehru, Pandit, 662, 734
Indian and Maltese contingents, 177
Indian Army Service Corps, 46
Indian forces in Burma, 1931
Indian forces in Malaya, 495
Indian infantry, 713
Indian National Army, 2170
Indian National Congress Party, 2157
Indian Ocean, 520, 680, 1939
Indian parachute regiment, 1931
Indian transport column, 590
Indian troops, 255, 563, 592, 716
—In Burma, 1620
—In Italy, 1268
"Indianapolis," 2426
Indo-China, 495, 2001, 2157
Indonesia, 2170
Indonesian People's Army, 2096
Indonesians demand independence, 2096
Infantry moves ahead on Hollandia, 1242-1243
Infantrymen in Luzon, 2455
Infantrymen in St. Malo, 2455
Infra-red ray principle, 2466
Ingram, Adm. Jonas H., 2102, 2259
Inland Sea, 1794
Insterburg, 1543, 1737
International High Tribunal, 2126
Internment camps, Canada, 188
Intramuros, 605
Ionosphere rocket, 2498
Ipoh, 611
Iran, 260, 507, 540
—Maps, 507
—Oil fields, 507
—United Nations Security Council, 2199, 2201
Iran—Political leaders
—Ala, Hussein, 2199
—Daftari, Akbar, 2199
—Mohammed, Prince, 260
—Riza, Shah, 260
—United Nations Security Council, 2199
Iraq, 260, 444, 459
Iraq—Political leaders
—Ali, Raschid, 444
—Gailani, Raaschid Ali Beg, 260
—Mohammed, Prince, 260
Ireland, 620
Iron Guard, 264
Iron Guard legionnaires, 264
Ironside, Gen. Sir Edmund, 2284
"Ironsides," 208
Irrawaddy River, 636, 638, 653, 674, 1939
Ishan, 1544
Isigny, 1314, 1325
Isitt, Vice Marshal Leonard M., 2042
Italian Air Force, 313
Italian air attacks on Sofia, 1132
Italian airborne landings, 467
Italian armies retreat before the Greeks in Albania, 310
Italian armistice, 1062
Italian artillery, 275
Italian battle scene, 1122-1123
Italian battleships, 196
Italian cavalry riding into Greece, 301
Italian colonial troops, 541
Italian convoys, 259

Italian cruiser, 365
Italian desert spotter, 275
Italian East Africa, 8, 259-260
Italian Fascists, 1552
Italian fighter planes, 840
Italian Fleet, 196, 225, 259, 406, 512, 1195
—Surrenders, 1040-1041
Italian forces driven from Sidi Barrani and Sollum, 340
Italian front, 1031, 1032, 1033-1045, 1054-1055, (Cancello entered) 1071-1073, 1076-1077, 1086-1087, 1119, 1121-1125, (Nettuno-Anzio beachheads open drive for Rome) 1126-1131, 1132, 1134-1135, 1144, 1148-1153, 1156, 1158-1159, (Cassino) 1164, 1175, 1179, 1189, 1206-1207, 1210-1211, 1221, 1230, 1238, 1246, 1248, 1253-1255, 1257-1259, 1263, 1265, 1268-1270, (Rome entered) 1271-1281, 1387-1389, 1426-1428, 1462-1463, 1544, 1550, 1572-1573, 1589, 1594-1595, 1624, 1629, 1641, 1665, 1668, 1728, 1790-1791, 1793-1794, 1797, 1799, 1903, 1920, 1924, (Allied victory in Italy) 1932, (additional scenes) 1938, 2267, 2270, 2297, 2302, 2401, 2407, 2486
—See also under names of cities, towns, etc.
Italian Front—Maps
—After four months, 1135
—Italy invaded, 1033
Italian garrison at Wolshefit surrenders, 541
Italian-German-Japanese treaty, 285, 1121
Italian infantry, 706-707
Italian islands, 934-937
Italian machine gunners, 275
Italian mainland, 942
Italian merchant ships, 415
Italian mobile corps, 691
Italian mortars, 311
Italian Navy, 225, 314, 406, 967, 1040-1041
Italian news agency, 196
Italian partisans, 1427, 1794, 1922-1923
Italian planes over Britain, 313
Italian prisoners, 340, 568-569, 890-891
Italian prisoners of war in America, 1080
Italian raids on Greek towns, 333
Italian Riviera, 1246
Italian Somaliland, 260, 380
Italian students, 101
Italian submarine, 802-803
Italian troops, 152, 272-273, 305
—in Sicily, 964-965
Italian ultimatum to Greece, 301
Italian victory parade in Greece, 438
Italian war industry, 800
Italian warships, 196, 225
Italian-Yugoslav border commission, 2192
Italians greet American troops, 1273
Italians invade Egypt, 272-273
Italians looting buildings in Catania, 990-991
Italy
—(1939) 8, (1940) 101, 153, 171, 172, 229, 232, 274, 285, 300, 322, 331, 338-339,

Italy (cont'd)
—(1941) 362, 376-377, 379,
—(1942) 700, 800-801
—(1943) 858, 970-971, 984-985, 1031, 1032
—(1944) 1195, 1234, 1445, 1449, 1552-1553
—(1945) 1922-1924
—Advance in Greece (map), 443
—Albanian campaign (map), 362
—Armistice agreement with Allies, 1031
—Bases in Albania, 259
—Black market, 2208
—Campaign in Italy, 1033-1045, 1054-1055, (Cancello entered) 1071-1073, 1076-1077, 1086-1087, 1119, (Nettuno-Anzio beachheads open drive for Rome) 1126, 1131, 1132, 1134-1135, 1144, 1148-1153, 1156, 1158-1159, (Cassino) 1164, 1175, 1179, 1189, 1206-1207, 1210-1211, 1221, 1230, 1238, 1246, 1248, 1253-1255, 1257-1259, 1263, 1265, (Rome entered) 1271-1281, 1387-1389, 1426-1428, 1462-1463, 1544, 1550, 1572-1573, 1589, 1594-1595, 1624, 1629, 1641, 1665, 1668, 1728, 1790-1791, 1793-1794, 1797, 1799, 1903, 1920, (Allied victory in Italy 1932, (additional scenes) 1938, 2144, 2149, 2267, 2270, 2297, 2302, 2401, 2407, 2417, 2486
—Declares war on France, 8
—Declares war on Great Britain, 8
—Declares war on the Allies, 152
—Declares war on the U. S., 578
—Four months after the initial landing, 1135
—Invades Greece, 259, 300-301
—Post war border discussions, 2234-2235
—Ships, see Ships
—Trieste border dispute, 2192
—Troops on French border, 8
Italy—Military leaders
—Aosta, Duke of, 416, 456
—Badoglio, Marshal, 173, 1031, 1035, 1041, 1195
—Cavagnari, Adm., 173
—De Bono, Marshal Emilio, 1121
—Gonella, Col., 541
—Nasi, Gen., 569
—Pricolo, Gen., 173
—Roatta, Gen., 173
Italy—Political leaders
—Badoglio, Marshal, 173, 1031, 1035, 1041, 1195
—Ciano, Count, 173, 285, 385
—Mussolini, Benito, 65, 152-153, 161, 163, 296, 984-985, 991, 1044-1045, 1087, 1121, 1280, 1794, 1922-1923
Iwamaura, Michiyo, 2105
Iwo Jima, 1544, 1764-1778, 1786, 1789, 1794, 1798, 2330, 2334-2335, 2383, 2458, 2474
—Cemetery, 2383
Izyum, 704
Izyum-Barenkovo area, 688
Izzi, Basil Dominic, 894

J

Jackson, Robert H., 2123, 2126
"Jamaica," 1113
James, Rembert, 2296
Japan, 285, 519, 574, 576-577, 1097, 1322, 1393, 1544, 1652, 1784, 1794, 1814, 1830, 1967, 1978, 1987, 2015-2017, 2021, 2038, 2070, 2075
—American occupation, 2038, 2060-2064, 2072, 2085, 2093
—American occupation forces, 2080, 2094
—At the end of the Second World War, 2046
—Black Dragon Society, 2113
—Demobilization, 2064
—Food, 2086
—Higashi-Kuni cabinet, 2093
—Invades the Philippines, 584-585, 591
—Maps, 2046-2047
—Maps, see also Maps and diagrams—Pacific Theater
—Offers to surrender, 2024
—Omori prison camp, 2105, 2108
—Post war, 2060, 2086, 2095
—Post war Cabinet, 2093
—Post war Diet, 2137
—Post war housing, 2185
—Shinagawa prison camp, 2087
—Ships, see Ships
—Sugamo prison, 2106
—Surrender, 1794, 2025-2035, 2041
—Surrender at Kerama Retto, 1943
—Surrender at Nanking, 2066
—Surrender delegation, 2032
—Surrender delegation arrives at Manila, 2033
—Surrender is official, 2027
—Surrender message, 2027
—Surrender of southern armies, 2078
—Surrender on Namur Island, 1160-1161
—Surrender on Saipan, 2145
—Surrender on Wake Island, 2059
—War crimes investigations, see War crimes investigations—Pacific
—War victims, 2088-2089
—**See also** China-Burma-India Theater; Pacific Theater
Japan—Military leaders
—Hata, Field Marshal Shunroku, 2146
—Homma, Lt. Gen. Masaharu, 2081, 2175-2177
—Kuroda, Lt. Gen. Shigenori, 2081
—Miyakazi, Lt. Gen. Shuichi, 2043
—Nogano, Adm., 1170, 1173
—Nomura, Adm., 576
—Sakaibara, Rear Adm. Shigematsu, 2143
—Suguyama, Field Marshal, 1170, 1173
—Tachibaba, Lt. Commander Soichi, 2143
—Takahashi, Adm. Sankichi, 2146
—Yamashita, Gen. Tomoyuki, 2058, 2104, 2151
Japan—Political leaders
—Araki, Gen. Sadao, 2110
—Hiranuma, Baron Kiichiro, 2146
—Hirohito, Emperor, 577, 2085, 2137, 2185

Japan—Political leaders (cont'd)
—Hirota, Koki, 2146
—Iwamura, Michiyo, 2105
—Koiso, Gen. Kuniaki, 1393
—Kurusu, Saburo, 285, 519, 576
—Suzuki, Adm, Baron Kantaro, 2105
—Tereshima, Adm. Ken, 2105
—Tojo, Gen. Hideki, 576, 1170, 1173, 1393, 2076, 2106, 2214
Japan—Political leaders—Post war
—Ashida, 2093
—Shidehara, Baron Kijuro, 2093
—Tsagita, 2093
Japanese advance in Burma (map), 673
Japanese advance in Malaya (map), 621
Japanese Air Force, 1214
Japanese aircraft carrying submarines, 2478
Japanese Army, 1170
Japanese Army in China, 2066
Japanese armistice mission, 2035
Japanese at Lorient, 1461
Japanese atomic research, 2158
Japanese atrocities, 1520
Japanese Baka bomb, 1994
Japanese balloons released against U. S., 2425
Japanese Banzai charge, 1982-1983
Japanese bomb Mandalay, 653
Japanese Cabinet, 1393
Japanese cargo ship sinking, 809
Japanese carrier in flames, 1334
Japanese children, 2315
Japanese cyclotrons, 2158
Japanese civilians in the Karama Islands, 1852
Japanese commit hari-kiri, 1418
Japanese convoy, 1562-1563
Japanese defeated in Papua, 844-845
Japanese emperor, 2025
Japanese escort vessel, 1867
Japanese Fifth Kwantung Army Group, 2037
—Surrenders to Russians, 2036-2037
Japanese Fleet, 682, 696, 1334
—Home Fleet, 1794
—Imperial Fleet, 1544, 1614-1615, 1619
Japanese forces enter Manila, 605
—in Burma, 626-627
—on Cebu, 2083
Japanese-German-Italian treaty, 285, 1121
Japanese gun, 2448
Japanese hari-kari, 732
Japanese Imperial Iron and Steel Works, 1322
Japanese Imperial Staff, 2035
Japanese in Burma, 1839, 1939
Japanese infantry and tanks, 625
Japanese jungle fighters, 732
Japanese land on the Aleutian Islands, 705
Japanese landing craft, 1748-1749
Japanese landing party, 619
Japanese landings on Singapore Island, 624
Japanese launch attack on Malaya, 582-583
Japanese light tanks, 624
Japanese loss at Saipan, 1333
Japanese Marines, 733
Japanese naval bases in the Pacific, 642-643

Japanese Navy, 736, 1170, 1544
Japanese nurses on Cebu, 2083
Japanese occupy Lashio, 672
Japanese officers on a mission to Germany, 285
Japanese prison camps, 2087, 2105, 2106, 2108
Japanese prisoners, 659
Japanese prisoners on Guam, 2030
Japanese retreat in New Britain, 1235
Japanese set-back in New Guinea, 757
Japanese shipping, 640-641
Japanese sink the U.S.S. "St. Lo," 2403
Japanese soldiers repatriated from Korea, 2147
Japanese suicide boats, 1849
Japanese suicide planes, 1917
Japanese tank column, 627
Japanese tankette, 2495
Japanese tanks, 1727, 2473
—and motor vehicles, 611
Japanese 37 mm anti-tank gun, 1217
Japanese transport aflame, 736
Japanese troops, 674
Japanese twin-engined bomber, 640-641
Japanese "Zero" float plane, 1992
Jarabub, 400, 563
—Jardov, Gen., 2286
Jassy falls to the Russians, 1476
Jato, 2454
Java, 519, 637, 1262, 2096
"Jean Bart," 818
"Jean de Vienne," 833
Jebel Achkel, 909
Jebel Mansour, 885
Jedabia, 812
Jeep, 748
Jena, 1880
Jerran, Guardsman T., 941
Jeschonnek, Gen., 309
Jet planes, 1889
Jet propelled bomber, German, 2452
Jet propelled fighter plane, 2172
—German, 2452
—U. S., 2460
Jet propelled pilotless aircraft, 2454
Jet propelled pilotless miniature plane, 1118
Jet propelled planes, American, 2449
Jet propelled torpedoes, 1339
Jews, 871
—Post war problems, 2117
Jibuti, 172
Jibuti-Addis Ababa railway, 280
"JM-1 Marauder," 2451
Jodl, Col. Gen. Alfred Gustav, 1944-1945, 1946, 2124-2125, 2237
Joessing Fjord, 55
Johnson, Jr. Hewlett, 695
Johore Bahru, 624
Joint Task Force One, 2218, 2220-2221, 2225
Joyce, William, 1981
"Ju 52," 811
Juda, King, 2210, 2211
"Judy," 1917
Juelich, 1781-1782
Juin, Gen. Alphonse Pierre, 1254-1255
Juliana Canal, 1726
Jumbo, 380
Jungle warfare, 778-779, 1031, 2424, 2479
Junkers dive bombers, 214

K

K-9 replacements, 1466
Kaczmarczyk, Alexander, 808
Kagi, 778
Kaiser Wilhelm Canal, 282
Kalach, 737
Kalamas, 362
Kalewa, 1660, 1689
Kalinin, 549, 586-587, 614, 646-647
Kallio, President, 62
Kaltenbrunner, 2237
Kaluga, 549, 587, 614
Kamaing, 1471
Kamaishi, 2006
Kamikaze, 1959, 2263, 2332-2333, 2370-
    2371, 2375, 2406, 2439
"Kanaris," 988
Kandy, 1953
Kantemirovka, 714
Karama Islands, 1852
Karelia, 1310
Karelian Isthmus, 8, 62, 260, 523, 545
Kase, Shunichi, 2043
Kasserine Pass, 884, 890-891, 911
Kastoria, 333
Kastornaya, 872
Katakolon, 1593
Katena, 1859
Katowice, 7
Kattegat, 8
Kaufbeuren, 2115
Kaunas, 1179
Kawabe, Lt. Gen. Takashiro, 2032-
    2033, 2035
Kazvin, 507
Kehsi Mansam, 672
Keitel, Field Marshal Wilhelm, 1395,
    1947-1948, 2124-2125, 2129, 2237
Kelantan River, 582-583
Kell, 2396
"Kelly," 334-335
Kelly, Capt. Colin, 2282
Kelly, Mrs. Colin, 2282
Kendleigh, Ensign Jane, 1798
Kennedy, Joseph P., 386
Kenney, Gen. George C., 1225, 2283
Kent, 262, 290
Kent, Duke and Duchess of, 756
Kenya, 260
Kerama Retto, 1943
Kerch, 580, 685
Kerch Peninsula, 688
Kerch Straits, 580, 604, 1032
Keren, 372, 403
Kerr, Maj. Robert M., 2104
Kesselring, Field Marshal Albert, 1129,
    1263, 1955
—Surrenders, 1955
Ketcham, Rear Adm. Dixwell, 2068
Keyes, Maj. Gen. Geoffrey, 960, 1272
Kharkov, 547, 554-555, 686-688, 704,
    771, 872, 1008-1009, 1010-1011
Kharlamov, Rear Adm., 490
Kahrtum, 368
Kherson, 546, 1194, 1219
Kholm, 548
Kiel, 282, 527
Kiev, 260, 506, 531, 536-539, 1032, 1085,
    1218
—Evacuation, 536
Kimmel, Rear Adm. Husband E., 2168,
    2250
"King George V," 369

King, Adm. Ernest J., 791, 1173, 2250,
    2298
King, Mackenzie, 1568
King's African Rifles, 568-569
Kinkaid, Vice Adm. Thomas G., 1544,
    1615, 1704, 1705, 2274
Kirchenpauer, Gen. Maj. Wilhelm,
    2140-2141
Kirk, Rear Adm. Alan G., 1283, 1306-
    1307, 2301
Kiska, 705, 772, 918, 1014-1019
Kismayu, 380
"Kittyhawk," 854
Kletskaya, 737, 754
Klein, Dr. Fritz, 2121
Kleist, Gen. von, 420, 725
Klin, 573, 586, 614
Klisura, 362
Klooga, 1588
Kluge, Field Marshal von, 1447
Knapsack Power Station, 501
Knightsbridge, 692
Knot, John, 1503
Knox, Col. Frank, 211, 2168, 2248, 2251
Knox, Elyse, 2303
Kobe, 664
Koelnischer Gummifaden Fabrik, 694
Koenig, Gen. Joseph, 1484
Koenigsberg, 1875
Koenigsberg Falls, 1875
Kohima, 1232, 1931, 1939
Koiso, Gen. Kuniaki, 1393
Kokoda, 782
Kokoda Gap, 779
Kolombangara Island, 1031
Konev, Marshal Ivan, 1200, 1202, 1781,
    1793, 1905, 2291
Konz-Karthaus Bridge, 1635
Korea, 2147
Koritza, 259, 311, 322, 331
Korsun, 1194
Kota Bahru, 582
Kotelnikovo, 754, 769
Kotelva, 1013
Kounine Hills, 902
Kramer, Joseph, 2121
Krasnodar, 725, 737
Krasnogorsk, 848
Krause, Maj. Gen., 907
Kremenchug, 531
Kretschmer, Commander Otto, 411
Krueger, Gen. Walter, 1705, 2274
Kuala Lampur, 611
Kuban, 725
Kuban River, 725
Kuestrin, 1544, 1747, 1793, 1808, 1818,
    1824, 1854, 1902
—Falls to the Russians, 1818
Kuhn, Fritz, 2196
Kukri, 1257
Kulai, 621
Kulmbach, 1919
Kunkel, John C., 1904
Kunming, 1636, 1733
Kunzel, Gen., 1941
Kupiansk, 704
Kurgis, Lt. Col. Howard G., 2145
Kuroda, Lt. Gen. Shigenori, 2081
Kursk, 547, 710, 772, 872, 886
Kuruso, Saburo, 285, 519, 576
Kuschev, 725
Kutno, 7
Kuusamo, 8
Kuzuu, 2113

Kwajalein, 1032, 1136-1141, 1176-1177, 1249, 2316, 2317, 2376
—Bombarded, 1138
—War crimes trials, 2143, 2153
Kweilin, 1544, 1636
Kyungon, 639, 653
Kyushu, 1180, 1322, 1963
Kyushu Imperial University, 2070

L

La Boix des Allies, 1359
La Galissonnaire, 833
La Marseillaise, 833
Labuan Island, 1992
Lacarte, Julio A., 2167
Ladoga, Lake, 8, 523, 647
Lae, 619, 641, 683, 1015, 1046-1047, 1049, 1102-1103
—Falls to the Americans and Australians, 1046-1047
Lager Nordhausen concentration camp, 1880
Lagone, 1122-1123
LaGuardia, F. H., 1375
La Haye de Puits, 1414-1415
Lake Achkel, 909
Lake Chad, 860, 1496
Lake Como, 1922-1923
Lake Ilmen, 629
Lake Ladoga, 8, 523, 647
Lamnos, 437
Lamy, 1496
Lake Tungting, 1106
Lakunai Airfield, 1050-1051
Lamone River, 1665
"Lancaster," 800, 916, 963, 1229, 1639
"Lancastria," 214-215
Landing at Biak, 1266
Landing at Nettuno, 1129
Landing Craft
—At Anzio, 1131
—Barge approaches Tarawa, 1093
—"Ducks," 959, 970-971, 1130-1131, 1492
Land based LST's in Normandy, 1296-1297
—Landing Craft—Infantry, 968-969, 970-971, 1238, 1261, 1705
—Landing Craft— Mechanized, 970-971
—Landing Craft—Personnel, 970-971, 1082-1083
—Landing Craft—Tanks, 970-971, 1149
—Landing Craft—Vehicle—Personnel, 1293, 1842
—Landing Ship—Tanks, 920-921, 938-939, 1017-1019, 1126-1127, 1238, 1240, 1296-1297, 1380, 1657, 2474
Landsberg, 1918
Langres Plateau, 160
Langsdorff, Capt., 43
Lansley, Pvt. Robert E., 1104-1105
Laon, 151, 1524
La Presse, 1485
Larissa, 434
La Roche, 1708
Las Banos internment camp, 1809
Lashio, 672, 1931, 1939
Lashio-Mandalay railway, 674
Latvia, 260, 1179, 1379, 1413, 1425, 1473, 1543, 1697

Laval, Pierre, 194, 663, 1431, 1505, 2011, 2092, 2098
Lawrence, Prof. Ernest Orlando, 2020
Lawrence, Sir Geoffrey, 2126
Leahy, Adm. William D., 1411, 1754, 2027
Lebanon, 260, 1984
Le Bourget Airfield, 224
Le Clerc, Gen. Jacques, 860, 1291, 1452, 1484, 1496, 2042, 2271
Ledo, 1972
Ledo Road, 1145, 1174, 1227, 1577
Ledo-Burma Road, 1544
Ledo-Burma Road re-opens, 1732
Leeb, Gen. von, 522
Leende, 1632
Leese, Gen. Sir Oliver, 1255, 1258, 1629, 2267
Legentilhomme, Gen., 477
Leghorn, 1179, 1387-1389 1422, 1462
—Falls to the 5th Army, 1388
—Harbor, 1387
Le Gleize, 1688
Legnano, 1572-1573
Le Havre, 377, 1565
—Bombed, 550
Leichester Square, 303
Leipzig, 1793, 1897
LeJeune, Camp, 1116
Lek River, 1586
Le Luc, Adm., 165, 173
Le Mans, 1180, 1507
Lend-Lease, 219, 265, 267, 386, 392, 498, 519, 1891
Leningrad, 260, 480, 506, 510, 519, 521-523, 544, 581, 628, 647, 1032, 1143, 2374
Leonforte, 964-965
Leoni, Raul, 2099
Leopold, King, 8, 125
Levant, 1984
"Lexington," 520, 682-683
Ley, Dr. Robert, 1970, 2100
Leyte, 1544, 1609-1611, 1615, 1656-1657, 1768, 2260, 2274, 2494
Leyte Gulf, 1544
Lgov, 886
Liao Yau Siang, Maj., 2265
"Liberator," 862, 986-987, 1015, 1183, 1186, 1269, 1332, 1596, 1763, 2318
Libya, 8, 221, 229, 232, 259, 268, 338, 343, 373, 374-375, 400-402, 413-414, 435, 520, 562-565, 590, 598-599, 602-603, 606-609, 690-691, 701, 703, 717, 804, 807, 810-811, 840, 858, 861
—Maps, 374-375, 598-599
Licanan airfield, 1983
Licata, 962
Liege, 105, 110, 112, 1558, 1569
Liege-Louvain-Brussels railway, 104
Liesneux, 2409
Light artillery, 2458
Lille, 699
Lillehammer, 79
Lily, 2463
Limburg, 1866
Lindenberg, Hans, 1927
Lindbergh, Charles, 224
Lindfort, 2421
"Lindsey," 2309
Lingayen Gulf, 591, 1544, 1704-1705, 1707, 1709
Lingkas, 1925

Linnich, 1779
Liquid flame, 1776
Li Shui riverbed, 1636
Lisichansk, 714
List, Gen., 439
Lithuania, 260, 1179, 1473, 1543, 1729
Lithuanian farm, 1729
Lithuanian peasants welcome the Russians, 1729
Littoria, 1128, 1179
Liuchow, 1544, 1794
Livorno, 1388, 1422, 1462
Lockheed "Hudson" coastal command planes, 142
Lockheed reconnaissance bombers, 33
Lockwood, Vice Adm. Charles A., 2012
Loerzer, Gen., 309
Lofoten, 387, 390
Lombardy, 1920
London, 58, 174-175, 200-201, 259, 262-263, 265, 1180, 1402, 1502
—Air war over London, 178-179, 230, 237-238, 244, 246-251, 261, 271, 286-291, 297, 302-303, 326-327, 346-357, 427-429, 448-451, 764-765, 1623
London Bridge, 261
London dockland area, 290
London policeman, 100
"London Range" German gun, 1514
London Times office, 302
Londoners, 10, 59
Longmire, Air Marshal, 413
Long-range guns, German, 243
"Long Tom," 1156, 2494
Looting in Catania, 990-991
"Lord Haw Haw," 1981
Lorengau, 1203
Lorient, 802-803, 1461
Lorraine, 167
Lothian, Lord, 369
Louis, Staff Sgt. Joe, 1409
Louvain, 112-113
Low Countries, 132, 1795
Low level attack on enemy convoy, 470-471
Luce, Claire Booth, 1904
Ludendorff Bridge, 1793, 1802-1803, 1804
—Collapses, 1831
Luebeck, 644-645, 669, 720
Luftwaffe, see German Air Force
Luga, 522
Luitpold, 1181
Lunan, Capt. Cordon, 2189
Luneburg, 1981, 2121
Luneburg Heath, 1941
Luneville, 167
Lutsk, 1143
"Lutzow," 283
Luxembourg, 8, 94, 1511, 1543, 1546, 1591, 1680, 1684
—Map, 1684
Luxembourg forest, 2319
Luzon, 584-585, 591, 605, 658, 1544, 1704-1705, 1709, 1712, 1723, 1727, 1748-1749, 1768, 1794, 1812, 1822, 2381, 2424, 2455, 2473
Lwow, 1179, 1396, 1528
—Again in Russian hands, 1528
"Lying In" Home at Bad Weisse, 1976
Lyon, 1455, 1543, 1560

M

M-18 tank destroyers, 2461
M29-C, 2492
Maaloy, 601
Maas, 103, 1726
Maas River, 1716
Maastricht, 103
MacArthur, Arthur, 651
MacArthur, Gen. Douglas, 519, 652, 772, 1047, 1410-1411, 1544, 1574, 1609, 1745, 1768, 2004, 2035, 2038-2039, 2040, 2041, 2042, 2045, 2060, 2085, 2252, 2260
—And his forces arrive in Japan, 2038
—Lands at Hollandia, 1241
—Takes over in Australia, 650
MacArthur, Mrs., 2252
MacArthur's son at Corregidor, 651
MacArthur's troops gain control of Buna Mission, 854-855
Macedonia, 434
MacFarland, Ernest W., 1904
Machinato airfield, 1896
Machine gun, 2468, 2479
Mackeig-Jones, Capt., 18
Macmillan, Harold, 941
Madagascar, 520, 680-681
Madang, 1032, 1243
"Madman of St. Malo," 1456
Magdeburg, 1897
Maginot Line, 8, 57, 129, 163, 285, 1526, 1564, 2431
Mahoney, Pvt. John V., 1105
Maikop, 723
—Evacuated, 737
Mail for the Pacific, 1525
Main River, 1842, 1843, 1863
Maisky, M., 490, 689
"Major of St. Lo," 1386
Makalapa, 1096
Makambo, 727, 759
Makin, 1031, 1089, 1163
Makow, 1722
Malabang, 1895
"Malaya," 323
Malaya, 495, 519, 582-583, 610, 625
—Evacuated, 621
Maldiba, 569
Maleme, 459, 460-461
Maletti, Gen., 338
Malinovski, Col. Gen., 875, 1231
Malmedy, 1694
Malmedy massacre, 1694
Malta, 153, 225, 512, 656, 934-935, 942, 964-965, 1040-1041, 1195, 2284
Maltese, 177
Mamers, 1454
Manaka, Tatanichi, 2153
"Manchester," 589
Manchester, 363
Manchuria, 1097, 1323, 2024, 2030, 2037-2038, (1945) 2154-2155
—Russian occupation, 2190
Mandalay, 642-643, 653, 673, 674, 1823, 1838
Manhattan Project, 2016, 2019, 2020
Manila, 519, 585, 591, 597, 1544, 1753, 1757, 1759-1760, 1785, 1812, 1822, 1977, 2030, 2431, 2493
—Evacuated, 605
—1195 Singalong Street, 2112
—Red Cross, 2104

Manila (cont'd)
—War crimes trials in, 2104, 2109, 2112, 2175-2177
Manila Bay, 584-585, 605
Manila Harbor, 1642-1643, 1762-1763, 2487
Mannerheim Line, 8, 62
Mannheim, 1863
Manstein, Gen. von, 685
Manus Island, 1203
Maps and diagrams—General
—Air war over England, 290-291
—Air war over Europe, 1228-1229
—Albanian campaign, 362
—As the fifth year ended, 1534-1535
—Axis campaign in Greece, 443
—Battle of the Atlantic, 408-409
—Convoy routes to Britain, 408-409
—Crete (1941), 468-469
—Enemy chart of small English war vessels, 1376
—Europe after one year of war, 256 257
—European areas debated at Paris Peace Conference, 2235
—German advance in Belgium (1940), 132-133
—German advance in France (1940), 132-133, 154-155
—Germany occupies half France, 166
—Iran, 507
—Russo-German division of Poland, 26
—"Scharnhorst" sunk in the Arctic, 1112
Maps and diagrams — African campaign
—British advance into Libya, 374-375
—British drive from Bengasi into Tripolitania, 812-813
—Cape Bon peninsula, 911
—East African campaign, 457
—Eighth Army breaks through Mareth Line, 897
—July 1942, 719
—In 1940, 257
Maps and diagrams — China-Burma-India Theater
—Allies take Mandalay, 1838
—Burma, 673, 1838
—May of 1944, 1232
Maps and diagrams—Eastern Fr
—After eight weeks, 506
—Allied junction in Germany, 1910-1911
—April of 1945, 1885, 1910-1911
—As the third year ended, 769
—As the third year opened, 521
—Finland, 506
—German retreat in the Caucasus, 830
—Germany invades Russia, 478-479
—March of 1944, 1220
—Russian drive on Baltic and Balkan states, 1671
—Russian drive to the Oder, 1747
—Russian winter advance (1941-1942), 684
—September of 1943, 1010
—Stalingrad, 799
Maps and diagrams—Italian Front
—After four months, 1135
—Italy invaded, 1033
Maps and diagrams — Mediterranean Theater
—Aircraft operational range, 934-935

Maps and Diagrams — Mediterranean Theater (cont'd)
—Campaign in Sicily, 964-965
—Middle East, 489
Maps and diagrams—Pacific Theater
—After three months, 642-643
—At the end of the war, 2046-2047
—August of 1944, 1429
—February of 1945, 1768
—Malaya, 621
—November of 1943, 1102-1103
—Second battle of the Philippine Sea, 1619
—September of 1944, 1535
—Singapore, 621
—U. S. actual and proposed post war bases, 2178-2179
Maps and diagrams—Western Front
—April of 1945, 1885, 1910-1911
—Battle for France, 1414-1415, 14
—Battle for Germany, 1581
—Battle of the Bulge, 1684
—September of 1944, 1534, 1581
Maquis, 1431, 1460, 1500, 1532, 1548
Maramas airstrip, 1982-1983
"Marauder," 942, 1414, 1572-1573, 1635
—Bomb Siegfried supply line, 1635
"Marching through New Georgia," 947
Mareth Line, 771, 842, 861, 892-893, 896, 897
Margaret, Princess, 1951
Marianas, 1170, 1173, 1180, 1316, 1326, 1333, 1418, 1652, 2298, 2488
Marine Corps Women's Reserve, 1912
Marines battle for Cemetery Ridge, 1975
Maritime Alps, 1439
Marko Jail, 2186
Marne, 1180, 2416
Mariupol, 546
Marseille, 1180, 1480
Marshall, Gen. George C., 930, 1173, 1307-1308, 1754, 2138, 2156, 2250
Marshall Islands, 622-623, 1032, 1137-1141, 1146, 1169, 1171, 1176, 1249, 2248
Martaban, 626
Martin "B. 26 Marauder," 942, 1414, 1572-1573, 1635
"Maryland," 576-577, 2400
Mascarenhas de Moraes, Gen. Joao Batista, 1799
Mashbir, Col. S. F., 2033
Mason, Frank, 582-583
"Massachusetts," 2006
Massacre Bay, 918-919
Massawa, 372
Massicault, 909
Matanikau River, 788
Matapan, 406-407
Mateur, 834, 909, 913
Matford Works, 635
"Matildas," 713
Matmata, 893
Matmata Hills, 897
Matruh, 520
—**See also** Mersa Matruh
Maturba, 811
"Mauritius," 1283
May, Dr. Alan Nunn, 2189
May, Andrew J., 2226
Mazerall, Edward Wilfred, 2189
McAfee, Capt. Mildred H., 2279
McCreery, Lt. Gen. Sir Richard, 1629

McLain, Maj. Gen. Raymond S., 1781
McNarney, Gen., 2196
McNaughton, Maj. Gen., 84
McNutt, Paul V., 2213
Mechanized forces, 22
Mechanized units, 12
Medenine, 861, 881, 891
Medenine-Gabes road, 892-893
Mediterranean Theater, 170, 196, 225,
    232, 259, 284, 294, 324, 376, 459,
    461, 484, 512, 542, 656, 772, 802-
    803, 806, 934-935, 938-939, 952-
    973, 988-997, 1022-1023, 1033-1045,
    1062-1063, 1253, 1453, 1544, 1984,
    2266
Mediterranean Theater—Maps
—Aircraft operational range, 934-935
—Campaign in Sicily, 964-965
—Middle East, 489
Medjez-el-Bab, 821, 822, 909
Meendsen-Bohlken, Adm. Wilhelm,
    1956
Meiktila, 1838, 1839, 2378
Meitner, Dr. Lise, 2171
Mejerda, 909
Mekili, 590
Memel, 1543, 1729, 1744
Mentone, 172
Menzies, 399
Mercer, Capt. P. V., 1096
Merchant vessels
—"Altmark" (Ger.), 54-55
—"Arandora Star" (Brit), 189
—"Athenia" (Brit), 11
—"Columbus" (Ger), 44
—"Conte Biancamano" (Ital), 415
—"Doric Star" (Brit), 39
—"Eisenach" (Ger), 415
—"Empress of Britain" (Can), 298-299
—"Fella" (Ital), 415
—"Gripsholm" (Swe), 1223
—"Idarwald" (Ger), 336
—"Lancastria" (Brit), 214-215
—"Neosho" (U.S.), 683
—"Washington" (U.S.), 159
Meretskov, Marshal, 2036-2037
Merezhkov, Gen., 581
Merkers, 1868
Merkstein, 1592
Merrill, Brig. Gen. Frank, 1174, 1192,
    2272
Merrill's Marauders, 1075
Mersa Brega, 813
Mersa Matruh, 706-707, 807
Merseyside, 394
Messerschmitt, 110, 236, 245, 454
—"262A-1," 2452
Messina, 772, 964-965, 992-993, 996-
    997
—Falls to the Americans, 996-997
Messina, Strait of, 1031, 1033, 1034-
    1035
Metaxas, Gen., 301
Metsovo, 362
Metz, 160, 1543, 1547, 1555, 1644, 1648
Meuse River, 104, 110, 1549, 1556-1557,
    1826
Michael (Mihai) King, 264, 1179, 1478
Middle East, 176, 268, 712-713
Middle Temple Hall, 303
Midget submarine, 2481
Midway, 696, 697, 2298
Mihailovitch, Gen. Draja, 1108, 1110,
    2195, 2257

Mikolajczyk, M. J., 187
Milan, 800, 1920, 1922-1923
Milch, Field Marshal, 1395
Military law overtakes Nazi spies,
    1996
Military leaders—Canada
—Crerar, Lt. Gen., H. D. G., 2287
—Moore-Cosgrove, Col. L., 2042
Military leaders—China
—Ho Yin-chen, Gen., 2281
—Hseuh Yeuk, Gen., 1106
—Hu, Gen., 1233
Military leaders—France
—Abrial, Adm. Jean, 143
—Allard, Maj. Jacques, 1120
—Bergeret, Gen., 165, 173
—Catroux, Gen., 413, 472, 477, 489,
    932
—Darlan, Adm. Jean, 455, 771, 818,
    839
—De Gaulle, Gen. Charles, 186, 197,
    268, 281, 292, 413, 857, 930, 932,
    941, 1325, 1374, 1474-1475, 1484,
    1487, 1497, 1498, 1638, 1951, 1984,
    2011, 2246
—De Laborde, Adm., 832
—Dentz, Gen. Henry, 260, 477, 488
—de Tassigney, Gen. de Latre, 1647,
    2277
—Gamelin, Gen. Maurice Gustave, 16,
    116
—Gensoul, Adm., 192
—Giraud, Gen. Henri Honore, 119,
    839, 857, 925, 930, 932, 941, 1062
—Juin, Gen. Alphonse Pierre, 1254-
    1255
—Koenig, Gen. Joseph, 1484
—Le Clerc, Gen. Jacques, 860, 1291,
    1452, 1484, 1496, 2042, 2271
—Legentilhomme, Gen., 477
—Le Luc, Adm., 165, 173
—Muselier, Adm., 186
—Parisot, Gen., 173
—Sevez, Gen. Francois, 1944-1945
—Weygand, Gen. Maxine, 116
Military leaders—Germany
—Basseage, Maj. Gen., 907
—Beck, Col. Gen. Ludwig, 1394, 1395
—Bieldwius, Gen., 907
—Bock, Gen. von, 536, 688, 760
—Borowletz, Maj. Gen., 907
—Doenitz, Grand Adm. Karl, 1395,
    1928-1929, 2124-2125, 2237
—Dostler, Gen. Anton, 2144
—Fiedler, Gen. Maj. Erich, 2140
—Friedeburg, Gen. Adm. Hans Georg,
    1941, 1944-1945, 1946, 1948, 1971
—Goering Reichsmarshal Herman, 163,
    165, 309, 1394, 1957, 2124-2125,
    2127, 2128-2129, 2139, 2194, 2236,
    2237, 2239, 2459
—Jeschonnek, Gen., 309
—Jodl, Col. Gen. Alfred Gustav, 1944-
    1945, 1946, 2124-2125, 2237
—Keitel, Field Marshal Wilhelm, 1395,
    1947-1948, 2124-2125, 2129, 2237
—Kesselring, Field Marshal Albert,
    1129, 1263, 1955
—Kirchenpauer, Gen. Maj. Wilhelm,
    2141
—Kluge, Field Marshal von, 1447
—Krause, Maj. Gen., 907
—Kretschmer, Commander Otto, 411
—Kunzel, Gen., 1941

Military leaders—Germany (cont'd)
—Loerzer, Gen., 309
—Manstein, Gen. von, 685
—Meendsen-Bohlken, Adm. Wilhelm, 1956
—Milch, Field Marshal, 1395
—Neuffer, Maj. Gen., 907
—Oxenius, Maj. Gen. Wilhelm, 1944
—Quast, Gen. von, 907
—Raeder, Grand Adm. Erich, 165, 2124-2125, 2237
—Rommel, Field Marshal Erwin, 520, 563, 567, 691, 700, 702, 768, 813, 851, 1109, 1209
—Rundstedt, Field Marshal Karl von, 536, 1543, 1680, 1684, 1695, 1741, 1937, 2312
—Theissen, Gen. Karl, 2140
—Vaerst, Maj. Gen. von, 907
Military leaders—Great Britain
—Alexander, Gen. Sir Harold R. L. G., 638, 925, 930, 1254, 2267
—Anderson, Gen., 821, 834, 930
—Auchinleck, Gen., 712, 718
—Cunningham, Lt. Gen. Sir Alan, 563
—Cunningham, Adm. Sir Andrew, 316, 914, 956, 1041
—Dempsey, Lt. Gen. Sir Miles, 1598, 1739, 2268
—Fraser, Adm. Sir Bruce, 2042
—Gort Gen., 16, 60, 143, 2284
—Harwood, Rear Adm. Henry, 41, 42-43, 58
—Ironside, Gen. Sir Edmund, 2284
—Leese, Gen. Sir Oliver, 1255, 1258, 1629, 2267
—Longmire, Air Marshal, 413
—McCreery, Lt. Gen. Sir Richard, 1629
—Montgomery, Field Marshal Sir Bernard L., 700, 804, 813, 847, 859, 892, 900, 930, 960, 962, 991, 1033, 1035, 1037, 1135, 1255, 1283, 1294, 1325, 1398, 1531, 1545, 1600, 1793, 1926, 1941, 2253
—Mountbatten, Adm. Lord Louis, 1192, 1382, 1939, 2078, 2281
—Percival, Lt. Gen. A. E., 2045
—Phillips, Adm. Sir Thomas, 583
—Ramsay, Adm. Sir Bertram, 2287
—Spears, Gen., 413
—Sturges, Maj. Gen., 681
—Syfret, Rear Adm., 681
—Wavell, Gen. Sir Archibald, 307, 338, 371, 413, 2299
—Wilson, Gen. Sir Henry Maitland, 2266
—Wingate, Maj. Gen. Orde Charles, 2289
Military leaders—Holland
—Helfrich, Adm., 2042
Military leaders—Italy
—Aosta, Duke of, 416, 456
—Badoglio, Marshal, 173, 1031, 1035, 1041, 1195
—Cavagnari, Adm., 173
—De Bono, Marshal Emilio, 1121
—Gonella, Col., 541
—Nasi, Gen., 569
—Pricolo, Gen., 173
—Roatta, Gen., 173
Military leaders—Japan
—Hata, Field Marshal Shunroku, 2037, 2146
—Homma, Lt. Gen. Masaharu, 2081, 2175-2177

Military leaders—Japan (cont'd)
—Kuroda, Lt. Gen. Shigenori, 2081
—Miyakazi, Lt. Gen. Shuichi, 2043
—Nogano, Adm., 1170, 1173
—Nomura, Adm., 576
—Sakaibara, Rear Adm. Shigematsu, 2143
—Sugiyama, Field Marshal, 1170, 1173
—Tachibaba, Lt. Commander Soichi, 2143
—Takahashi, Adm. Sankichi, 2146
—Yamashita, Gen. Tomoyuki, 2058, 2104, 2151
Military leaders—New Zealand
—Freyberg, Gen., 847
Military leaders—Poland
—Sikorski, Gen. Wladyslaw, 220
Military leaders—Russia
—Batov, Col. Gen., 1571
—Budenny, Marshal, 503, 508
—Chermiaeff, Lt. Gen. Ivan, 1944-1945, 1946
—Golikov, Gen., 490
—Golubov, Gen., 634
—Jardov, Gen., 2286
—Kharlamov, Rear Adm., 490
—Konev, Marshal Ivan S., 1200, 1202, 1781, 1793, 1905, 2291
—Malinovski, Col. Gen., 875, 1231
—Meretskov, Marshal, 2036-2037
—Rokossovsky, Marshal Konstantin, 1926, 2291
—Rusakov, Maj. Gen., 1906
—Timoshenko, Marshal S. K., 686, 704, 2291
—Vasilevsky, Marshal Alexander, 2037, 2038, 2291
—Zhukov, Field Marshal Gregory, 1544, 1747, 1793, 1947, 1948, 2261
Military leaders—South Africa
—Pienaar, Gen., 811
Military leaders—U. S.
—Ainsworth, Rear Adm. W. L., 1621
—Arnold, Gen. Henry H., 1307, 2254, 2278
—Berkey, Rear Adm. Russell, 1817
—Blandy, Vice Adm., W. H. P., 2219, 2224, 2227
—Bradley, Lt. Gen. Omar N., 1284, 1294, 1399, 1484, 1531, 1545, 1600, 1861, 1893, 2258
—Buckner, Lt. Gen. Simon Bolivar Jr., 1985, 2294, 2300
—Carney, Rear Adm. Robert B., 1621, 2296
—Chamberlain, Maj. Gen. S. J., 2035
—Chennault, Maj. Gen. Claire, 1098, 1226, 2264
—Clark, Lt. Gen. Mark, 818, 826-827, 1031, 1033, 1038, 1179, 1254, 1258, 1265, 1272, 1277, 1281, 1388, 1422, 1793, 1799, 2267, 2270
—Doolittle, Lt. Gen. James H., 664, 666, 1180, 2276
—Eichelberger, Lt. Gen. Robert I., 1817
—Eisenhower, Gen. Dwight D., 773, 814, 839, 902, 925, 930, 941, 1041, 1107, 1284, 1307, 1398, 1399, 1484, 1600, 1781, 1861, 1904, 1996, 1998, 2253
—Gavin, Maj. Gen. James, 2297
—Geiger, Maj. Gen. Roy, 1859, 2300
—Halsey, Adm. William F., 1544, 1562, 1615, 1621, 2038, 2264

Military leaders—U. S. (cont'd)
—Hewitt, Adm. H. K., 818, 1038, 1441
—Hill, Rear Adm. Harry W., 1092
—Hodge, Maj. Gen. John R., 1859
—Hodges, Gen. Courtney H., 1524, 1600, 1861, 1905, 2286
—Ingram, Adm. Jonas H., 2102, 2259
—Kenney, Gen. George C., 1225, 2283
—Keyes, Maj. Gen. Geoffrey, 960, 1272
—Kimmel, Adm. Husband E., 2168, 2250
—King, Adm. Ernest J., 791, 1173, 2250, 2298
—Kinkaid, Vice Adm. Thomas G., 1544, 1615, 1704, 1705, 2274
—Kirk, Rear Adm. Alan G., 1283, 1306-1307, 2301
—Krueger, Gen. Walter, 1705, 2274
—Leahy, Adm. William D., 1411, 1754, 2027
--MacArthur, Gen. Douglas, 519, 650, 652, 772, 1047, 1241, 1410-1411, 1544, 1574, 1609, 1745, 1768, 2004, 2035, 2038-2039, 2040, 2041, 2042, 2045, 2252, 2260
—Marshall, Gen. George C., 930, 1173, 1307-1308, 1754, 2250
—Merrill, Brig. Gen. Frank, 1075, 1174, 1192, 2272
—Mitscher, Adm. Marc A., 1173, 1857, 2263
—Nimitz, Adm. Chester W., 1089, 1096, 1193, 1410, 1411, 1778, 2038, 2041, 2255, 2300
--Patch, Lt. Gen. Alexander, 1556, 1957, 2275
—Patton, Gen. George S. Jr., 856, 960, 962, 989, 1180, 1399, 1526, 1531, 1545, 1566, 1637, 1695, 1988, 2290
—Reinhardt, Maj. Gen. Emil F., 1906
—Shepherd, Maj. Gen. Lemuel C., 1985, 2294
—Simpson, Lt. Gen. William, 2262
—Smith, Lt. Gen. Walter Bedell, 1944-1945
—Spaatz, Gen. Carl A., 1186, 1944-1945, 1948, 2278
—Spruance, Adm. Raymond A., 1193, 1859, 2248, 2298
—Stark, Adm. Harold R., 1360
—Stilwell, Lt. Gen. Joseph W., 676-679, 1145, 1174, 1191, 1192, 1227, 1232, 1233, 2247, 2265
—Stratemeyer, Lt. Gen. George E., 2066
—Truscott, Lt. Gen. Lucian K., 1920, 2302
—Wainwright, Lt. Gen. Jonathan, 650, 658, 2040, 2045, 2269
—Whitehead, Maj. Gen. Ennis, 2283
—Vandergrift, Lt. Gen. A. A., 728, 2256
Military leaders—Yugoslavia
—Mihailovitch, Gen. Draja, 1108, 1110, 2195, 2257
—Simovich, Gen., 404
—Tito, Marshal Josip Broz, 1108, 1109, 2257
Military Railway Service, 1972
Mille Atoll, 2153
Millerovo, 722, 836
Millerovsk, 714
Milne Bay, 757, 778
Milo, 942

Mindanao, 591, 1562-1563, 1677, 1794, 1816-1817, 1895, 1982-1983, 2440
Mindoro, 1544, 1674-1678, 1768
Mine detector, electrical, 1230
Minsk, 260, 481, 482-483, 486-487, 1366, 1367
"Miss Spark-Plug," 2273
"Mississinewa," 2349
"Missouri," 1794, 2041
Misurata, 851
Mitscher, Adm. Marc A., 1173, 1857, 2263
Miyakazi, Lt. Gen. Shuichi, 2043
Mobile guns, 2461
Mobile rocket unit, 2474
Mogadishu, 380
Mogaung River, 1471
Mogaung Valley, 1215
Mogok, 1838
Mohammed, Prince, 260
Mohammedan troops with the Fifth Army, 1120
"Mohawk," 31
Mohne Dam, 916-917
Mojaisk, 548, 573, 586, 614-615
Molotov, V. M., 7, 26, 203, 689, 755, 1084, 1100-1101
"Molotov Cocktails," 202-203
Mongasha, Ras, 368
Mono, 1081-1083
Mons, 1554
Montevideo Harbor, 41
Montgomery, Field Marshal Sir Bernard L., 700, 804, 813, 847, 859, 892, 900, 930, 960, 962, 991, 1033, 1035, 1037, 1135, 1255, 1283, 1294, 1325, 1398, 1531, 1545, 1600, 1793, 1926, 1941, 2253
Mont Le Ban, 1741
Montreau, 1508, 1529
Montreuil, 1519
Moon, radar signal directed to, 2169
Mooney, Cardinal Edward, 2180
"Moonstone," 170
Moore-Cosgrove, Col. L., 2042
Morgan, Lt. Gen. Sir F. E., 1944-1945
Morgan, Gen. W. D., 1924
Morgenthau, Henry, 1374
Morocco, 771, 814, 1120
Morotai Island, 1544, 1574, 1578, 1579, 2313
—Invasion, 2313
Morrison, Herbert, 325
Morriss, Elmer, 2205
Mortar, 2467
Moscow, 260, 500, 506, 510, 519, 521, 548, 572-573, 1384, 1907, 1952
—citizens digging anti-tank ditches, 572-573
—defenses, 511
—radio, 798, 982
Moscow agreement, 1084
Moscow-Leningrad railway, 510
Moscow-Rostov railway, 710
Moselle River, 1795, 1829
"Mosquito," 1183, 1625
Motion picture entertainers, 1878
Motor gun boats, 1056-1057
Moulmein, 519, 616, 626
Mount Hemeimat, 768
"Mt. Mckinley," 2224, 2227
Mount Suribachi, 2330
Mount Peschio, 1179
Mountbatten, Adm. Lord Louis, 1192, 1382, 1939, 2078, 2281

Moyne, Lord, 386
Mozdok, 830, 848-849
Muenchen-Gladbach, 1788, 1796
Mukden, 2190
Mulhouse, 1647, 1663
Munda, 944, 948
Munich, 34, 1929, 1976
—falls to Seventh Army, 1921
Munich pact, 7
Munster, 2318
Murmansk, 519, 797
Muroc Field, 2460
Murphy, Robert, 941
Murzouk, 860
Muselier, Adm., 186
Mussolini, Benito, 65, 152-153, 161, 163, 296, 984-985, 991, 1087, 1121, 1280, 1794, 1922-1923
—released by Germans, 1044-1045
"Mustang," 1182-1183, 1987, 2334-2335
Myawaddi, 616
Myitkyina, 1179, 1405, 1464-1465
—airfield, 1232
Myola, 778

N

Nagasaki, 1794, 2021-2023, 2070
"Nagato," 2227
Nagoya, 664
Naha, 1794, 1966, 1969, 1975, 1985, 2294
—City, 1599
Nalchik, 771, 829, 848
Namsen Fjord, 80
Namsos, 8, 80, 88
Namur, 111, 1160-1161, 1203, 1549
Nancy, 1555
Nanking, 2066
Nantes, 1180
Naples, 1031, 1054-1055, 1221
—Harbor, 1124-1125
Narew River, 1722
Narva, 1143
Narvik, 8, 83, 124, 220, 387
—Fjord, 69
—Harbor, 83
Nasi, Gen., 569
National Liberation Army of Yugoslavia, 1601
Naval Air Transport Service, 1809
Naval Civil Engineer Corps, 1979
Navigator, British, 2441
Near East, 53, 170
Negro 92nd Division, 1550, 1624
Negro troops, 1356, 1403, 1409, 1149, 1589, 1645
—and officers, 2293
—in France, 1403
Negros, 1570
Nehru, Pandit, 662, 734
"Nelson," 542, 1035, 1037
Nelson, Capt. Henry, 838
"Neosho," 683
Netherlands, 512, 618, 699, 1208, 1566, 1580, 1582-1587, 1598, 1626-1627, 1631-1632, 1779
—Naval bases in the Pacific, 642-643
—See also Holland
Netherlands East Indies, 519, 636-637, 642-643, 1242-1243, 1262, 1266, 1429, 1925

Netherlands East Indies uprisings
—British intervention, 2096
—Indonesians declare war on Netherlands, 2096-2097
Netherlands New Guinea, 1239-1245, 1261
Nettuno, 1032, 1129-1130, 1230
Neuffer, Maj. Gen., 907
Neurath, Constantin von, 2125
Neutrality law, U. S., 32
Neva, 522
"Nevada," 1283, 1290, 2219, 2225, 2227
New Britain, 519, 618, 642-643, 654-655, 727, 736, 1031, 1032, 1050-1051, 1102-1103, 1235
New Caledonia, 292
New Delhi, 662
New Georgia, 944, 948-949
New Guinea, 519, 619, 641, 642-643, 717, 738, 757, 772, 778, 780, 784, 785, 854-855, 944, 1014-1015, 1032, 1046-1047, 1049, 1065, 1102-1103, 1170, 1179, 1225, 1239-1245, 1261, 1406, 1429
New Ireland, 618, 642-643, 727
"New York," 1767, 2227
New York City, 2459
New Zealand, 61, 174, 269, 396, 741, 859
New Zealand—Military leaders
—Freyberg, Gen., 847
New Zealand forces, 1081
New Zealand infantry, 566, 713, 719
New Zealand troops, 563, 847, 1544
New Zealanders, 612
"Newcomb," 2375
Newfoundland, 228
Nibeiwa, 338
Nice, 1180, 1439
Nichols airfield, 585, 597
Niederbronn, 1662
Nielsen, Capt., 2159
Nieman River, 1730
Night bombers, 2472
Nijmegen, 1543, 1580, 1582, 1583, 1587, 1632, 2297
Nikolayev, 503, 508, 1179, 1194, 1218
Nile River, 177
Nimitz, Adm. Chester W., 1089, 1096, 1193, 1410, 1411, 1778, 2038, 2041, 2255, 2300
Nimitz, Mrs. Chester W., 2255
19th Army Corps, 1781
9th Air Force, 1068, 1284, 1324, 1331, 2372
Ninth Army, 1796, 1853, 2324
—Enters into Muenchen-Gladbach, 1796
—Glider troops, 1877
—See also American Ninth Army
9th Division, 1338, 1349
9th Infantry Division, 1750
90mm gun, 1644
92nd Division, 1550, 1624
94th Division, 2396
94th Division, Third Army, 2323
95th Infantry Division, 1942
96th Division, 2330
Nippon Times building, 2060
Nobel Prize, 2475
Noble, Carazon, 2104
Noel, M. Leon, 164-165, 173
Nogano, Adm., 1170, 1173
Nomura, Adm., 576
Nordhausen, 1880

"Norfolk," 462, 1112
Normandy, 1180, 1283-1309, 1295, 1325, 1327, 1329, 1330, 1342, 1344, 1356, 1358, 1360, 1369-1371, 1383, 1386, 1403, 1433, 1468, 2268, 2287, 2293, 2297, 2301, 2314, 2422-2423, 2441, 2463, 2470
—Wounded, 1287
Normandy Beach in 1946, 2216
North Africa, see Africa, North
North-German Lloyd Line, 44
North Sea, 50, 1056-1057
Northrop "Flying Wing XB-35," 2447
Norway, 8, 68-83, 88-89, 124, 387-391, 601, 645, 1639, 1954, 1981
—German invasion of, 8, 69-70
—Ships, see Ships
Norway—Political leaders
—Quisling, Vidkun, 8, 70, 1954, 1981
Norwegian campaign, 78
Norwegian forces, 390, 528
Norwegian Navy, 113
Norwegian squadrons over Dieppe, 741
Norwegian territorial waters, 55
Norwich, 669, 670
Notre Dame Cathedral, 1497
Noumea, 292
Novgorod, 522, 1032
Novlya, 1009
Novorossisk, 737, 829
Novy Oskol, 872
Numa-Numa Trail, 1104
Nuremburg, 1793, 1874, 1897, 1900-1901, 2136
—Congress (1936), 1181
—Palace of Justice, 2123
—Surrenders, 1900-1901
—Trials, 2122-2129, 2135, 2139, 2236-2237, 2238-2239
   See also War crimes investigations
—Europe
Nurse Corps—Brazilian Expeditionary Force, 1797
Nurses
—U. S. Navy, 1798, 1809

O

Oak Ridge, Tennessee, 2019
Oba, Capt. Sakae, 2145
Obersalzburg Mountain, 1909
Obliteration bombing, 1832-1833
O'Brian, John Lord, 2199
Oder River, 1544, 1747, 1781, 1793, 1818, 1824, 1902
Odessa, 260, 503, 551, 1179, 1231
Office of Scientific Research and Development, 2020
Ohta, Lt. Col., 2108
Okinawa, 1599, 1794, 1849, 1852, 1858-1860, 1869, 1871-1873, 1881, 1894, 1908, 1953, 1966, 1969, 1975, 1977, 1985-1986, 1989, 1990, 1994-1995, 1999, 2294, 2298, 2300, 2309, 2315, 2330, 2370, 2392-2393, 2397, 2400, 2406, 2415, 2450, 2453, 2466, 2495
—Casualties, 1896
—Civilians, 2002
—Landings, 1860
"Oklahoma," 574, 577
Old Kent Road, 238
Oliver, Col. A. C., 1745

Omori prison camp, 2105, 2108
100th Division, 7th Army, 2373
100th Infantry Battalion, 1422
100th Japanese Army Division Headquarters, 2440
108D pillbox, 2489
101st Airborne Division, 1682, 1909, 1955, 1970
130 mm guns, French, 843
155 mm gun, 1512
155 mm howitzers, 1663
155 mm Long Tom, American, 1156
155 mm self-propelled guns, 2461, 2494
Onega lake, 523
Operation Crossroads, 2218-2225
—"B-29," 2219
—Blandy, Vice Adm., W. H. P., 2219, 2224, 2227
—"Dave's Dream," 2219
—"Independence," 2227, 2229
—Joint Task Force One, 2218, 2220-2221, 2225
—"Mt. McKinley," 2224, 2227
—"Nevada," 2219, 2225, 2227
—Swancutt, Maj. Woodrow P., 2219
—Wood, Maj. Harold, 2219
Oppeln, 1543, 1734
Oran, 172, 192, 771, 818, 820-821
Orel, 548, 772, 977, 978-979, 981-983, 1008, 1011
Orel-Byelgorod sector, 976-977
Orel-Kursk-Byelgorod sector, 978-979
"Orion," 1283
Ortona, 1119, 1134, 1265
Osaka, 664, 1987
Osato, Sono, 2187
Oslo, 8, 70, 1981
Osmena, 2213
Ossetian military highway, 829, 848
Ostend, 377
Osuriecim concentration camp, 2121
Ottawa, 2189
Owen Stanley Mountains, 757, 772, 778, 780-781, 782, 1103
Oxenius, Maj. Gen. Wilhelm, 1944

P

"P-38," 1406, 1675
"P-40," 946-947
"P-47," 2456
"P-80" jet propelled fighter plane, 2172
PT boats, 1618, 2471
PWB sound truck, 1449
Paan, 626
Pachino, 957, 959, 963
Pacific atoll invaded, 752
Pacific fleet, 2011
Pacific Fleet Train, 2348-2349
Pacific submarine fleet, 2012-2013
Pacific submarine task force, 2012-2013
Pacific Theater
—(1941) 574-579, 600, 605
—(1942) 610, 618-619, 640-643, 650-652, 654-655, (end of U.S. resistance on Bataan) 658-661, 664-667, (Battle of the Coral Sea) 682-683, (Battle of Midway) 696-697, 717, (U.S. Marines land in the Solomons) 726-733, 736-739, 746-753, 757-759, (Guadalcanal) 772, 778-791, 808-809, 838, 844
—(1943) 854-855, 866-869, 944-949, 1031

Pacific Theater (cont'd)
   (Lae falls) 1047, 1032, 1047, 1059,
   1060-1061, 1064-1065, 1081-1983,
   1088-1090, (Tarawa) 1091, 1092-
   1095, 1096, 1102-1106
—(1944) (landing in Marshall Islands)
   1137-1141, 1146-1147, 1154-1155,
   1157, 1160-1161, 1163, 1166-
   1167, 1176-1177, 1188, 1198, 1201,
   (landings in Admiralty Islands)
   1203, 1235-1237, (Hollandia) 1239-
   1245, 1247, 1249, 1252, 1260, 1266,
   1316, 1322, (Saipan) 1326, 1337,
   (Guam landings) 1390-1392, 1397,
   1408, 1418-1419, 1429, 1432, 1464,
   1518, 1520, 1525, 1530, 1562-1563,
   1574-1579, (Americans return to
   the Philippines) 1608-1611, (Second
   battle of the Philippine Sea) 1615,
   1618, 1619, 1621, 1652-1653, 1656-
   1658, (landings at Mindoro) 1674.
—(1945) 1714, 1724, 1746, 1748-1749,
   1752-1753, (storming Manila) 1759-
   1761, 1762-1763, (Iwo Jima) 1764-
   1776, 1784-1786, 1789, 1798, 1814,
   1830, (Okinawa) 1857-1859, 1860,
   1869-1873, 1894-1896, 1912, 1917,
   1925, 1943, 1958-1961, 1963, 1966-
   1969, 1978, 1985-1987, 1989-1995,
   2002, 2004-2007, 2012-2018, 2021-
   2047, (Allied victory over Japan)
   2030-2031
—(additional scenes) 2145, 2246, 2252,
   2256, 2263, 2274-2276, 2282, 2285,
   2294-2296, 2310-2311, 2313, 2316-
   2317, 2330-2335, 2370-2371, 2376-
   2377, 2382, 2383, 2385, 2386-2387,
   2391-2393, 2397-2398, 2402-2403,
   2420, 2426-2427, 2429, 2431, 2439-
   2440, 2458, 2465-2467, 2469, 2473,
   2476, 2479, 2484, 2486-2488,
—Okinawa, 1599, 1849, 1852, 1857-
   1859, 1881, 1908, 1953, 1975, 1999,
   2298, 2300, 2309, 2315, 2400, 2406,
   2415, 2450, 2453, 2495
—Philippine Islands, 582-585, 591, 594-
   597, 658-661, 675, 1406, 1608-1611,
   1642-1643, 1674-1678, 1704-1705,
   1709, 1712, 1720, 1727, 1736, 1757,
   1809, 1816-1817, 1822, 1834, 1982-
   1983, 2260, 2269, 2306-2307, 2381,
   2424, 2455, 2493-2494
—Allied invasion armada at Lingayen
   Gulf, 1704
—**See also** China-Burma-India Theater;
   names of islands, places, etc.
Pacific Theater—Maps
—After three months, 642-643
—At the end of the war, 2046-2047
—August of 1944, 1429
—February of 1945, 1768
—Malaya, 621
—November of 1943, 1102-1103
—Second battle of the Philippine Sea,
   1619
—September of 1944, 1535
—Singapore, 621
Palau Islands, 1212-1214, 1544, 1574,
   1575, 1658, 1768, 2313
Palawan, 1677
Pallazzo degli Uffizi, 1426-1427
Pallazzo Venezia, 1280
Palermo, 772, 960, 964-965
Palestine, 53, 445, 472
—Riots, 2117

Palmi, 1035, 1037
Palmyra, 484
Panama Canal, 66, 1979
Panay, 1794, 1834
Pantelleria, 934-935, 941
Panzer Divisions, 118
Papen, Franz von, 1877, 2124-2125,
   2129
Papen, Franz von, Son of, 1877
Papua, 717, 757, 779, 844-845, 854
Parang, 1895
Paratroopers
—Allied, 784-785
—American, 1299, 1763, 1324
—British, 29, 631, 820, 1587, 1602, 1670,
   1933
—Enemy, 884
—Escaping from Arnhem pocket, 1587
—German, 835, 1044-1045, 1263
—Indian, 1933
—Japanese, 584
—Russian, 540
Parachuted bombs, 1978
Parafrags, 1720, 1978
Paris, 8, 148, 151, 154-157, 158, 166,
   224, 632-633, 635, 1180, 1196, 1474,
   1484-1498, 1516, 1523, 1638, 2011
—Action in Paris before the libera-
   tion, 1498
—Civilians, 1485, 1498
—Greets her liberators, 1493
—High Court of Justice, 2092
—Liberation, 1484-1498
—Occupied by Germans, 156
—Peace Conference, 2234-2235
—Treason trial opens, 2011
Paris Peace Conference, 2234-2235
Parisot, Gen., 173
Parker, John, 2126
Parry, Capt. 61
Parshin, 837
Parsons, Capt. William S., 2018
Pasaleng Bay, 1748
Pasay, 595
Pas de Calais, 1180, 1510, 1547
Pasig River, 1759
Patch, Lt. Gen. Alexander, 1566, 1957,
   2275
Patiala, 255
Patras, 1593
Patterson, Robert P., 1439, 1453
Patton, Gen. George S. Jr., 856, 960,
   962, 989, 1180, 1399, 1526, 1531,
   1545, 1566, 1637, 1695, 1988, 2290
Peace
—Foreign Minister's Council meets in
   London, 2074
—Paris Peace Conference, 2234-2235
—United Nations Security Council,
   2165, 2198-2201
Pearl Harbor, 519, 574-579, 1096, 1410-
   1411, 2028-2030, 2250, 2251, 2255
—Investigations, 2134, 2138, 2168
Peck, Maj. Gen. DeWitt, 2116
Pegu, 626
Peiping-Hankow-Canton Railway, 1337
Peleliu, 1544, 1574-1576, 1578, 1658,
   2300, 2420, 2426, 2485, 2486
Penicillin, 2475
"Pennsylvania," 579, 2227
"Pensacola," 2227
Perak, 611
Percival, Lt. Gen. A. E., 2045
Perekop Isthmus, 547, 551, 556
Permovaisk, 503

Peron, Juan D., 2184
Pershing, Gen. John J., 218, 1375
Persian oil fields, 507
"Perth," 66
Pescara, 1127
Petacci, Clara, 1922-1923
Petain, Marshal Phillipe, 160, 161, 296,
     455, 663, 1446, 2246
—government, 190
—on trial, 2011
Peter Beach, 1152
Peter, King, 1110
Petsamo, 2235
Philadelphia Navy Yard, 218
Philippine Islands
—(1941) 519, 584-585, 591, 594-597
—(1942) 642-643, 651-652, 658-661, 675
—(1944) 1334, 1406, 1410, 1544, 1570,
     1608-1610, 1614-1615, 1642-1643,
     1656-1657, 1674-1678
—(1945) 1704-1705, 1707, 1709, 1712,
     1720, 1723, 1727, 1736, 1752, 1757,
     1759-1760, 1762-1763, 1768, 1785,
     1794, 1809, 1812, 1816-1817, 1822,
     1834, 1895, 1977, 1982-1983, (Al-
     lied victory over Japan) 2030-2031,
     2040, 2058, 2081, 2083, 2260, 2264,
     2269, 2274, 2306-2307, 2381, 2424,
     2440, 2455, 2487, 2493-2494
—Map, 1768
—prison camp, 1753
—War crimes trials in Manila, 2104,
     2109, 2112, 2175-2177
—See also under Filipino
Philippine Islands—Political leaders
—Osmena, 2213
—Roxas, Manuel A., 2213
Philippine Sea, 2426
—Second battle of, 1544, 1615, 1618,
     1619, 1621, 2264, 2403, 2439
Philippines, Eastern, Sea Battle, 1334
Phillips, Adm. Sir Thomas, 583
Photographers, 1261, 1392, 1778
—Coast Guard Combat, 1261
—Russian, 1808
Piacenza rail bridge, 1641
Piatigorsk, 737
Piazza del Popolo, 1278
Pichon, 911
Pienaar, Gen., 811
Pillbox, German, 2489
Pilotless aircraft, 2454
Pindus, 331
Pinsk, 1413
Pipelines, 2487
Piraeus, 1602-1603
Pisada, 861
Pistoia, 1589
Pistoria, 1797
Pitti Palace, 1426
Pius XII, Pope, 2180
Piva trail, 1104
Plabennec, 1472
Ploesti, 986-987, 1179, 1220, 1229, 1478
Plymouth, 360, 398
Po River, 2486
Po Valley, 1793, 1903, 2270
Pofi, 1463
Pogradets, 331, 362
Pointe de la Tour, 843
Poison gas shells, 1106
Poissy, 635
"Pola," 406
Poland, 20, 187, 220, 260, 446, 480,

Poland (cont'd)
     870-871, 1032, 1099, 1117, 1143,
     1528, 1543, 1571, 1715, 1717-1719,
     1721-1722, 1742, 1747, 1819
—Division of, 26
—German advance, 12
—German-Russian agreement, 26
—Government in London, 871
—Russo-German division of Poland,
     (map), 26
—Surrender to Germany, 7
—Western, 21
Poland—Military leaders
—Sikorski, Gen. Wladyslaw, 220
Poland—Political leaders
—Mikolajczyk, M. J., 187
—Sikorski, Gen. Wladysyaw, 220
Polish armored train, 23
Polish Corridor, 26, 1543
Polish forces, 612
—in Italy, 1263
Polish ghettos, 871
Polish Highland Brigade, 220
Polish infantry, 13
Polish Patriot Army, 1613
Polish soldiers, 187
Polish squadrons, 741
**Polish troops parade in liberated War-
     saw,** 1718-1719
Political leaders—Argentina
—Farrell, Gen. Edelmiro J., 1187, 2184
—Peron, Juan D., 2184
—Ramirez, Pedro, 1197
—Tamborini, Jose P., 2184
Political leaders—Australia
—Menzies, 399
Political leaders—Austria
—Seyss-Inquart, Arthur, 2125, 2237
Political leaders—Belgium
—Leopold, King, 8, 125
Political leaders—Brazil
—Dutra, Gen. E. G., 1799, 2174
Political leaders—Bulgaria
—Filoff, Prof., 385
Political leaders—Canada
—Athlone, Earl of, 85
—King, Mackenzie, 1568
Political leaders—China
—Chiang Kai-shek, Generalissimo,
     888, 1032, 1097-1098, 1340, 2001,
     2247
—Fu Ping-sheung, 1084
—Quo Tai-chi, Dr., 2198
—United Nations Security Council,
     2198
Political leaders—Czechoslovakia
—Benes, Dr. Eduard, 216
Political leaders—Denmark
—Christian, King, 8
Political leaders—Egypt
—Farouk, King, 1756, 2212
Political leaders—Finland
—Kallio, President, 8
Political leaders—France
—Daladier, M., 2011
—Laval, Pierre, 194, 663, 1431, 1505,
     2011, 2092, 2098
—Petain, Marshal Phillipe, 160, 161,
     190, 296, 455, 663, 1446, 2011, 2246
—Reynaud, Paul, 160, 2011
Political leaders—Germany
—Frank, Hans, 2125, 2237
—Frick, Wilhelm, 2125, 2237
—Fritzsche, Hans, 2125, 2237
—Funk, Walther, 2125, 2237

Political leaders—Germany (cont'd)
—Goebbels, Joseph Paul, 193, 270
—Hess, Rudolph, 165, 454, 2124-2125, 2127, 2128-2129, 2139, 2236
—Himmler, Heinrich, 1394-1395, 1971
—Hitler, Adolf, 7, 34, 65, 160-161, 163-165, 193, 259, 296, 983, 984, 1045, 1181, 1194, 1248, 1394-1395, 1494, 1659, 1794, 1909, 1928-1929, 2118-2119
—Ley, Dr. Robert, 1970
—Neurath, Constantin von, 2125, 2237
—Papen, Franz von, 1877, 2125, 2129, 2237
—Ribbentrop, Joachim von, 7, 8, 26, 165, 285, 385, 404, 2125-2129, 2139, 2237
—Rosenberg, Alfred, 2125, 2127, 2237
—Schacht, Hjalmar, 2125, 2237
—Shirach, Baldur von, 2125, 2237
—Speer, Albert, 2125, 2237
—Streicher, Julius, 2125, 2237
Political leaders—Great Britain
—Attlee, Clement, 1794, 2010, 2114, 2242
—Beaverbrook, Lord, 195
—Bevin, Ernest, 1949, 2010, 2117, 2165
—Bracken, Brenden, 100
—Cadogan, Sir Alexander, 2198, 2199
—Chamberlain, Neville, 9, 60, 100
—Churchill, Winston, see under Churchill
—Cranborne, Lord, 386
—Cripps, Sir Stafford, 490, 662, 734
—Eden, Anthony, 53, 204, 689, 930, 1084, 1100-1101
—George, Lloyd, 792
—George VI, King, 271, 325, 386, 916, 925, 940-941, 1041, 1306, 1439, 1600, 1951, 2268
—Halifax, Lord, 64, 369, 447
—Henderson, Sir Neville, 7
—O'Brian, John Lord, 2199
—United Nations General Assembly, 2165
—United Nations Security Council, 2198, 2199
—Wavell, Gen. Sir Archibald, 307, 338, 371, 413, 2299
Political leaders—Greece
—Metaxas, Gen., 301
Political leaders—Hungary
—Baky, 2203
—Bardossy, MM., 426
—Endre, Laszlo, 2203
—Imredy, Bela, 2186
Political leaders—India
—Bose, Subhas Chandra, 2170
—Gandhi, 662, 734
—Nehru, Pandit, 662, 734
Political leaders—Iran
—Mohammed, Prince, 260
—Riza, Shah, 260
Political leaders—Iraq
—Ali, Raschid, 444
—Gailani, Raaschid Ali Beg, 260
Political leaders—Italy
—Badoglio, Marshal, 173, 1031, 1035, 1041, 1195
—Ciano, Count, 173, 285, 385, 1121
—Mussolini, Benito, 65, 152-153, 161, 163, 296, 984-985, 991, 1044-1045, 1087, 1121, 1280, 1794, 1922-1923
Political leaders—Japan
—Araki, Gen. Sadao, 2110

Political leaders—Japan (cont'd)
—Hiranuma, Baron Kiichiro, 2146
—Hirohito, Emperor, 577, 2085, 2137, 2185
—Hirota, Koki, 2146
—Iwamaura, Michiyo, 2105
—Koiso, Gen. Kuniaki, 1393
—Kurusu, Saburo, 285, 519, 576
—Suzuki, Adm. Baron Kantaro, 2105
—Tereshima, Adm. Ken, 2105
—Tojo, Gen. Hideki, 576, 1170, 1173, 1393, 2076, 2106, 2214
Political leaders—Japan—Post War
—Ashida, 2093
—Shidehara, Baron Kujuro, 2093
Political leaders—Norway
—Quisling, Vidkun, 8, 70, 1954, 1981
Political leaders—Philippine Islands
—Osmena, 2213
—Roxas, Manuel A., 2213
Political leaders—Poland
—Mikolajczyk, M. J., 187
—Sikorski, Gen. Wladyslaw, 220
Political leaders—Rumania
—Antonescu, Gen., 264
—Carol, King, 264
—Michael (Mihai) King, 264, 1179, 1478
Political leaders—Russia
—Gromyko, Andrei, 2198, 2199, 2200-2201
—Maisky, M., 490, 689
—Molotov, V. M., 7, 26, 203, 689, 755, 1084, 1100-1101
—Stalin, Marshal Joseph, 25, 549, 755, 857, 978, 1032, 1100-1101, 1568, 1669, 1754, 1907, 1934, 1952, 2008, 2242-2244
—United Nations General Assembly, 2165
—United Nations Security Council, 2198, 2199
—Vishinsky, Andrei, 2165
Political leaders—South Africa
—Smuts, Gen., 255, 304, 755, 792
Political leaders—Spain
—Franco, Gen. Francisco, 161, 296, 2187
Political leaders—U. S.
—Biddle, Francis, 1883, 2123, 2126
—Byrnes, James F., 2008, 2027, 2074, 2114, 2198, 2199, 2234
—Connally, Tom, 2165
—Dewey, Thomas E., 2198
—Forrestal, James V., 1422, 1439, 1441, 2248
—Hull, Cordell, 1084, 1375, 2027, 2134
—Knox, Frank, 211
—Roosevelt, Mrs. Eleanor, 2165, 2209
—Roosevelt, Franklin D., see under Roosevelt
—Stettinius, Edward R. Jr., 1883, 1891, 2000, 2165, 2198, 2199
—Stimson, Henry L., 1399, 2249, 2288, 2417
—Truman, Harry S., 1883, 1891, 1949, 2000, 2016, 2027, 2045, 2102, 2114, 2138, 2191, 2213, 2215, 2242, 2255
—United Nations General Assembly, 2165
—United Nations Security Council, 2198, 2199
Political leaders—Yugoslavia
—Cincar-Markovich, 404, 426
—Peter, King, 1110
—Simovich, Gen., 404

Polotsk, 1368
Pomerania, 1854
—East, 1543
Pompeii, 1076
Pont De Claiz, 1501
Ponte alla Carraia, 1427
Ponte alle Grazie, 1426-1427
Ponte di Ferro, 1427
Ponte Olivo, 963
Ponte Vecchio, 1427
Pontine marshes, 1265
"Pop Inn, The," 1378
Pope Pius XII, 2180
Port Arthur, 2036-2037
Port Moresby, 519, 772, 778, 1031, 1102-
  1103
Portable ports in Normandy, 1370-1371
Portland, 262, 2405.
Porto, Col. Marcus, 1799
Porto Edda, 259
Portsmouth, 252, 262, 360
Post war, see Atomic bomb; specific
  countries; War crimes investiga-
  tions
Potsdam, 425, 2008
Potsdam Conference, 1794, 2008, 2242
Potsdam ultimatum, 2025
Pourville, 741
Poznan, 1742, 1819
Pozorrubio, 1727
Praga, 1571
Pratt, Maj. Harry D., 2151
Prefrabricated harbors, 1370-1371
Premeti, 331, 362
"President Coolidge," 838
Pricolo, Gen., 173
Prien, Lt., 29
Priest gun-howitzer in action, 881
"Prince of Wales," 462, 504-505, 582-
  583
"Princeton," 1616
"Prinz Eugen," 463, 588-589, 2227
Pripet Marshes, 1099, 1133
Prisoners of war
—Allied in Japan, 2068
—Axis, 807
—British, 706-707
—Camp in North Africa, 906
—Camp in United States, 1080
—French, 663
—German, 188, 893, 910, 1042-1043,
  1056-1057, 1066-1067, 1194, 1278,
  1302, 1318-1319, 1350, 1404, 1434,
  1499, 1892-1893, 2418
—German wounded, 1287
—German in Moscow, 1384-1385
—Italian, 172, 826-827, 890-891, 1080,
  1318-1319
—Japanese, 753, 944, 1201
—Negotiations for exchange, 543
—North African, Axis, 898
—North African campaign, 925
—Prison ship, 55
—Sicily, 963
—Tunisia, 900
"Privateer" patrol bombers, 2438
Professional entertainers, 1878
Prome, 638, 653
Propaganda, 1596, 1943
—German, 11, 1779, 1981, 2197
—Italian, 196
—Japanese, 2071
"Provence," 833
Pruem, 1543

Prussia, East, 260, 1179, 1366, 1396,
  1430, 1473, 1543, 1669, 1730, 1737,
  1747, 1751, 2291
Prut River, 1179, 1216
Pskov, 1379
Pultusk, 1722
Puntarenas, 415
Push button bombs, 2483
Puys, 741
Pyawbwe, 2378
Pyle, Ernie, 1871
—and buddies, 1871
Pyu, 638

Q

Quast, Gen. von, 907
Qattara Depression, 712
Quebec Conference, 1569
Queen Victoria Street, 302
"Quincy," 731
Quineville, 1311
Quisling, Vidkun, 8, 70, 1954, 1981
Quo Tai-chi, Dr., 2198
Quotations
—Chamberlain, Neville, 9
—Churchill, Winston, 915, 1024, 2191,
  2245
—Clark, Gen. Mark W., 1793
—Ingram, Adm. Jonas H., 2259
—MacArthur, Gen. Douglas, 2060,
  2252

R

R. A. F. see Royal Air Force
R. A. A. F., see Royal Australian Air
  Force
Rabaul, 519, 618, 641, 654-655, 1031,
  1049, 1050-1051, 1065, 1102-1103,
  1235, 1237
Radar, 2169, 2437, 2471-2472, 2482,
  2491
—Photo, 2472
—Signal beamed at the moon, 2169
—"Umbrella," 2491
—Unit, portable, 2491
Radarguided bomb, 2438
Radio, 2071
Radio controlled bombs, 2483
Radio controlled cameras, see Cam-
  eras, Radio-controlled
Radio Corporation of America, 2451
Radio navigational system, 2441
"Radio proximity fuze," 2476
Radio shell fuze, 2476
Radiolocation, 453
Radiolocation station, German, 631
Radom, 1543
Radome bulb, 2471
Radomsko, 1717
Raeder, Grand Adm. Erich, 165, 2124-
  2125, 2237
Ragusa, 959, 962, 964-965
Raids on Berlin protested, 1184
Rajlovac (Serajevo) airfield, 998
Ramirez, Pedro, 1197
Ramsay, Adm. Sir Bertram, 2287
Ramu Valley, 1065
Randazzo, 964-965, 996

Rangoon, 519, 627, 630, 1787, 1794, 1930-1931, 1933, 1939, 2379
—Evacuated, 636-637
Rangoon-Prome railway, 638
Rangoon railway, 1405
Rapido River, 1127
Red Banner Baltic fleet, 1310
Red Barricade Factory, 798
Red Beach, 1774
Red Cross, 127, 138, 1153, 1340, 1363, 1369, 2396
Red Cross in Manila, 2104
Red October Factory, 798
Red October works, 798
Red Sea, 176
Redin, Galina, 2202
Redin, Lt. Nicolai G., 2202
Re-education begins in Germany, 1963
Refueling at sea, 2014
Refugee children, 2149
Regalbuto, 991, 996
Reggio Calabria, 1033, 1036-1037
Réichart, Johann, 2152
Reichbank, 1868
Reichstag, 270
Reims, 1944-1946
Reinhardt, Maj. Gen. Emil F., 1906
Reisling gun, 731
Remagen, 1793, 1802-1803, 1805, 1831, 1853
Remmiville, 1713
Remizov, Gen., 571
Remote-control cameras, see Cameras-Radio-controlled
Rena, 77
Renault plant, 632-633
Rendova Island, 946-949
—Occupied, 944
Rennes, 1180
"Renown," 323, 376
"Renshaw," 2102-2103
Republic "XP-84," 2460
"Repulse," 583
Revolt against Fascism in Italy, 984-985
Reynaud, Paul, 160, 2011
Reynolds, Maj. Gen. Russell B., 2150-2151
Rezekne, 1697
Rezhev, 771
Rheims, 1793, 1794
Rhine River, 1543, 1585, 1587, 1782, 1793, 1795, 1800, 1802-1807, 1810, 1813, 1825, 1827, 1831, 1835, 1841-1842, 1843, 1846, 1850, 1879, 2408
Rhine valley, 1666
Rhineberg, 2421
Rhineland, 7, 130, 150, 501, 694
Rhone River, 1180, 1443
Rhone valley, 1543
Ribbentrop, Joachim von, 7, 8, 26, 165, 285, 385, 404, 2124-2125, 2139, 2237
Ribeauville, 1666
Richards, Commander R. J., 1956
Richland, Washington, 2019
Rickenbacker, Capt. Edward V., 808, 2288
Riga, 1379, 1413, 1543, 1671
Rigney area, 2467
Rimberg Castle, 1592
Rimini, 1544, 1572, 1589, 1629
River Plate, 40-43
—Battle Heroes Honored, 58
Riviera, 1180, 1440-1441, 1444, 1450
Riza, Shah, 260

Road building through the New Guinea jungle, 1064-1065
Roatta, Gen., 173
Robot bombs, 1180, 1320, 1336, 1381, 1502, 1703
—American, 1696
—Jet propulsion engines, 1696
—Lair on the Normandy coast, 1354
—Launching sites, 1533
Robot planes, 1118, 1339, 1354, 1402, 1547
Robot tanks, 1328
"Roc," 2483
Rocket bombs, 1622, 1705, 1766, 1927, 2474, 2004, 2456, 2459
—Equipment, 2474
—Launcher, multiple, 1645
—Projectiles, 1993
—Run on Okinawa, 1993
Rockets, Ionosphere, 2498
"Rodney," 1035, 1037
Roer River, 1750, 1758, 1779, 1782
Roermond, 1716, 1739
Roetgen, 1564
Rogov, Lt. Col., 2198
Roi, 1137
Rokossovsky, Marshal Konstantin, 1793, 1926, 2291
"Roma," 1041
Rome, 101, 152, 172, 984, 1032, 1129, 1254-1255, 1271-1281, 1544, 1552
—Allied entry into, 1271
—Anti-Fascists, 1279
—Beachhead, 1131
—Colosseum, 1274-1275
—Fascists, 1279
Rome-Berlin-Tokyo Pact, 1121
Romilly 155
Rommel, Field Marshal Erwin, 520, 563, 567, 691, 700, 702, 813, 851, 1109, 1209
—Launches a new attack on Egypt, 768
Romsdals Fjord, 82
Rongerik Atoll, 2211
Rooney, Pfc. Mickey, 1878
Roosevelt, Mrs. Eleanor, 2165, 2209
Roosevelt, Franklin D., 32, 211, 369, 392, 577, 578, 1057, 1067, 1107, 1195, 1375, 2242, 2243, 2250
—Atlantic Charter, 504-505
—Cairo Conference, 1032, 1097
—Casablanca Conference, 856-857
—Churchill visits Roosevelt, 915
—Death of, 1794, 1882
—Funeral of, 1884
—Middle East conference, 1756
—Quebec Conference, 1568
—Shrine dedicated to, 2209
—Teheran Conference, 1032, 1100-1101
—Yalta Conference, 1754-1756
Roosevelt, Theodore, 1383
Roosevelt, Brig. Gen. Theodore, Jr., 1383, 2290
Rosenberg, Alfred, 2124-2125, 2127, 2237
Rosenthal, Joe, 1778
Roslavl, 548
Ross, Marine Lt. Col. R. P., 1986
Rossosh, 711
Rostock, 669
Rostov, 519, 552, 570-571, 714-715, 722, 772, 875, 1058
Rostov-Baku railway, 737
"Rosyth," 31
Rotterdam, 90, 108, 493, 1952

Rotterdam Harbor, 493
Rovno, 1143
Roxas, Manuel A., 2213
Roxas, Maria R., 2213
Royal Air Force
—(1940) 74, 78, 92, 130, 142, 150, 153,
    178, 181, 185, 212-213, 224-225,
    229, 232-236, 245, 253, 259, 266,
    270, 276-279, 282-284, 290, 293, 339
—(1941) 372, 377, 379, 439, 453, 464,
    491, 493, 501, 526, 550, 563, 567,
    588-589
—(1942) 617, 626-627, 630, 632-633,
    644-645, 669, 678, 693, 694, 699,
    720, 741, 811, 840
—(1943) 895, 925, 934, 988, 992, 996,
    1004, 1006-1007, 1068, 1077, 1114,
—(1944) 1183, 1185, 1228-1229, 1364-
    1365, 1402
—(1945) 1750, 2369
—Attacks German dams, 916-917
—Bombs sink the Tirpitz, 1639
—In Greece, 307
—In Rangoon, 1939
—Over Norway, 74-75, 78
—Raid On Waalhaven, 92
—Raids Stavanger and Bergen, 74
—Role in the withdrawal from Greece,
    442
—Strikes at Italy's war industry, 800-
    801
—Tactical Air Force, 1625
Royal artillery, 1512
Royal Australian Air Force, 253, 566-
    567
Royal Canadian Air Force, 48
Royal Dragoons, 592
Royal Marine Commandos, 1626-1627
Royal Marines, 1503
Royal Navy, see British Navy
Royal Netherlands Indies Army, 1925
"Royal Oak," 29
Royal Scots Fusiliers, 1620
Royce, Maj. Gen. Ralph, 1098, 1284
Rubber boat, German, 102
Rubber decoys, 2442, 2443
Ruegenwalde, 1918
Ruhr, 150, 694, 1788, 1845, 1877
Ruhr valley, 916, 1833
Ruhrberg Dam, 1750
Rumania, 260, 264, 480, 986-987, 1179,
    1194, 1202, 1216, 1220, 1473, 1476
—Post war border discussions, 2234-
    2235
—Quits the Axis camp, 1478
Rumania—Political leaders
—Antonescu, Gen., 264
—Carol, King, 264
—Michael (Mihai) King, 264, 1179, 1478
Rumanian Army, 1179
Rumanian forces, 551, 685
Rumanian infantry, 831
Rumanian oilfields, 986-987, 1179
Rumanian troops, 260, 1231
—With German forces, 260
Runstedt, Field Marshal Karl von, 536,
    1543, 1680, 1684, 1695, 1741, 1937,
    2312
Runstedt, Lt. Hans von, 1937
Rupel Pass, 422
Rusakov, Maj. Gen., 1906
Russia, 26, 260, 478-479, 480, 482, 485,
    524, 534-535, 689, 796-797, 798,
    1179, 1195, 1794
—Celebrates peace, 1952

Russia (cont'd)
—Declares war on Finland, 37
—Delares war on Japan, 1794, 2024
—Germany declares war on, 260
—Invades Finland, 8
—Maps, see Maps and diagrams—
    Eastern Front
—Naval bases in the Pacific, 642-643
—Non-aggression pact with Germany,
    7
—Peace treaty with Finland, 8, 62-63
—Post war border discussions, 2234-
    2235
—Russian-German agreement on Po-
    land, 26
—Russo-German pact, 1528
—White Russia, 260, 519, 1032
—**See also** Eastern Front
Russia—Military leaders
—Batov, Col. Gen., 1571
—Budenny, Marshal, 503, 508-509
—Chermiaeff, Lt. Gen. Ivan, 1944-1945,
    1946
—Golikov, Gen., 490
—Golubov, Gen., 634
—Jardov, Gen., 2286
—Kharlamov, Rear Adm., 490
—Konev, Marshal Ivan S., 1200, 1202,
    1781, 1793, 1905, 2291
—Malinovski, Col. Gen., 875, 1231
—Meretskov, Marshal, 2036-2037
—Rokossovsky, Marshal Konstantin,
    1926, 2291
—Rusakov, Maj. Gen., 1906
—Timoshenko, Marshal S. K., 686, 704,
    2291
—Vasilevsky Marshal Alexander,
    2036-2037, 2291
—Zhukov, Marshal Gregory, 1544,
    1747, 1793, 1947, 1948, 2261
Russia—Political leaders
—Gromyko, Andrei, 2198, 2199, 2200-
    2201
—Maisky, M., 490, 689
—Molotov, V. M., 7, 26, 203, 689, 755,
    1084, 1100-1101
—Stalin, Marshal Joseph, 25, 549, 755,
    857, 978, 1032, 1100-1101, 1568,
    1669, 1754, 1907, 1934, 1952, 2008,
    2242-2244
—United Nations Security Council,
    2198, 2199
Russian advance across the River Don,
    836
Russian Air Force, 480, 604, 1070
Russian air raids on Finland, 38
Russian anti-aircraft, 1053
Russian anti-aircraft guns in action,
    500
Russian armored train, 523
Russian Army, 570-571, 684, 760, 828-
    829, 830, 831, 836-837, 848-849,
    872, 875, 976-978, 980-981, 1008-
    1009, 1079, 1133, 1194
—Anniversary, 628
—Counter-attacks near Stalingrad, 775
—In Germany, 1906
—Nurses, 1264, 1310
—Recaptures Kharkov, 1010-1011
—Retakes Orel and Byelgorod, 982-
    983
—Retakes Sevastopol, 1256
Russian battlefield, 646-647
Russian Black Sea Fleet, 708-709, 824
Russian bombing plane, 689

Russian-British mutual assistance pact, 490
Russian cavalry, 1052
—Attack in East Prussia, 1669
Russian civilians, 483, 524, 571, 777
Russian drive for Czechoslovakia, 1590
Russian entry into Rumania, 1224
Russian family returns home, 1013
Russian First Ukrainian Army, 1905
Russian guardsmen, 1824, 2425
Russian guerrillas, 570
Russian guns in action, 1070
Russian infantry, 614-615, 704, 831
—Equipped with automatic weapons, 714
Russian laborers in Germany, 1820
Russian marines, 829
Russian Navy, 829, 2202
Russian nurses, 2430
Russian 1941 winter advance, 684
Russian 1942 winter advance in the Caucasus, 848-849
Russian 1943 fall offensive, 1070
Russian 1943 summer offensive begins, 978-979
Russian 1944 northern offensive, 1142-1143
Russian 1945 winter offensive, 1737, 1783, 1824
Russian occupation in Germany, 1918, 1940
Russian peasants, 523, 874-877, 1002-1003
Russian prisoners, 549
Russian resistance in air raids, 776
Russian sappers, 629, 714-715
Russian Scouts Company, 634
Russian Second Army, 1793
Russian semi-automatic tank rifle, 1435
Russian siege of Warsaw, 1571
Russian ski troops, 848-849
Russian soldiers, 587
Russian soldiers hunting down German stragglers in Rostov, 570-571
Russian tanks, 485, 573, 685, 1855
Russian tommy-gunners, 1379, 1744, 1819
Russian troops, 685
—In the Vitebsk sector, 1343
Russian village, 534-535, 688, 872
Russian women soldiers, 836-837, 1725
Russian workers' battalion, 774
Russians advance on Stettin, 1854
Russians and Americans meet at Torgau, 1905
Russians capture Tallinn, 1588
Russians celebrate junction with Allies, 1907
Russians close in on East Prussia, 1430
Russians drive to the Oder, 1747, 1824
Russians encircle German Sixteenth army at Staraya Russa, 628
Russians enter Danzig, 1851
Russians evacuate Odessa, 551
Russians in Berlin, 1934-1936
Russians overrun Vienna, 1876
Russians push forward in Rumania, 1224
Russians reach the Baltic sea, 1413
Russians reach the Baltic, 1744
Russians recapture Mojaisk, 614-615
Russians recover Odessa, 1231
Russians retake Minsk, 1366
Russians retreat towards the Dnieper, 503

Russians sweep through Poland, 1722
Russians take Koenigsberg, 1875
Rutbah, 444
Ruweisat Ridge, 713, 718-719
Rybachi Peninsula, 8, 62
"Ryukaku," 683
Ryukyus, 1599, 1794, 1857-1860, 1881, 2300, 2332-2333, 2375
Rzhev, 646, 886

S

Saar-Moselle region, 51
Saar region, 1543, 1666
Saarebourg, 1543
Sacco River, 1463
Safi, 843
Saga General Hospital, 2070
Sahara, 860
St. Angelo, 1268
St. Clement Danes, 303
St. Joost, 1739
"St. Lo," 2403
St. Lo, 1180, 1386, 1400-1401, 1404
St. Lo-Carentan road, 2216
St. Malo, 1180, 1456-1457, 1509, 2327, 2455
St. Michel, Mont, 1424
St. Nazaire, 648-649
St. Paul's Cathedral, 230, 247, 289
St. Sauveur, 1362
St. Tropez, 2382
St. Vith, 1731
Saipan, 1172-1173, 1180, 1316, 1326, 1332, 1357, 1789, 2145, 2298, 2331, 2382, 2386-2387, 2391, 2465, 2488
Saishu Island, 2072
Saito, Maj. Gen., 2107
Sakai, Maj. Sakaji, 2142
Sakaibara, Rear Adm. Shigematsu, 2143
Saksin, Georgii, 2167
Salamaua, 519, 619, 683, 1031, 1047, 1102-1103
Salerno, 1031, 1033, 1038-1039, 1042-1043, 1069, 1248, 2297, 2407
Salla, 8
Salonika, 311, 422, 424
Salsk, 725
"Salt Lake City," 2227
Salvio Prison, 1121
Salween River, 626, 1227, 1232, 1250, 1337
Salzburg, 404
Salzwedel, 1964
Samland Peninsula, 1751
Samoa, 808
Samurai swords, 2034
San Clements, 1144
San Fernando, 584
San Francisco, 2000
San Giorgio, 364-365
San Giovanni, 1035, 1037
San Jose, 1675
San Pablo, 591, 596
Sanananda, 854, 944-945
"Sangamon," 2439
Sansapor, 1406, 1429
Santa Barbara, 1723
"Santa Fe," 1836-1837
Santa Maria Del Fiore, 1449
Santa Maria Degli Angeli Church, 1277
Santi Quaranta, 332, 362

Santiago, 2173
Santo Thomas concentration camp, 1753
Sarajevo, 430, 998
Sarandoporo valley, 362
"Saratoga," 2227, 2233
Sarawak, 618
Sardinia, 324, 934-935, 942, 1041
Sarmi, 1261
Sarrebourg, 1647
Sarreguemines, 1679
Sarterne, 1062
Saruzac, Capt., 860
Saukel, Fritz, 2124-2125, 2237
"Saumarez," 113
"Savage," 1113
Savo Island, 520, 730
Savona, 800
Sbeitla, 881
Sbiba, 882
Scafati, 1076
Scapa Flow, 29
Schacht, Hjalmar, 2125, 2237
"Scharnhorst," 282, 588
—Sunk in the Arctic (map), 1112
Scheldt estuary, 1627
Schepke, Capt., 411
Scherfede, 1840
Schillingen, 2384
Schirmeck, 1679
"Schleswig-Holstein," 15
Schleuse River, 1815
Schlieben, Lt. Gen. von, 1348
Schouten Islands, 1267
Schultze, Capt. 411
Schusselburg, 522
Schmidt, 1758
Schwammenauel Dam, 1758
Schweinfurt, 1888
Sciacca, 942
Scoglitti, 970-971
"Scorched earth" policy, 2330
—Burma, 636-637
—Russia, 725, 762-763, 831
"Scorpion," 1113
Scotland, 30, 454
Scots Guards, 712-713
Scottish division, 1850
Sea of Azov, 547, 552, 570, 772, 1013, 1032
Seabees, 1249, 1979
Seadrome, 2463
Sebha, 860
Sebretev, 837
Second Army, 1598
—See also British Second Army
Second battle of the Philippine Sea, 1544, 1615, 1618, 1619, 1621, 2264, 2439
2nd Corps—Fifth Army, 1272
2nd Division, 1094
2nd French Armored Division, 1291, 1417, 1484, 2271
Second Front, 814-815
2nd Marine Division, 1088-1089, 2377
Second Ukrainian Army, 1200
Second White Russian Army, 1722, 1751, 1926
"Secret weapons," 2476
—Allied, 1370-1371
—British, 453
—German, 1320, 2490
—Japanese, 2434-2435
—United States, 2454
Sedan, 8, 119, 132, 1543

Sedan-Rethel area, 114
"Seeing Eye," 2471
Seine River, 1180, 1416, 1470, 1484, 1508, 1539
Seipel, Johann, 2111
Seitz, Capt. George A., 1959
Self-propelled guns, 2461, 2494
Serbia, 424
Sevastopol, 520, 557, 580, 708-709, 1179, 1256
7.2 howitzer, 1519
7.62 mm gun, 1310
Seventh Army, 960, 962, 1451, 1459, 1480, 1566, 1645, 1662, 1666, 1863, 1866, 1874, 1878, 1897, 1955
—Infantrymen, 1874
—100th Division, 2373
—Storms Hulirich, 1874
—See also American Seventh Army
7th Division, 1139, 2376
7th Infantry Division, 1137
Seventh Fleet, 1615, 1704-1705, 1817, 1991, 2004
75 mm guns, French, 149
76 mm gun, 2461
77th Division, 1849, 2315, 2415,
77th Infantry Division, 1953
78th Division, 963, 989, 991
Sevez, Gen. Francois, 1944, 1945
Seyss-Inquart, Arthur, 2124-2125, 2237
Sfax, 898, 900
Sfax and Sousse fall to the Eighth army, 900-901
SHAEF, 1945
Shadazup, 1215
Shan states, 672
Shanghai, 577
Shanghai prison camp, 2087
"Shangri-La" is born, 664
Sharpnack, Lt. George L., 2204-2205
"Shaw," 574-575
Shawcross, Sir Hartley, 2126
"Sheffield," 1112
Shepherd, Maj. Gen. Lemuel C., Jr., 1985, 2294
Sherman, Capt., 682
Sherman, Rear Adm., 2035
Sherman tanks, 1706, 2470
Shidehara, Baron Kijuro, 2093, 2137
Shigemitsu, Mamoru, 2043, 2045
Shinagawa prison camp, 2087
Ships—Australia
—"Canberra," 731
—"Perth," 66
Ships—Canada
—"Empress of Britain," 298-299
Ships—France
—"Algerie," 833
—"Colbert," 833
—"Dunkerque," 192, 833
—"Dupleix," 833
—"Foch," 833
—"Jean Bart," 818
—"Jean de Vienne," 833
—"La Galissonaire," 833
—"La Marseillaise," 833
—"Provence," 833
—"Strasbourg," 192, 833
—"Surcouf," 191
Ships—Germany
—"Admiral Graf Spee," 39, 41, 42, 52, 58
—"Altmark," 54-55
—"Bismarck," 463
—"Columbus," 44

Ships—Germany (cont'd)
—"Eisenach," 415
—"Gneisenau," 588-589
—"Idarwald," 336
—"Lutzow," 283
—"Prinz Eugen," 463, 588, 2227
—"Scharnhorst," 282, 1112
—"Schleswig-Holstein," 15
—"Tirpitz," 1223, 1639
—"U-249," 2405
—"U-858," 1965
Ships—Great Britain
—"Achilles," 61
—"Ajax," 41, 294
—"Arandora Star," 189
—"Ark Royal," 317, 323, 464, 558-559
—"Athenia," 11
—"Belfast," 1112, 1283
—"Berkeley," 741
—"Berwick," 324
—"Black Prince," 1283
—"Campbeltown," 648-649
—"Cossack," 1283
—"Courageous," 31
—"Doric Star," 39
—"Dorsetshire," 464
—"Duke of York," 112-113
—"Eagle," 315
—"Edinburgh," 31
—"Exeter," 41, 52
—"Exmoor," 962
—"Gloucester," 406
—"Glowworm," 67
—"Grenville," 50
—"Hardy," 69
—"Hasty," 406
—"Hood," 462-463
—"Illustrious," 315
—"Jamaica," 112-113
—"King George V," 369
—"Lancastria," 214-215
—"Malaya," 323
—"Mauritius," 1283
—"Mohawk," 31
—"Nelson," 542, 1035, 1037
—"Norfolk," 112, 462
—"Orion," 1283
—"Prince of Wales," 462-463, 582-583
—"Renown," 323, 376
—"Repulse," 582-583
—"Rodney," 1035, 1037
—"Royal Oak," 29
—"Saumarez," 1113
—"Savage," 1113
—"Scorpion," 1113
—"Sheffield," 1112
—"Southampton," 31
—"Victorious," 464
—"Warspite," 1037, 1283
—"York," 294-295
Ships—Greece
—"Kanaris," 988
Ships—Italy
—"Artigliere," 295
—"Conte Biancamano," 415
—"Eugenio Di Savoia," 1195
—"Fella," 415
—"Fiume," 406
—"Galileo Galilei," 17
—"Giulio Cesare," 1041
—"Pola," 406
—"Roma," 1041
—"San Giorgio," 365
—"Vittorio Veneto," 406
—"Zara," 406

Ships—Japan
—"Nagato," 2227
—"Ryukaku," 683
—"Syukaku," 683
—"Yamato," 1615, 1870
Ships—Norway
—"Stord," 1113
Ships—Sweden
—"Gripsholm," 1223
Ships—United States
—"Arizona," 574, 577
—"Arkansas," 2227, 2231
—"Astoria," 731
—"Augusta," 504-505, 1283
—"Birmingham," 2322
—"Bunker Hill," 1958-1959, 2332-2333
—"California," 578-579
—"Cassin," 578-579
—"Charles S. Sperry," 1959
—"Coolidge," 2402
—"Downes," 579
—"English," 1959
—"Enterprise," 2406
—"Essex," 2406
—"Franklin," 1836-1837, 2368
—"Hammon," 696
—"Hancock," 2397
—"Hazelwood," 2370
—"Hornet," 664-666, 2340
—"Houston," 2402
—"Indianapolis," 2426
—"Intrepid," 2358
—"Langsley," 2354-2355
—"Lexington," 520, 682-683
—"Maryland," 577
—"Massachusetts," 2006
—"Neosho," 683
—"Nevada," 1283, 1290, 2219, 2225, 2227
—"New York," 1767, 2227
—"Newcomb," 2375
—"Oklahoma," 574, 577-578
—"Pennsylvania," 579
—"Pensacola," 2227
—"Princeton," 1616-1617
—"Quincy," 731
—"Renshaw," 2102-2103
—"St. Lo," 2403
—"Salt Lake City," 2229
—"Santa Fe," 1837
—"Saratoga," 2227, 2233
—"Sims," 683
—"South Dakota," 2039
—"Stembel," 1959
—"Stephen Potter," 2402
—"Tennessee," 577
—"Texas," 1319
—"Tuscaloosa," 1283
—"Vincennes," 731
—"Wahoo," 809
—"Washington," 159
—"Wasp," 786
—"West Virginia," 577
—"Wilkes-Barre," 1959
—"Yorktown," 520, 696
Shirach, Baldur von, 2124-2125, 2237
Short, Maj. Gen. Walter C., 2168
Showa Steel Works, 1323
Shuri, 1794, 1975, 1986, 2315, 2495
Shushi Shu, Dr., 2166-2167
Shuttle bombing, 1229
Shwebo, 1689
Siberia, 2024
Sibert, Maj. Gen. Franklin C., 676
Sibuyan Sea, 1544

Sicilian airfields, 952
Sicilian campaign, 952-973
Sicily, 294, 771, 772, 842, 934-935, 942, 952-973, 988-997, 1031, 1035, 1073, 2297, 2453
—Allied invasion of, 952-953
—Allied surface ships, 956
—Conquered, 996-997
Sidi Barrani, 8, 259, 338, 340, 707, 807
Sidi Omar, 563
Sidi Rezegh, 564-565, 691
Sidon, 474
Siegfried Line, 57, 132, 1543, 1564, 1566, 1581, 1635, 1741, 1758, 2489
Signal Corps, 1701
Sikh infantry, 1930
Sikh leaders, 662
Sikh troops, 2378-2379
Sikorski, Gen. Wladyslaw, 220
Silesia, 1735, 1742, 1783
—German Silesia, 1543, 1734, 1747, 1808
—Upper, 1543
Sima, Horea, 264
Simeto, 991
Simeto River, 991
Simferopol, 556, 557
Simmons, Sgt. Dave, 2227
Simon, Viscount, 792
Simovich, Gen., 404
Simpson Harbor, 1235
Simpson, Lt. Gen. William, 2262
Simpson, Mrs. Elizabeth Hood, 2262
"Sims," 683
Singapore, 519, 610, 621, 624-625, 1746, 2045, 2058, 2078-2079, 2281
—Prisoner of war camps, 2107
—Surrenders, 625
Siret River, 1476
Sirte, 847, 851
Sittang River, 627, 638
Sittard battle area, 1739
16 Evacuation Hospital, 1797
16 inch shells, 1872
6th Amphibious Group, 1816-1817
6th Armored Division, 1865
6th Armored Division infantrymen, 2399
Sixth Army Group, 2292
6th Marine Division, 1969, 2294
Skagerrak, 8
Skeen, Maj. J. H., Jr., 2176-2177
Slim, Gen., 1931
Slovak divisions on the Eastern Front, 552
Slovenia, 998
Smith, Lt. Gen. Holland M., 1764, 1789
Smith, Maj. Gen. Julian C., 1092
Smith, Lt. Gen. Walter Bedell, 1944, 1945
Smiyev, 687
Smolensk, 260, 500, 506, 525, 531, 628, 634, 886, 1013, 1032, 1052
Smuts, Gen., 255, 304, 755, 792
Smyth, Dr. H. D., 2020
Snooperscope, 2466
Sofia, 384, 1132
Soissons, 154, 1524
Sollum, 340, 358, 563, 592, 612-613, 707, 806-807
Solomon Islands, 520, 727-731, 746, 747, 750, 751, 757, 772, 783, 788-789, 838, 867, 946-947, 1031, 1082-1083, 1102-1103, 1198, 2275, 2296, 2300

Soluk, 592
Somaliland, 172, 280
—Camel Corps, 223
Somervell, Lt. Gen. Brehon, 1453
Somerville, Vice Adm. Sir James, 192
Somme, 1515
Sotojiro, Capt. Tatsuta, 2159
Sousse, 824-825, 900
South Africa, 255, 380
South Africa—Military leaders
—Pienaar, Gen., 811
South Africa—Political leaders
—Smuts, Gen., 255, 304, 755, 792
South African Air Force, 280, 563, 703
South African Field Force, 255
South African mechanized units in Kenya, 304
South African patrol, 693
South African Premier visits Britain, 792
South African 2nd Division, 811
South African soldiers, 255
South African troops, 304, 416, 563, 713, 719, 811, 1427
South Atlantic, 39
"South Dakota," 2038
South Pacific, 520
South Pacific force, 2296
South Seas, 1097
"Southampton," 31
Southampton, 262, 325
Soviet-British-American armistice, 1478
Soviet 58th Guards Division, 1906
Spain, 296
Spaatz, Lt. Gen. Carl A., 1186, 1944-1945, 1948, 2278
Spaatz, Mrs. Anna, 2278
Spain
—Franco regime, 2187
—French economic boycott, 2187
Spain—Political leaders
—Franco, Gen. Francisco, 161, 296, 2187
Spars, 2279
Spears, Gen., 413
Speer, Albert, 2124-2125, 2237
Spellman, Cardinal Francis J., 2180
Sperr, Ingeborg, 2135
"Charles S. Sperry," 1959
Spezia, 1041
Spies, see Espionage
"Spitfire," 236, 589, 1077
Spitzbergen, 528-529
Spree River, 1902
Spruance, Adm. Raymond A., 1193, 1859, 2248, 2298
"Squirt, The," 1118
Stahmer, Dr. Otto, 2194
Stalin, Marshal, 26, 549, 755, 857, 978, 1032, 1100-1101, 1568, 1669, 1754, 1907, 1934, 1952, 2008, 2242-2244
Stalin-Hitler pact, 1528
Stalingrad, 714, 737, 754, 760-763, 769, 771, 774-777
—Map, 799
Stalino, 552, 647
Stanley, Lt. Leon A., 1104
Stansund, 389
Staraya Russa, 646, 668
Stark, Adm. Harold R., 1360
Stary Oskol, 711
Stassen, Commander Harold E., 1621
Stationer's Hall, 303
Stauffenberg, Col. Count von, 1394
Stavanger, 8, 74

Stavelot, 1685-1686
Steinkjer, 79
"Stembel," 1959
"Stephen Potter," 2402
"Sterling," 589
Stettin, 1808, 1854
Stettinius, Edward R. Jr., 1883, 1891, 2000, 2165, 2198, 2199
Stilwell, Lt. Gen. Joseph W., 676-679, 1145, 1174
Stilwell, General, 1191, 1192, 1227, 1232, 1233, 2247, 2265
—March from Burma, 676-679
Stilwell Road, 1544, 1838
Stimson, Henry L., 1399, 2249, 2288, 2417
Stimson, Mrs. Henry L., 2249
"Stirling," 526, 550, 800, 720-721
Stone, Chief Justice Harlan, 1883
"Stord," 1113
"Stork" plane, 402
Storming Manila from assault boats, 1759
"Stormovik" dive bombers, 711
Strait of Dover, 185, 199
Straits of Messina, 992, 1031,1135
Straits Settlements, 625
Strand Theatre, Aldwych, 174
"Strasbourg," 833
Strasbourg, 192, 1649
Strasser, Franz, 2152
Strategic Air Force of Eastern Air Command, 1596
Stratemeyer, Lt. Gen. George E., 2066
Stratton, Capt. Dorothy C., 2279
Street fighting in Athens, 1628
Street fighting in Tunis, 910
Street scene in Anzio, 1159
Streeter, Col. Ruth Cheney, 2279
Streicher, Julius, 2125, 2237
Stritch, Cardinal Samuel A., 2180
Struma Valley, 422
"Stukas," 385, 1041
Stumpff, Col. Gen. Paul, 1948
Sturges, Maj. Gen., 681
Submarines, 11, 18, 29, 36, 77, 170, 189, 284, 405, 408-409, 411, 558, 802-803, 833, 862, 878, 894, 950-951, 1056-1057, 1066-1067, 1461, 1561, 1942, 1965, 2012-2013
—Anti-submarine measures, 802-803, 878
—Anti-U-Boat Warfare Committee, 803
—Anzio Harbor, 1207
—Base at Brest, 1561
—British midget, 1223
—"Galileo Galilei" (Ital), 17
—German submarine surrenders, 2405
—Italian, 1041
—Italian midget, 1195
—Japanese, 1015
—Japanese aircraft carrying, 2478
—Midget, 1015
—Nest at Bremen Harbor, 1942
—One-man, 1152
—"Surcouf" (Fr), 191
Surrenders to a bomber, 530
—"U-249" (Ger), 2405
—"U-858" (Ger), 1965
—"Wahoo" (U.S.), 809
Suda Bay, 467, 469
Sudetenland, 7
Suez Canal, 8, 53, 176, 259, 520, 700, 702
"Suffolk," 462

Suffolk, 313
Sugamo Prison, 2106
Sugiyama, Field Marshal, 1170, 1173
Suicide planes, Japanese, 2439
Sulpha compounds, 2462
Sulpha drugs, 2462
Sulu Seas, 1544
Sumatra, 519, 642-643, 1429
Sumida River, 1652-1653
Sunderland, 284, 862
"Superfortress," 1322, 1332, 1544, 1784, 1787, 1794, 1859, 2018, 2334-2335,
—Bomb Tokyo, 1652-1653
—In action, 1323
Supplies and supply routes
—Anzio, 1149
—Arctic convoy route, 797
—Bastogne, 1691
—Convoy routes to Britain, 408-409
—Genoa, 800
—German route through Balkans, 766
—Italy, 1132, 1594-1595, 2401
—Iwo Jima, 1775
—Leyte, 1656-1657
—Russia-bound, 797
—Western Front, 1848, 1879
—See also Burma Road; Ledo Road
Supreme Allied Command, 1944-1945
Surabaya, 637, 1180, 1262
"Surcouf," 191
Suribachi, Mt., 1764-1765, 1772-1773
Surigao Strait, 1677
Surrender at Cherbourg, 1348
Susloparoff, Gen. Ivan, 1945, 1946
Sutherland, Lt. Gen. Richard, 2035, 2252
Suzuki, Adm. Baron Kantaro, 2105
Swancutt, Maj. Woodrow P., 2219
Swedish diplomatic exchange ship, 1222
Swedish ships, see Ships
Swiss roll, 2463
Swiss soldiers, 167
Switzerland, 167
"Swordfish," 317
Sydney, 66, 168
Sydney Harbor, 397, 2481
Syfret, Rear Adm., 681
"Syokaku," 683
Syracuse, 959, 961, 963, 964-965
Syria, 260, 459, 474-475, 488, 494, 1984
—Capitulates to Allies, 488
—Comes under control of the Allied armies, 488
Syrian airfields, 455
Syrian armistice, 495

T

Tablac hospital, 1812
Tachibaba, Lt. Commander Soichi, 2143
Tacloban, 1544, 1609, 1657
Tactical Air Force, 898, 1572-1573
Taganrog, 552, 570-571, 722, 1013
Tahuna, 851
Takahashi, Adm. Sankichi, 2146
"Talamba," 961
Tallinn, 511, 522, 1543, 1588, 1671
Tamborini, Jose P., 2184
Tanahmerah Bay, 1240
Tanambogo, 727, 730, 759
Tanchuk, 1544

Tank battles in the Ukraine, 531-533
Tank destroyer, 2461
Tank hospital in France, 1702
Tanks, 2464, 2477, 2480
—AVRE, 1515
—Axis, 690-691
—Flame throwing, 2464
—In allied plans, 852
—Miniature, 1328, 2495
—Rubber decoys, 2443
—Tankette, Japanese, 2495
—U. S., 2477
Tannenberg, 1543, 1669, 1737
Taormina, 992-993
Tarakan, 618, 1794, 1925
Taranto, 259, 315, 1031, 1041
Tarawa, 1031, 1088-1095, 1252, 1789,
    2415, 2429, 2446
—Beach, 1090-1091
—Tent city, 1252
Tarnopol, 1194
Taroa, 623
Tasklaotos, 1629
Tatsyaskaya, 837
Taylor, Maj. Gen. Maxwell D., 1955
Tebessa, 882
Tebourba evacuated, 835
Tedder, Air Chief Marshal, 930, 941,
    1484, 1947, 1948, 2287
Teheran, 507, 1032, 1100-1101, 1107
Teheran Conference, 1100-1101, 2242
Tel Aviv, 2117
Tel el Eisa, 713, 718, 719
Telepte, 881
Television, 2451
Teller mines, 1230
Tempest Squadron, 1336
Tenaru River, 732
Tengchung, 1522, 1527, 1577
"Tennessee," 576-577
Tenth Army, 1894, 1985, 1997, 2294,
    2310-2311
10th Mountain Division, 1790, 1797,
    1938
Terek River, 829
Tereshima, Adm. Ken, 2105
"Texas," 1319
Thailand, 495, 519
Thala, 882
Thames, the, 146, 205
Thames Estuary, 252, 262
Tharawaddy, 638
Thebes, 437
Theissen, Gen. Karl, 2140
"There will always be an England,"
    2245
Thermopylae, 436
3rd American Division, 1073
3rd Armored Division, 2477
Third Army, 1399, 1526, 1566, 1637,
    1692, 1810, 1865, 1868, 1893, 1988,
    2275, 2319, 2323, 2326
—Captures German gold hoard, 1868
—Crosses the Rhine, 1841
—11th Armored Division, 1811
—Storms Andernach, 1811
3rd Division, 1438-1439, 2382, 2467
Third Fleet, 1615, 2006, 2007, 2038,
    2264, 2296
Third Ukraine Army, 1231
Third White Russian Army, 1730
13th Army Air Force, 1736, 1817, 1991
30th Division infantrymen, 2324
30th Infantry Division, 1887
31st Division, 2313

31st Infantry, 1982-1983
32nd Division, 2307
32nd Infantry Division, 2381
34th Division, 1462, 1903
35th Division, 2421
36th Division, 1440
38th Evacuation Hospital, 1799
Thompson, Capt. John, 2297
Thrace, 422
3.7 anti-aircraft gun, 1258
343rd Engineer Regiment, 2448
351st Infantry Regiment, 2486
"Thunderbolt," 1207, 2460
"Thunderjet," 2460
Thurstan, Edgar, 55
Tibbets, Col. Paul, Jr., 2018
Tiber River, 1553
Tiddim Road, 1620
Tientsin, 2090-2091
"Tiger of Malaya," 2058, 2151
Tiger tanks, 1038, 1512
Tikhoretsk, 725
Tikhvin, 581
Timoshenko, Marshal S. K., 686, 704,
    2291
Tinian, 1173, 1180, 1397, 1432
Tiny Tim, 2456
"Tirpitz," 1223, 1639, 2481
Tito, Marshal Josip Broz, 1108, 1109,
    2195, 2257
Tittingen, 2414
Tmimi, 811
Tobruk, 232, 259, 364-367, 435, 520, 564,
    566-567, 606, 691, 692, 702, 706-
    707, 771, 810-811
Tobruk Harbour, 365
Todt construction workers, 1314
Toguri, Iva, 2071
Tojo, Gen. Hideki, 576, 1170, 1173,
    1393, 2076, 2106, 2214
Tokashiki Island, 1849, 1852
Tokyo, 664, 666, 867, 1652-1653, 1761,
    1784, 1814, 1830, 2038-2039, 2086,
    2334
—Post War, 2060-2064
—Radio, 2025
Tokyo Bay, 1794
"Tokyo Rose," 2071
Tollo, 1156
Tolman, Dr. Richard C., 2020
Tomioka, Rear Adm. Todatoshi, 2043
Tommygun, 2480
"Tommy" sub-machine gun, 207
Tongres, 104
Torboli, 1938
Torgau, 1793, 1905
Toronto Scottish troops, 84
Torre Annunziata, 1076
Toujane, 893
Toul, 167
Toulon, 172, 771, 1451, 1455, 1481
Toungoo, 638, 653
Toungoo-Mandalay road, 639
Tower of London, 327
Transjordan, 472
Transjordan Arab Legion, 445
Transports remove wounded, 1869
Transvaal regiment, 417
Transvaal Scottish Regiment, 457
Transylvania, 264, 2235
Treasury Islands, 1081, 1082-1083
Trento, 1035
Trevieres, 1345, 1358
Tricycle landing gear, 2449
Trier, 1635

Trieste, 1793, 2192, 2235
Trigh Capuzzo, 691
Tripartite Pact, 404
Tripartite Treaty, 285, 1121
Tripoli, 771, 813, 847, 859-860, 861
Tripolitania, 813, 840, 850-851
Troina, 991, 996
Tromso Fjord, 1639
Tronheim, 8, 72
Trondheim Harbor, 72
Tropez, 1458
Troyes, 1524
Truk, 1032, 1102-1103, 1166-1167, 1168, 1247
Truman, Harry S., 1891, 1949, 2000, 2008, 2016, 2027, 2045, 2102, 2114, 2138, 2191, 2209, 2213, 2215, 2242, 2255
—Becomes President, 1883
Truman, Mrs., 1883, 1949
Truman, Mary Margaret, 1949
Truscott, Lt. Gen. Lucian K., 1920, 2302
Tsagita, 2093
Tsolakoglu, Gen., 434
Tsvetkovich, M., 404
Tsymlianskaya, 1058
Tsymlyansk, 722
Tuapse, 829
Tula, 573
Tulagi, 520, 726-729, 746, 759, 783, 788, 1102-1103
Tungting, Lake, 1106
Tunis, 172, 772, 820-821, 834, 902-903, 908-913, 924-925
Tunis and Bizerte fall to the Allies, 908
Tunisia, 771, 772, 820-826, 834, 842, 861, 880-885, 890-891, 898-903, 913, 924-925, 2462
Turin, 153, 800, 963
Turkestan, 1404
Turkey, 424, 1877
Turner, Adm. Richmond K., 1789
"Tuscaloosa," 1283
Tuyun, 1689
Twaddle, Maj. Gen. Harry L., 1877
12th Air Force, 1442-1443, 2401
12th Army Group, 1484, 1600, 1793, 1861, 1893
20th Air Force, 1322
20th Bomber Command, 1968
20 mm gun, 2301
21st Army Group, 1793, 1926
22nd Chinese Division, 1215
24th Division, 1895
27th Division, 1089
29th Division, American Ninth Army, 1796
Twining, Maj. Gen. Nathan F., 2411
240 mm howitzer, 1259, 2493
Tyrrhenian Sea, 1253
Tyrrhenian seacoast, 1265

U

"U-249," 2405
"U-858," 1965
UNRRA see United Nations Relief and Rehabilitation Administration
U. S. O., 1412
Ueno railroad, 1784
Uerdingen, 1807
Ukraine, 260, 480, 503, 506, 531-533,

Ukraine (cont'd)
536-539, 546, 552, 647, 872-877, 1012-1013, 1085, 1143, 1194, 1200, 1202, 1219, 1264, 1435
Ukraine Harvest, 1002-1003
Ukrainian Army, 1194
Ukrainian girls, 1679
Umberto, Crown Prince, 1234
"Umbrella" antenna, 2491
Umezo, Gen. Yoshijiro, 2043
Unalaska, 698
United Auto Worker's Union, 2133
United Nations Charter, 2000
United Nations
—Franco regime, 2187
—Palestine, 2117
—Paris Peace Conference, 2234-2235
—"Free Territory," 2235
United Nations Conference, San Francisco, 1794, 2000
United Nations General Assembly, 2165
—Bevin, Ernest, 2165
—Connally, Tom, 2165
—First session in London, 2165
—Roosevelt, Mrs. Eleanor, 2165
—Stettinius, Edward R., 2165
—Vandenberg, Arthur H., 2165
—Vishinsky, Andrei, 2165
United Nations Security Council, 2165, 2198-2201
—Ala, Hussein, 2199
—Byrnes, 2198, 2199, 2234
—Cadogan, Sir Alexander, 2198, 2199
—Daftari, Akbar, 2199
—Dewey, Thomas E., 2198
—First New York session, 2165, 2198-2201
—Gromyko, Andrei, 2198, 2199, 2200-2201
—Iranian question, 2199, 2200-2201
—O'Brian, John Lord, 2199
—Poland, 2201
—Quo Tai-Chi, Dr., 2198
—Stettinius, Edward R. Jr., 2198, 2199
United Nations site-inspection committee, 2166-2167
United Nations Pact, 520
United Nations Relief and Rehabilitation Administration, 2149, 2183
United Service Organization, 1412
United States
—Bases in the Pacific (map), 2178-2179
—Black market, 2208
—Casualties and losses, see Casualties and losses—Allied
—Defense, 211
—Demobilization, 2162-2164
—Fifty destroyers for Great Britain, 265
—Lend-Lease, 219, 265, 267, 386, 392, 498, 519, 1891
—Naval bases in the Pacific, 642-643
—Occupation forces in Europe, 2196
—Office of Price Administration, 2188, 2208, 2215
—Office of Strategic Services, 2144
—Pearl Harbor investigations, 2134, 2138, 2168
—Post-war housing shortage, 2206
—Ships, see Ships
—State Department, 519, 864
—Veterans, 2057, 2160, 2204-2205

United States (cont'd)
—War Department, 2249
—War profits investigations, 2226
United States—Military leaders
—Ainsworth, Rear Adm. W. L., 1621
—Arnold, Gen. Henry H., 1307, 2254, 2278
—Berkey, Rear Adm. Russell, 1817
—Blandy, Vice Adm., W. H. P., 2219, 2224, 2227
—Bradley, Lt. Gen. Omar N., 1284, 1294, 1399, 1484, 1531, 1545, 1600, 1861, 1893, 2258
—Buckner, Lt. Gen. Simon Bolivar, Jr., 1985, 2294, 2300
—Carney, Rear Adm. Robert B., 1621, 2296
—Chamberlain, Maj. Gen. S. J., 2035
—Chennault, Maj. Gen. Claire, 1098, 1226, 2264
—Clark, Lt. Gen. Mark, 818, 826-827, 1031, 1033, 1038, 1179, 1254, 1258, 1265, 1272, 1277, 1281, 1388, 1422, 1793, 1799, 2267, 2270
—Doolittle, Lt. Gen. James H., 664, 666, 1180, 2276
—Eichelberger, Lt. Gen. Robert I., 1817
—Eisenhower, Gen. Dwight D., 773, 814, 839, 902, 925, 930, 941, 1041, 1107, 1284, 1307, 1398, 1399, 1484, 1600, 1781, 1861, 1904, 1996, 1998, 2253
—Gavin, Maj. Gen. James, 2297
—Geiger, Maj. Gen. Roy, 1859, 2300
—Halsey, Adm. William F., 1544, 1562, 1615, 1621, 2038, 2264
—Hewitt, Adm. H. K., 818, 1038, 1441
—Hill, Rear Adm. Harry W., 1092
—Hodge, Maj. Gen. John R., 1859
—Hodges, Gen. Courtney H., 1524, 1600, 1861, 1905, 2286
—Ingram, Adm. Jonas H., 2102, 2259
—Kenney, Gen. George C., 1225, 2283
—Keyes, Maj. Gen. Geoffrey, 960, 1272
—Kimmel, Adm. Husband E., 2168, 2250
—King, Adm. Ernest J., 791, 1173, 2250, 2298
—Kinkaid, Vice Adm. Thomas G., 1544, 1615, 1704, 1705, 2274
—Kirk, Rear Adm. Alan G., 1283, 1306-1307, 2301
—Krueger, Gen. Walter, 1705, 2274
—Leahy, Adm. William D., 1411, 1754, 2027
—MacArthur, Gen. Douglas, 519, 650, 651, 652, 772, 1047, 1241, 1410-1411, 1544, 1574, 1609, 1745, 1768, 2004, 2035, 2038-2039, 2040, 2041, 2042, 2045, 2252, 2260
—Marshall, Gen. George C., 930, 1173, 1307-1308, 1754, 2250
—Merrill, Brig. Gen. Frank, 1075, 1174, 1192, 2272
—Mitscher, Adm. Marc A., 1173, 1857, 2263
—Nimitz, Adm. Chester W., 1089, 1096, 1193, 1410, 1411, 1778, 2038, 2041, 2255, 2300
—Patch, Lt. Gen. Alexander, 1566, 1957, 2275
—Patton, Gen. George S. Jr., 856, 960, 962, 989, 1180, 1399, 1526,

United States—Military leaders (cont'd)
1531, 1545, 1566, 1637, 1695, 1988, 2290
—Reinhardt Maj. Gen. Emil F., 1906
—Shepherd, Maj. Gen. Lemuel C., 1985, 2294
—Simpson, Lt. Gen. William, 2262
—Smith, Lt. Gen. Walter Bedell, 1944, 1945
—Spaatz, Gen. Carl A., 1186, 1944-1945, 1948, 2278
—Spruance, Adm. Raymond A., 1193, 1859, 2248, 2298
—Stark, Adm. Harold R., 1360
—Stilwell, Lt. Gen. Joseph W., 676-679, 1145, 1174, 1191, 1192, 1227, 1232, 1233, 2247, 2265
—Stratemeyer, Lt. Gen. George E., 2066
—Truscott, Lt. Gen. Lucian K., 1920, 2302
—Vandergrift, Lt. Gen. A. A., 728, 2256
—Wainwright, Lt. Gen. Jonathan, 650, 658, 2040, 2045, 2269
—Whitehead, Maj. Gen. Ennis, 2283
United States—Political leaders
—Biddle, Francis, 1883, 2123, 2126
—Byrnes, James F., 2008, 2027, 2074, 2114, 2198, 2199, 2234
—Connally, Tom, 2165
—Dewey, Thomas E., 2198
—Forrestal, James V., 1422, 1439, 1441, 2248
—Hull, Cordell, 1084, 1375, 2027, 2134
—Knox, Frank, 211
—Roosevelt, Franklin D., see under Roosevelt
—Roosevelt, Mrs. Eleanor, 2165, 2209
—Stettinius, Edward R. Jr., 1883, 1891, 2000, 2165, 2198, 2199
—Stimson, Henry L., 1399, 2249, 2288, 2417
—Truman, Harry S., 1883, 1891, 1949, 2000, 2016, 2027, 2045, 2102, 2114, 2138, 2191, 2213, 2215, 2242, 2255
—United Nations General Assembly, 2165
—United Nations Security Council, 2198, 2199
United States Air Forces, 641, 727, 741, 840, 934, 986-987, 993, 1114, 1165, 1182-1183, 1185, 1228-1229, 1307, 1967, 2254
—Airborne infantrymen, 1327
—Bomb Lakunai Airfield, 1050-1051
—Buzz bomb, 1703
—8th Air Force, 1184, 1294, 1561, 1788, 1848, 2318
—5th Air Force, 1530
—14th Air Force, 1544, 2001
—In China, 1106, 2066
—9th Air Force, 1068, 1331, 1635
—Secret Weapon, 2454
—Testing base, 2460
—12th Air Force, 1641
—**See also** 1st Airborne Division; 5th, 9th, 13th, 14th, 15th Air Force, etc.
United States arms her merchant ships, 560-561
United States Army, 826-827, 867, 948-949, 970-971, 1137-1141, 1146, 1238 1242-1243, 1260, 1346-1347, 1397, 1418

United States Army (cont'd)
—Armies, see under Allied Fourteenth Army; American Eighth, Fifth, First, Ninth, Seventh, Sixth, Tenth, Third, Twelfth
—Engineers, 780, 1124-1125, 1529, 2409
—5th Infantry Division, 1648
—1st Cavalry Division, 1753
—1st division, 826-827
—In India, 1972
—In Italy, 1259
—Medical corps, 1153
—Mortar squad, 2414
—Nurses in France, 1309
—Service forces, 1227
—Signal Corps, 1659
—Trucks, 1589
—Women's Army Corps, 1115, 1559, 1658, 1700, 1714, 1822, 1953, 1977, 2273
—**See also** names of companies, divisions, etc.
United States-Canadian joint defense board, 864
United States carrier planes lash at Okinawa, 1599
United States citizens recalled from Britain, 159
United States clergy protest air raids on Germany, 1184
United States Coast Guard, 1017, 1018, 1171, 1611, 1772-1773, 2428
—Cemetery on Ie Shima, 2385
—Combat cameramen, 752, 1261
—Cutter, 2471
—In the Pacific, 1146
—Landing barge, 1344
—Reserve, 2279
—Women's Reserve, 2279
United States combat engineers, 2419
United States Congress, 32, 915
United States Counter-Intelligence, 2197
United States Fleet, 772, 1761
—At Pearl Harbor, 519
—Atlantic fleet, 2102
—Before Kwajalein, 1140-1141
—Fifth Fleet, 1859
U. S. 1st Armored Division, 902-903
—Rifle Brigade, 902-903
United States fliers return to Cavite, 1736
United States forces, 918-919
—Cross the Moselle River, 1829
—In Iceland, 497-498
—Invade Okinawa, 1857
—Invade the Karama Islands, 1849
—Land in French North Africa, 814-815
—Land in the Ryukyus, 1860
—Take Panay, 1834
United States 41st Division, 1816-1817
United States 4th Division, 1769
United States heavy bombers, 1015
United States
—Industry, 32, 267, 2447
—Post war strikes, 2082, 2132-2133, 2188, 2193
United States Labor
—Post war, 2065
—Post war strikes, 2082, 2132-2133, 2188, 2193
United States landing in the Marshalls, 1136-1137

United States landings in the Admiralty Islands, 1203
United States leases British bases, 386
United States legislators investigate Nazi atrocities, 1904
United States Marines
—(1941), 520
—(1942), 658, 726-727, 728, 730-732, 747, 750, 758-759, 772, 783, 788-791
—(1943), 867, 944, 948-949, 1031, 1061, 1088-1095, 1104-1105
—(1944), 1136-1138, 1147, 1154-1155, 1160-1161, 1171, 1204, 1249, 1390, 1397, 1418, 1530, 1544
—(1945), 1764, 1769, 1778, 1794, 1860, 1871, 1881, 1894, 1977, 1990, 1995, 2002
—(additional scenes), 2061, 2256, 2315, 2330, 2382, 2446
—Burial at sea, 1147
—Demolition squad, 1578
—Establish a beach head in the Solomons, 758-759
—F. Company, 28th Marines, 1773
—5th Division, 1774
—1st Division, 1574-1575, 1975, 1986, 1997, 2090-2091
—4th Division, 1764, 1774
—4th Marine Wing, 2059
—Marine howitzer, 1432
—Iwo Jima cemetery, 2383
—Land in the Solomons, 726-727
—Occupation forces in China, 2090-2091, 2116
—Rescue Formosa prisoners of war, 2068
—2nd Division, 1094, 2377
—6th Marine Division, 1985
—Storm Peleliu, 1574-1575
—3rd Amphibious Corps, 2300
—28th Regiment, Fifth Division, 1778
—Women, 1116
—Women's Reserve, 2279
—**See also** under names of divisions, places, etc.
United States Military Cemetery in China, 1968
United States Naval guns hurl steel at Okinawa, 1872-1873
United States Navy
—(1941), 519
—(1942), 622-623, 640-641, 682-683, 696-697, 728-729, 731, 787, 816-817, 818, 843
—(1943) 863, 941, 1031, 1047, 1059, 1081, 1088, 1096, 1103, 1111
—(1944) 1137-1141, 1146, 1166-1167, 1168-1173, 1176-1177, 1204, 1212-1214, 1225, 1243, 1283, 1306, 1328, 1334, 1390, 1562-1563, 1608-1609
—(1945) 1836-1837, 1870, 1872-1873, 1895, 1963
—(additional scenes) 2250, 2255, 2259, 2405, 2450
—Aircraft, 697
—Aircraft carrier, 1917
—Beach battalion, 1300
—Bombs Truk, 1166-1167
—Camp in the Pacific, 1157
—Combat photographers, 1266
—Cub hospital plane, 2485
—Develops airborne television, 2451
—Flight nurse on Iwo Jima, 1798
—Medical Corps, 751

United States Navy (cont'd)
—Naval Reserve Training School, 1116
—Navy Day, 2102-2103
—Nurses, 1809, 2279
—Pilotless aircraft, 2454
—Raids the Marshall and Gilbert Islands, 622-623
—Task force, 1249
—Task Forces in Normandy, 2301
—War fleet at Kwajalein, 1176-1177
—Women's Reserve, 1111, 2279
United States Neutrality Act revised, 560-561
United States neutrality law, 32
United States occupation of Japan, see Japan, American occupation
United States offers to mediate Russo-Finnish dispute, 8
United States Pacific Fleet, 697, 727, 730, 1081, 1089, 1096, 1193, 1562-1563, 1570, 1599, 1616-1617, 1619, 1621, 1767, 2255
—Aircraft carrier crew, 1225
—Hits Palau, 1212
United States Price control, 2215
United States Public Roads Administration, 864
United States raid on Tokio, 664-667
United States rehabilitation of war wounded, 2204-2205
United States 2nd Army corps, 898
United States 2nd Corps, 909, 913
United States Senate, 32
United States Senate War Investigating Committee, 2228
United States Seventh Fleet, 1544, 1619, 2274
United States 7th Infantry Division, 921
United States southwest Pacific air force, 2283
United States submarines help strangle Japan, 2012-2013
United States tactical air forces, 1832-1833
United States Tactical and Strategic Air Force, 1945, 2278
United States task force, 1306
—Off Saipan, 1172-1173
United States 3rd Amphibious Corps, 1859
United States Third Fleet, 1544, 1619
United States troops, 738, 752
—Build a road in Sicily, 972-973
—Find desolation on Saipan, 1332
—In India 735
—In Sicily, 964-965
United States 12th Air Force troop carrier command, 1602-1603
United States 12th Army Group, 2258
United States 24th Army Corps, 1858-1859
United States 26th Division, 1815
United States Veterans' Administration, 2258
United States victory on Guadalcanal, 868
United States warships visit Australia and New Zealand, 396
University of California, 2020
Upper Thames Patrol, 205
Urquhart, Maj. Gen. R., 1586
Uschi, 2118-2119
"U-249," 2405
"U-858, 1965

V

V-bombs, 1650, 1655
V-E Day, 1949-1950
V-E Day in the Far East, 1953
V-E Day in Russia, 1952
V-for-Victory sign, 1272
V-J Day, 2027, 2045
V-2 bomb, 1927
V-bomb over Belgium, 1655
V-2 rocket, 1927, 2445, 2459
Vaagso Islands, 601
Vaerst, Maj. Gen. von, 907
Valdes, Maj. Gen. Basilo J., 2176
Valence, 1443
Valletta, 657, 1041
Valona, 259
Vatutin, Gen. Nikolai, 875, 1219
Vandenberg, Arthur H., 2165
Vandenberg, Lt. Gen. Hoyt S., 1904
Vandergrift, Lt. Gen. Alexander A., 728, 2256
Vardar Valley, 424
Varengeville, 741
Vargas, Maj., 2099
Vasilevsky, Marshal Alexander, 2036-2037, 2291
Vegesack, 720
Velikie Luki, 771
Velizh, 524
Velletri, 1270
Venezia Alpini, 362
Venezia Giulia, 2235
Venezuela, 2099
Venice, 1920
"Venturas," 1991
Verde Trail, 2306-2307
Verdun, 155, 1526
Verona, 984, 1121
Versailles, 663
Versailles, Treaty, 7
Vesuvius in eruption, 1221
Veterans Administration, United States, 2258
Via Casilina, 1135, 1271
Vian, Capt., 54
Vian, Rear Adm. Sir Philip, 1283
Viborg, 63
Vichy, 166, 194, 455, 472, 663, 1431
Vichy French, 260
Vichy-French forces, 520
Vichy government, 296, 2011
Vickers guns, 716
Victor Emmanuel, King, 1234
Victoria, 1992
Victoria League Club, 175
Victoria Station, 271
"Victorious," 464
Victory parade in Paris, 1490-1491
Vienna, 385, 1543, 1793, 1808, 1876, 2472
Vietinghoff-Sheel, Col. Gen. Heinrich von, 1793, 1924
Vietri, 1248
Vigan, 584
Viipuri, 8
Villa Inchesa, 172
Village of Hate, 1973
Villard, Oswald Garrison, 1184
Vilna, 1179
"Vincennes," 731
Vinegar Joe, 2265
Viper, 2490
Vishinsky, Andrei, 2165

Vistula River, 1715
Vitebsk, 1343
"Vittorio Veneto," 406
Vlookolamsk, 573
Voelkischer Beobachter, 2125
Volchansk, 686, 710
Volga River, 714, 771
Volkssturm, 1667
Volkssturm parade in Berlin, 1667
Volturno River, 1031, 1032, 1071
Voronezh, 710-711, 714-715, 771, 872
Voronezh-Rostov railways, 837
Voroshilovgrad, 715, 875
Vosges Mountains, 1663, 1646-1647, 1679
Vunakanau airfield, 654-655
Vunapope, 1235
Vyazma, 549, 886

W

W.A.A.F., 453
WAC, see Women's Army Corps
"Wac Corporal," 2498
Waal River, 1584
Wada, Lt., 2440
Wadi Bei-el-Kebir, 851
Wadi el Assiub, 897
Wadi Halfaya, 275
Wadi Matratin, 847
Wadi Zemzem, 851
Wadi Zigzau, 896
"Wahoo," 809
Wainwright, Lt. Gen. Jonathan, 650, 658, 2040, 2045, 2058, 2269
Wagner, Kontur Adm., 1941
Wakde Island, 1260-1261
Wake Island, 591, 642-643, 1060-1061, 2143
—Japanese surrender, 2059
Walcheren Island, 1565, 1626-1627
Waldau, 1815
Wallace, Henry A., 1340
Walter Reed Hospital, 1375
Wana Ridge, 1975
War brides, 2148
—Italian, 2182
Warburton-Lee, Capt., 69
War correspondents, 1388, 1871, 2296
War crimes investigations — Courts — Europe
—International High Tribunal, 2126
War crimes investigations — Courts — Pacific
—International Military Tribunal for the Far East, 2214
War crimes investigations—Europe
—Baky, 2203
—Belsen concentration camp, 2121
—British Army court at Luneberg, 2121
—Doenitz, Grand Adm. Karl, 2125, 2237
—Dostler, Gen. Anton, 2144
—Endre, Laszlo, 2203
—Frank, Hans, 2125, 2237
—Frick, Wilhelm, 2125, 2237
—Fritzsche, Hans, 2125, 2237
—Funk, Walther, 2125, 2237
—Goering, Reichsmarshal Herman, 2125, 2128, 2129, 2139, 2194, 2236-2237
—Grese, Irma, 2121
—Guyon-Witzschel, Louise, 2135

War Crimes Investigations—Europe (cont'd)
—Hangings, 2238-2239
—Hess, Rudolph, 2125, 2128, 2129, 2139, 2236
—Himmler, Gudron, 2135
—Himmler, Mrs. Margaret, 2135
—Hungary, 2186, 2203
—Imredy, Bela, 2186
—Jodl, Col. Gen. Alfred Gustav, 2125, 2237
—Kaltenbrunner, 2237
—Keitel, Wilhelm, 2125, 2129, 2237
—Klein, Dr. Fritz, 2121
—Kramer, Joseph, 2121
—Laval, Pierre, 2092
—Ley, Dr. Robert, 2100
—Mihailovitch, Gen. Draja, 2195
—Neurath, Constantin von, 2125, 2237
—Nuremberg trials, 2122-2129, 2135, 2139, 2194
—Oswiecim concentration camp, 2121
—Papen, Franz von, 2125-2129, 2237
—Raeder, Grand Adm. Erich, 2125, 2237
—Ribbentrop, Joachim von, 2125, 2129, 2139, 2237
—Rosenberg, Alfred, 2125, 2237
—Sauckel, Fritz, 2125, 2237
—Schacht, Hjalmar, 2125, 2237
—Seipel, Johann, 2111
—Seyss-Inquart, Arthur, 2125, 2237
—Shirach, Baldur von, 2125, 2237
—Speer, Albert, 2125, 2237
—Sperr, Ingeborg, 2135
—Strasser, Franz, 2152
—Streicher, Julius, 2125, 2237
—Verdict, 2236-2237
—Wolf, Johanna, 2135
—Yugoslavia, 2195
War crimes investigations—Pacific
—Araki, Gen. Sadao, 2110
—Black Dragon Society, 2113
—Doolittle raiders' executions, 2159
—Hata, Field Marshal Shunroku, 2146
—Hiranumara, Baron Kiichiro, 2146
—Hirota, Koki, 2146
—Homma, Lt. Gen. Masaharu, 2081, 2175-2177
—Iwamura, Michiyo, 2105
—Kuroda, Lt. Gen. Sigenori, 2081
—Kuzuu, 2113
—Manaka, Tatanichi, 2153
—Ohta, Lt. Col., 2108
—Okawa, Shumei, 2214
—Saito, Maj. Gen., 2107
—Sakai, Maj. Sakaji, 2142
—Sakaibara, Rear Adm. Shigematsu, 2143
—Singapore, 2107
—Sotojiro, Capt. Tatsuta, 2159
—Suzuki, Adm. Baron Kantaro, 2105
—Tachibaba, Lt. Commander Soichi, 2143
—Takahashi, Adm. Sankichi, 2146
—Tereshima, Adm. Ken, 2105
—Tojo, Gen. Hideki, 2076, 2106, 2214
—Trials at Omori prison camp, 2105
—Trials in Manila, 2104, 2109, 2112, 2150-2151, 2175-2177
—Trials on Kwajalein Island, 2143, 2153
—Yamashita, Gen. Tomoyuki, 2104, 2151
"Warhawks," 1207

Warsaw, 20, 26, 871, 1179, 1543, 1571, 1613, 1715, 1718-1719, 1721
—Ghetto, 2130-2131
—Resistance, 22
—Surrender, 24
—Victory Parade, 27
Warship anti-aircraft guns, 2488
Warships shell Japanese homeland for first time, 2006
"Warspite," 1036-1037, 1283
"Washington," 159
Wasile, 1530
"Wasp," 1510
Wasp, 786
Wavell, Gen. Sir Archibald, 307, 371, 413, 2289
WAVES, 1111, 2279
Weapons, 2433-2495
—**See also** Bombs; Radar; Rockets; Tanks, etc.
"Weasel," 2492
Wehrmacht, 260, 1032, 1350, 1793
Welles, Sumner, 64
"Wellington," 130, 233, 800
Werfthafen, 1942
Wesel, 1793, 1800, 1832-1833, 1846-1847, 1879
Wesel-Geldern road, 1845
Western Canadian infantry, 1134
Western desert air force, Allied, 851
Western Front
—(1944) (D-Day) 1282-1285, 1360-1365, 1433-1434, 1450-1451, 1454-1459, 1479, (Toulon) 1480-1482, 1483, (liberation of Paris) 1484-1498, 1499-1501, 1508-1516, 1547, 1551, 1554-1561, 1564-1567, 1580, (Battle for Germany opens) 1581, 1582-1587, 1591, 1598, 1600, 1627, 1635, 1637, 1644, (Belfort Gap) 1646-1647, 1648-1649, 1651, 1654, (Battle of the Bulge begins) 1680-1684, 1690-1695, 1698-1699
—(1945) 1701-1702, 1710, 1716, 1726, 1735, 1738-1739, 1741, 1743, 1795, (Muenchen-Gladbach) 1796, 1825-1829, 1835, 1850, 1853, 1874, (Ruhr pocket) 1892-1893, 1937, (Germany surrenders unconditionally at Rheims) 1944
—(additional scenes) 2268, 2275, 2286-2287, 2292-2293, 2301, 2302, 2308, 2312, 2314, 2319, 2323-2329, 2369, 2373, 2384, 2390, 2396, 2399, 2404, 2408, 2409, 2414, 2416, 2418-2419, 2421-2423, 2431, 2457, 2467-2468, 2470, 2473
—(Belgium) 1524, 1543, 1546, 1549, (Brussels liberated) 1551, (Battle of the Bulge begins) 1680-1684, 1685-1688, 1706, 1708, 1711, 1713, 1731, 1886-1887, 2297, 2476
—(France) 1180, 1282-1309, 1311-1315, 1324, 1325, 1327, 1329, 1338, 1342, (Cherbourg) 1346-1353, 1358, 1369-1371, 1377-1378, 1380, 1386, 1398-1401, 1403-1404, 1407, 1414-1417, 1420-1421, 1423, (invasion of southern France) 1436-1444, 1446-1448, 1467-1470, (Toulon) 1480-1482, (liberation of Paris) 1484-1498, 1504, 1519, 1521, (Chateau-Thierry) 1524, 1526, 1531, (Le Havre) 1565, 1662-1664, 1666, 2455, 2493

Western Front (cont'd)
—(Germany) (Battle for Germany opens) 1581, 1592, (Aachen surrenders) 1605-1607, 1659, 1750, 1758, 1779-1782, (Cologne) 1800-1801, 1802-1807, 1810, 1813, 1815, 1831-1833, 1840-1848, 1861, 1863-1866, 1877-1879, (map of drive in Germany) 1885, 1897, 1900-1901, 1921, (Berlin falls to the Russians) 1934-1936, (north German forces surrender) 1941, (Germany surrenders unconditionally at Rheims) 1944-1945, 2336, 2461, 2489, 2494
—Russian-American junction, 1905-1906
—Russian-British junction, 1926
—**See also** Eastern Front (for Russian campaign from the East); names of cities, towns, etc.
Western Front—Maps and diagrams
—April of 1945, 1885, 1910-1911
—Battle for France, 1414-1415, 1468
—Battle for Germany, 1581
—Battle of the Bulge, 1684
—September of 1944, 1534, 1581
Westerplatte, Fort, 14
Westphalian plains, 1850
Westkapelle, 1626-1627
Westminster, 288, 792
Westminster Abbey, 449, 450-451
"West Virginia," 576-577
Westwall, 1317, 1319, 1564, 1581, 1635, 1735
Wewak, 1180, 1243
Weygand, Gen. Maxime, 116
Wegand Line, 151
Wheeler, Burton K., 1904
Wheeler, Gen. R. A., 2078
Whitehead, Maj. Gen. Ennis, 2283
Wiesloch, 2461
Wildcat Infantry Division, 1574
Wilhelmshaven, 720
Wilhelmina, Queen, 512
"Wilkes-Barre," 1959
Willkie, Wendell, 363, 392
Willoughby, Maj. Gen. C. A., 2035
Wilsher, Kathleen, 2189
Wilson, Gen. Sir Henry M., 472, 477, 489, 1439, 1446, 2266
Winant, John G., 386
Windischleuba, 2399
Wingate, Maj. Gen. Orde Charles, 923, 1205, 2289
Wingate's raiders, 2272
Winged wind tunnel, 2460
Wismar, 1926
Wittenberg, 1182-1183
Wolf, Johanna, 2135
Wolff, Gen. Karl, 1924
Wolshefit, 541
Women
—American, 1111, 1115-1116, 1559, 1591, 1912, 2273, 2279
—Chinese, 888
—English, 210, 382, 393, 793
—Filipino, 1712, 1723
—French, 1373, 1505, 1517
—German, 1004-1005
—Russian, 777, 836-837, 1058, 1725, 1740
Women's Army Corps, 1115, 1559, 1658, 1700, 1714, 1822, 1953, 1977, 2273
—Arrives in Peleliu, 1658

Women's Auxiliary Air Force, 453
Women's Reserve, United States Navy,
 1111, 2279
Wood, Col. George T., 1799
Wood, Maj. Harold, 2221
World's biggest bomb, 2436
World War II Ends, 2027
Worms, 1835
Wotje, 623
Wright Field, 2483
Wuerzburg, 1863
Wunthe, 677

X

"XB-35," 2447
"XP-84," 2460

Y

Y Force, 1227, 1250
YMCA War Prisoner Aid, 2087
Yalta Conference, 1754-1756
Yamashita, Gen. Tomoyuki, 627, 2058,
 2104, 2151
"Yamato," 1614-1615, 1870
Yangtze River, 888-889, 929
Yanina, 311, 333, 431
Yap, 1214
Yap City, 1212-1213
Yawata, 1322
Ye, 1596
Yenang Yaung, 653
Yervada Palace, 734
Yokohama, 664, 2040
Yonai, Adm. Mitsumasi, 1393
Yontan, 1859
"York," 294
York, 669, 670-671
Yorkshire, 122
"Yorktown," 520, 696
Young, Sir Mark, 600
Young, Lt. Richard, 676
Young Men's Christian Association
 War Prisoner Aid, 2087
Younger, Maj. K. S., 2167
Ypres, 123
Yu Cheng-Wan, Gen., 1106

Yugoslav Air Force, 420
Yugoslav civilians, 766-767
Yugoslav guerrillas, 766, 998-999, 1109,
 2195
Yugoslav infantrymen, 418
Yugoslav patriots, 766-767, 998-999,
 1793
Yugoslav Partisans, 1108, 2195
Yugoslavia, 260, 404, 418, 420, 426, 998-
 999, 1108-1110, 1543, 1601, 2257
—Government in exile, 1110
—Post war border discussions, 2234-
 2235
—Surrenders to Germany, 430
—Trieste border dispute, 2192
—United Nations Relief and Rehabili-
 tation Administration, 2183
—War crimes investigations, 2195
Yugoslavia—Military leaders
—Mihailovitch, Gen. Draja, 1108, 1110,
 2195, 2257
—Simovich, Gen., 404
—Tito, Marshal Josip Broz, 1108, 1109,
 2195, 2257
Yugoslavia—Political leaders
—Cincar-Markovich, 404, 426
—Peter, King, 1110
—Simovich, Gen., 404
—Tsvetkovich, M., 404
Yukhnov, 634
Yukon, 864
Yunnan, 638

Z

Zaghouan, 913
Zahringen, 283
Zakharov, Col. Gen., 1781
Zamboanga, 1816-1817
Zaporozhe, 1032, 1074
"Zara," 406
Zarat, 892
Zeebrugge, 147
Zellin, 1544
Zelten, 861
"Zero," 746, 1675
Zhitomir, 1032
Zhukov, Field Marshal Gregory K.,
 1544, 1747, 1793, 1947, 1948, 2261
Zuara, 861